Endorsements

"Few books can matc ...g spirit of *Hard Knocks & Di...* .. ɪ inesilver teaches how grit, intelligence, and compassion help define not only what you do, but who you truly are. Coach cared. Not only about how I performed on the field, track, or mat, but about how I did in class and in life. If you meet a couple of people like that in a lifetime, consider yourself lucky."

—Kevin Corke, White House News Correspondent

"It wasn't what Coach Finesilver said, it was what I watched you do and be every time I was around. That's what I fell in love with! A man with a passion for young men no matter race, creed, color, or socioeconomic background. I just saw a man that cared for young men that look like me around the program."

—Ray Jackson, VP of Player Development, Denver Broncos

"I am grateful for the Lord putting you in my life as a young man. I am thankful for the stern life lessons that went far beyond athletics. These life lessons have stuck with me to this very day. May the Lord continue to richly bless you and keep you in his loving arms."

—William A. Lyle Jr., Class of '82

"Coach Finesilver is a living legend! As a kid growing up in Montbello, he inspired us, cared about us, and told us we had greatness ahead of us. It is my privilege to know him, and I congratulate him on being memorialized with this book."

—Sheriff Elias A. Diggins
Denver Sheriff Department

"Thank you Coach Finesilver for your support and mentorship at Montbello High School. Having educators like you was critical to my success!"

—Javon Jackson, Professor of Jazz
Director, Jackie McLean Institute of Jazz
The Hartt School, University of Hartford

"Legendary teacher, mentor, activist, and friend for over four decades. Coach has inspired many of us to be well-rounded and to take care of the family and our community."

—RA Pablo, Retired Law Enforcement Officer
Pres. of Denver Sheriff Fraternal Order of Police
Pres. of the Latin American Law Enforcement Assoc.
Restorative Justice Councilor for DPS

"No one commands the respect of all constituencies more than Steve Finesilver, DPS teacher and coach. His ability to inspire, motivate, serve, and lead produces champions in life. He has put action into the rhetoric and knows that racial and social justice are indispensable for closing the achievement gap. This servant-leader has a proven record of success."

—Bonnie G. Guggenheim, DPS Teacher, Retired
Colorado History Day Teacher of the Year
Boettcher Foundation Teacher Award
Richard T. Farrell Teacher of Merit Award, National Finalist

"Coach Finesilver is one of those guys who you look back on fondly and say, 'If there was one teacher who truly gave a damn, it was that guy.'"

—Theo E. J. Wilson
Speaker, Writer, Author

"Every athlete that goes to GW knows Coach Fino. Many of us came from troubled homes and brought difficult attitudes to his class. Especially me. But Coach Finesilver had limitless patience and, over time, instilled in me a no-excuse attitude that has paid dividends in my soccer and military careers. He taught me how to channel my anger into something productive and changed the course of my life by helping me get into West Point. He has transformed so many lives in his career, and I'm endlessly grateful for his patience, loyalty, and presence in mine."

—CPT Lauren McGovern, West Point Graduate
Currently stationed at Fort Riley, Kansas
First Infantry Division

"To know Coach Steve Finesilver is to know that you are supported, mentored, and part of a special community. While I wasn't an athlete, Coach still took a special interest in my interests in music and performance. He has always had a special way of making me feel like family and has acknowledged me for what I have to offer the world, even at this stage of my life. He is a gift, and I'm honored to not only know him, but also to be supported by him."

—Kenya M. Johnson
Certified Health and THRIVE Coach

"I was blessed with many positive male role models in my life, without whom I would not have survived childhood. Among those is Steve Finesilver, who I call Coach to this day. I have carried his lessons on character and integrity with me as I live into the example he consistently demonstrated. It is no mean feat to turn the tide in a young person's life. It requires commitment, trustworthiness, respect, accountability, and above all, care. Coach has given me and thousands of other kids all the above—kids who so desperately needed the tides to change in their lives."

—Stephen Brackett, Musician
Flobots

"Bless you for your work. The phrase, "To whom much is given, much is required," has burned in my soul, along with my teachers who spoke life into me. I quickly learned the importance of giving back to my community. The community helped mold and create me, which is why I do my work."

—Malcinia "Nina" Toombs-Conley
Career Educator; Mentor

"You had such impact in my life I had to find you and reconnect. If you taught at Gove Junior High in 1979-1980 and you once wrestled a bear, you're the teacher and coach I've been searching for. I have so much to tell you."

—Robert Hayden
Business Owner

"Coach Finesilver sets a standard of excellence and a community environment where people are acknowledged, affirmed, celebrated, encouraged, and consistently cared for and where they experience a sense of belonging. We all (students and athletes) felt safe and belonged under Coach Finesilver; his leadership, teaching, and care was intergenerational."

—Oscar Joseph III, Ph.D., D. Mgt.

Hard Knocks
and
Dirty Socks

Through the Eyes of Coach

Steve Finesilver

Stella Nova Publishing

Overland Park, KS

This book is dedicated first to Papa, my daddy, who left us in October 2006. Without a doubt, he was the most imperfect/perfect man of all time. He singlehandedly changed the lives of thousands. My next book is about him.

Next, this is dedicated to the flashing-eyed beauty I fell for like a ton of bricks thirty-five years ago. Brenda, my *much* better half, is the motivation for me to persist and continue to do what I know is very important.

Almost last...the Village! The most beautiful collection of children ever raised under one roof.

Felly, our dear oldest, who is battling the real world and holding her own in her early thirties. The proud mother of two beautiful children.

Mary, our rebel, who continues to amaze with her spirit and passion. Married and new mother to an adorable little girl.

Becca, who never met a stranger. Like my Bubie (Jewish grandmother), she always finds the good in every person and every situation.

My Zach-Zach, the oldest son by two minutes, who is blessed with his Papa's toughness and compassion and cursed with his impulsivity and mule-like stubbornness.

Mitchie, who is the most driven, competitive soul I have ever been around. His heart and loyalty will bring one to tears.

Matt, who bears my old nickname (Big Fino). The most energy-bound wild-child who carries one identity at school, "Schoolboy," and a different identity at home, which is a cross between pugilist and caretaker.

J.J.—our Josh. He is the deepest soul ever and was at my side for countless amazing hours. He always has a dream to chase and no doubt corral.

Olivia, Emmy, and Marzanna—our newest additions. No, Mama didn't get pregnant again. Felly has two beautiful babies who have a spirit and love of life that can't be contained. Marzanna is Mary's first.

Lastly, the kids. The students of The Denver Public Schools. The oath of poverty I took when I signed my first contract to begin teaching in 1979 has been well worth it. I salute you, all of you!

I wear my name
I've got my grind
I'm chasing dreams
To Life!

—OUR CHANT, SPOKEN AFTER WRESTLING PRACTICES

CHILDREN IN SCHOOL OFTEN TAKE THEIR GIVEN NAMES AND AMERICANIZE
THEM. WE RESPECT THE NAME AND PRONOUNCE IT PROPERLY.
THE KIDS ARE PROUD OF THE CULTURES THEY CAME FROM AND SHOULD BE.
THEY COME TO SCHOOL EVERY DAY
TO CHASE THEIR DREAMS,
FIND THEIR GRIND,
AND BE SOMEBODY.
THEY WORK HARD TO ACCOMPLISH SOMETHING THEY CAN BE PROUD OF.

These kids remind me to do the chant.
It is repeated in every native language represented.

CONTENTS

Adrian Green

A loud, deep voice booms through the George Washington High School wrestling/dance room to start off our 6 a.m. Saturday morning wrestling practice. "Unless it's raining there'll be no complaining!" The young but seasoned coach points to the mirrors that run along the wall of the room and declares, "We will end practice when I cannot see myself in the mirror!"

In 1987 Coach Steve Finesilver returned to his alma mater to teach and coach after a seven-year tenure at Montbello High School. During those first years in the profession, Coach gained a reputation for being a hard-nosed teacher and football and wrestling coach who set high expectations and pushed his students to meet them, as could be seen when he led his Montbello wrestling team to a very unexpected league title a few years prior. Neither my teammates nor I were surprised by Coach's challenge. We were, however, very concerned about how long it would take to generate enough heat to make the mirrors so foggy that our coach could not see himself, and whether or not we could survive that process.

I was a Freshman from North Denver. George Washington High School was not my assigned school. My parents thought GW's International Baccalaureate (IB) program would provide me better opportunities than my home school. They never imagined one man would be the reason that sending me to GW was the best decision they could have made. My parents, disillusioned with the educational system, felt the entity was failing low income students and students of color, and they hoped GW would provide an education that would open doors for me.

They were right, but my success was not because of the IB program. Coach Fino was the instructor who made that happen for me.

But on that fateful Saturday morning I was not so sure how things would go.

After some hard drilling and a grueling live wrestling session, Coach led the team through conditioning.

"That was not good enough! Start over!" he commands.

"Okay, you want to miss a rep, let's start again."

"If 'ifs and buts' were candy and nuts, I'd open a 7-11!" he'd say.

He blows his whistle unexpectedly. We look at each other with dismay and wonder *what now*. Coach smiles, walks to the mirror, and swipes his finger over it, removing a line of steam. He proudly declares, "We are done! I can't see myself. Get out of here and use deodorant!"

This was the moment I discovered what Coach was all about. His reaction to us successfully meeting his challenge showed he believed in us. He knew he was making a big ask, but he also knew we would meet his challenge and, based on his reaction, I think we met it quicker than he expected. From that point on, I knew why so many students trusted and adored him.

Over my remaining four years of high school, I experienced and witnessed Coach's relentless, tireless, and loyal dedication to his students. He ate at Denny's every morning at 4:30 a.m., promising to pay for any student who got up early and met him there—and he did. He always had snacks in his office for students. He worked to acquire donations for programs, including a huge donation of shoes that he shared with students and coaches for years. He worked the phones, calling college coaches to help students get scholarships. He invited students to his family events. When Coach Finesilver gave out t-shirts to his teams that said "family" on them, you knew he meant it.

I always hoped to wrestle in college, but I did not perform well my senior year. When I returned to school feeling dejected the Monday after the season ended, Coach greeted me with a smile, some encouraging words, and a plan to write letters to college coaches. I did not think it was possible to generate interest after my performance, but Coach believed someone was going to give me a chance. After Coach and I wrote many letters and called many schools, I realized my dream of wrestling in college and did it without paying a dime. He found ways to get me scholarships and grant money to cover my education. If I had gone to any other school, I know I would not have received the type of commitment I got from Coach Fino.

You may chalk this up to the common story of player/coach relationships where a coach takes a strong interest in an athlete and provides extra support. But Coach does this for many students every year. Over forty years of encouraging, preparing, and supporting students through the college application and financial aid processes, Coach Finesilver has changed the courses of many young people from every background, over and over again. All he asks in return is that you meet your potential.

A high school teammate of mine, Brian Olson, now an engineer, said, "Coach Fino was and is a mentor for all. He mentored me as a student, athlete, and coach. I would not have the passion for helping others without this influence. "And," Olson adds, "thanks to his matchmaking skills, I have the family I have today." This is one of many examples of how Coach made connections with his students and influenced their lives in a positive way.

In 1997, I completed my college degree and decided I wanted to be the next Coach Fino. I wanted to be a teacher and coach. I did not get an education degree, however, which made it difficult to get into the education field. So I called Coach Finesilver. Coach employed me in his summer work program, Jobs by George, as supervisor of a crew. He started this program in the early 1990s with Marsha Pointer, a GW teacher and coach, and a handful of students. They went to construction sites, swept houses, and dug window wells. By the time I returned to the program as a college graduate, Coach employed over fifty students. He hired college students, teachers, and staff members to supervise crews.

As a supervisor, I got to work at construction sites, on landscaping projects, at a meat-packing plant, and at a large bread-baking company over the course of a few summers. Jobs by George continues to this day. Many students have had the opportunity to learn valuable employable skills and experience a variety of jobs. Coach has provided opportunities for students and staff members to earn a fair wage over summer break.

Beyond helping me with summer employment, Coach once again worked the phones for me. His research and contacts led me to the alternative licensing program for teachers without education degrees. This program allowed me to gain employment as a teacher and earn my licensure while employed by the district. Coach also served as my mentor-teacher throughout the program. I became a fully certified teacher and am currently in my twenty-sixth year in education.

I never became the next Coach Finesilver. Coach is a legend, and I'm not sure there will ever be another like him. However, thanks to his support and mentorship, I have had the pleasure to teach and coach many great young individuals and have hopefully made a similar impact on some. I attribute my success to having learned so much from Coach.

Coach Randy Gallegos, wrestling coach at East High School for over twenty years, had a similar experience, despite being one of Coach's students. Coach Fino and Coach Gallegos met in the early 2000s. Coach Randy said, "Coach Finesilver is the epitome of what a high school coach should be. He inspired me, supported me, and continues to encourage me as a coach. George Washington High School is blessed to have him as a part of Team DPS."

Over my twenty-six-year career as teacher and coach, I have tried to carry on his traditions by instilling in my students and athletes many of the values he drove home to me and others. I have worked to instill discipline, work ethic, and integrity. I have shared his coined team motto, "The Pride Starts Here," with the teams I have coached. I am a good coach because of what I learned from him.

But his story doesn't end there. In addition to supporting his former students, he is doing the same for their children. Some are his current students and some are not. His loyal commitment to his students now spans multiple generations. Coach made calls for my son, now a college student-athlete.

This book shares highlights of all Coach Finesilver has contributed over his forty-three-year tenure and includes individual stories of how his influence positively guided his protégés. What makes Coach's undying commitment to young people even more impressive is the fact that he raised seven children of his own during this time. I know no one with such energy, commitment, loyalty, and conviction. I'm proud and honored to be part of his legacy.

The educational system has evolved since Coach started in 1979. While many things have changed, Coach Finesilver continues to do what he always has done—build authentic relationships with students and families, set high expectations, inspire students to reach their goals, and loyally support them in all their endeavors.

Most school districts claim to be defenders of equity and set high expectations for their students. Ironically, this "new" focus and the policies that came with it has put obstacles in the way for Coach and many other great educators. Coach has not compromised but continues to fight for what he knows is right. In turn, he has questioned why students are not held to a higher standard and why students do not have equal access and representation in the educational system. He wonders why there are not more teachers in the classroom that look like the students in front of them and who share common experiences with them. He aspires to figure out ways that schools can become pillars of their community and offer resources that stakeholders need.

Due to the injustices and malpractices Coach witnessed over the years and those made more obvious during the pandemic, Coach started the Denver Youth Initiative in 2020. He created a plan that would close educational gaps, promote equity, and support students outside of school by going into the communities to find out what the kids, and sometimes their families, needed. He spent months walking neighborhoods, visiting parks, recreation centers, churches, and community meetings to listen to the district's constituents. He reached out to the DPS superintendent and board to share his findings and the plan he created. After many phone calls, the district finally met with him but graciously brushed aside his ideas.

Coach is an expert in his field and prides himself on maintaining the highest level of integrity. He has committed his career to developing contributing members of our community while providing the best opportunities possible for students to help them get where they want to go. He has maintained relationships with many former students from Montbello and GW over the years. He has walked the streets and spoken to members of the communities that make up the DPS. He works to get donations for food, furniture, clothing, toiletries, and other items on a weekly basis to provide church food banks and donation centers, and many other things not covered here.

Coach has built his career on setting a high bar for himself, his peers, and his students. Now he asks his school district and others in both the state and the nation to do the same. He did not compromise his values and approach when challenged by the powers that be, because he knew the students would meet his expectations while the pundits feared they would have to field parent complaints instead of maintaining high expectations for our youth. He does all of this because he wants us to succeed.

After reading what Coach Finesilver has lived and learned, I hope you will be inspired to challenge our school systems to provide all students with what they desperately need and deserve.

—ADRIAN GREEN
FORMER GW TEACHER AND COACH

Zach Finesilver

If you know Coach Finesilver, he's probably already on a first name basis with you and telling you he loves you every time before you hang up the phone. I grew up watching my dad wake up every single morning—early. He was a man of consistency and habit and gave his very best, not just for our family, but for the many kids who needed him. That part was apparent. We practically grew up in the halls of George Washington High School. There was always a waitlist for my dad's classes (not just the PE ones, the science ones too), and student assists who weren't even given credit for it. It was in each of these interactions that I was able to learn how to truly care for someone. How to truly make them feel heard and special. That's a scarce skill nowadays. And if it's scarce in general, you can only imagine how many inner city and at-risk kids are feeling heard and special. I love my dad. He's my hero. I cherish the fact that he has been able to be there for so many other kids who needed a mentor, a dad, a hero, or a friend.

It's necessary to use an anecdote to fully understand our level of closeness. Wrestling is a big part of our family's lives. And for those of you unfamiliar with wrestling, it is a very emotional sport. It takes a lot of emotional fortitude to walk out on the mat and perform in front of people. For me, it was daunting, and it took a lot of practice to get better. My dad made that daunting experience seem manageable and even enjoyable. We often talked through performance anxiety moments or the sadness of losses, conversations no one would understand or appreciate unless they were me or my dad. Some took place in the back room at a wrestling tournament with both of us sobbing. Before every match, I'd look to my dad for confidence and composure. And after each match I won, I'd look for him in the crowd. As the ref raised my hand, I would wink at him, only the two of us understanding the struggle that took place to overcome that fear of mine. Even more important was the closeness between us. That look and (hopefully) wink if I won was one of extreme friendship and love. The kind of love that accepts the other for their faults, their shortcomings, and their anxieties. In recent years, I have worked to do the same for him. To show love, understanding, and complete acceptance for who he is and our relationship. More than understanding and respect, our relationship is that of complete love and honest admiration.

For that very reason I am baffled. How could I have had such an amazing relationship with my dad? That's kind of a weird question, isn't it? But if you know or have heard of Coach Finesilver, you have heard how he is a father to many more than his own kids. So I wonder again how he and my mom have the energy, time, or even money to provide the parenting me and my many other siblings required. For over forty-five years this man has been a father figure to kids who needed some kind of mentorship, some kind of structure, some kind of discipline, and some kind of love. He gave so many kids the love they so desperately needed because of broken families, hard situations, or just struggling identities. What he has done and continues to do for so many around him astonishes me and those who know him.

My father has a deep care for the people and communities he serves. To say anyone truly cares for people more than Coach Finesilver is to lie. On one occasion Costco agreed to give him all their unsold produce and other items so he could distribute them to needy families in Denver. I tagged along on this delivery to help. We unloaded the food and supplies into a large family's small apartment unit. They had a bed in the living room and were clearly doing their best, but they were in a tough situation. My dad unloaded the supplies and gave the mom and each of the kids a hug. Not only did he help provide them with much needed items for their everyday lives, but he made them feel special and that they mattered, no matter where or how they lived. He has the skill to make someone, no matter who they are, feel like they're the only person in the room.

From all these relationships, we have many non-biological brothers and sisters who have become family, people who needed someone like Coach Finesilver to save them. These relationships show the power of moments and experiences. If you ever get the chance to talk to my dad, you'll find his speech riddled with stories and anecdotes, times of laughter, and times of grieving. In these stories you can see how immense this man's memory box must be. But it's also in these stories that you learn how important it is to cherish your own life experiences and powerful moments. I hope that in this book you will understand the exceptionality of a moment. It is something to be cherished, and although fleeting, the feelings and the people who experience a moment with you will live with you always.

In light of this, the immense frustration I imagine my father has toward the school system is entirely justified and well intentioned. The school system in the DPS is convoluted, and the administration cares about paychecks over people. We have a systematic rat race where "educators" wear suits and sit at an oak desk in their ivory towers. For over forty-five years, Coach Finesilver has been a staple of the DPS education system, and more importantly, the communities around the DPS school district.

Now let's back up a second. Why did I have to say education system and community as two separate entities? Shouldn't these be integrated into one another seamlessly? Coach Finesilver has worked tirelessly to do just this. Let's join in and make people proud to attend GWHS and proud to be a community. Countless former students see him on a daily basis because he is not only a leader for the Denver inner-city communities, but also a friend for many.

The exact solution to giving the power back to the people and communities as opposed to the administration looking for their next six-figure paycheck is unknown to me. I haven't done the time as an educator and leader for the inner city of Denver. But I do know my dad, more than anyone else on God's green earth. From knowing him, as well as from my understanding of his explanations, I learned that the solutions lie in people who truly care for our kids. We can create initiatives like the Denver Youth Initiative, with known and trusted leaders to delegate money toward helping students expand their resources. We can bring in teachers who are trained well and get them to stay by paying them a little bit more. We can expect discipline among students and not let the school run rampant with misbehavior angled toward gang violence. That last one is easier said than done, but by bringing in trusted leaders, that can be nipped in the bud. Above all, let's empower the people who have done the time and who *want* to help. We can't afford to turn a blind eye toward capable people with a desire to make a difference. Written qualifications are great, but when it comes down to it, we must look for those with people skills and genuineness. I'm excited for all of you to read through my father's experiences, many of which, growing up, I have heard stories about. I ask that you foster a deep relationship with your local school and lend your hand in any way you can.

—ZACH FINESILVER
DUKE GRADUATE AND COACH

PREFACE

My career spanning more than four decades has gone by in the blink of an eye. Several years ago, my phone rang. Dan C. was returning my call. I had spoken with his mom the week before. He took leave from medical school to pursue his dream. After earning his degree from the University of Pennsylvania, he started medical school. He was always into music and played in some of the small venues and coffee shops. He recently had one of his songs on iTunes, and even though he's not sure he's going to hit the big time, he loves his music. Let's say he falls a bit short for that, then he'll finish med school. Either way, he'll be great at whatever he does. He is now a neurosurgeon after a decade of training.

A while ago, I got a call. "Hi Coach, this is Tony." I knew instantly who it was. Tony played on my first championship team in 1983. I'm lucky that I rarely forget a name, a voice, or a face. It seems like I have taught or coached half of Denver. Tony had a big job opportunity. He knew I'd help, with pleasure. They always come back! Some of my former kids are darn near fifty-eight years old. Hundreds call and come by, either to my house or where I work now at George Washington High School. I am damn lucky. I now am teaching and coaching the children from more than forty-two graduating classes. It's been a great run and I'm having a great time.

Now you can be sure there have been some tough times, but overall, it has been rewarding. That is why I get up at 4:30 a.m. every day and challenge the kids on my watch. That's all I know. I am tough as heck on them. I've coached football nearly forty years, spent a bunch coaching wrestling, had a decade or so as the dean of students, eight or nine years teaching science, and a multitude teaching physical education. I'm now finishing my thirty-fourth year at George Washington High School, my alma mater. I'm also a parent of seven great kids. They are not angels, but they work very hard. They are respectful and well adjusted.

Am I an expert? Heavens no! I'm just a guy who changed from a pre-veterinary medicine major to education nearly forty-five years ago. No regrets. I don't profess to having all the answers—hell, I probably have more questions than answers. My hope is that teachers will read this.

Teaching is a noble profession, but I'm saddened by the number of bright lights who enter teaching and leave disheartened after only a few years. *We need you!* Maybe you can latch on to one tip or one story and be able to manage kids a little better. Teaching can be rewarding, relatively stress-free, and fun. It isn't liver surgery. Maybe you parents can pick up some pointers from the wonderful parents who have reared some of the great kids I've worked with. And last, maybe a few students will gain some inspiration from the real stories of kids who are kicking butt in the real world, many of whom were raised in lower- and middle-income families, yet they transcended barriers and set goals to succeed. Some were just plain poor, existing at the poverty level. Yet somehow, they found hope and attended or are still attending our nation's finest colleges. Some have chosen to represent our country. Some have died.

As you read, be assured I won't hold back. I won't get too graphic with the language, as some students, both present and former, will read these pages. Some of this will make you laugh; other parts will make you cry. Everything you read is real, not fiction or fairy tales. You will be troubled by the sadness of kids who chose gangs. Yes, I've been exposed to the stark reality of gang life. You may be elated by stories of a few who survived gang life and made it out, some after being shot, stabbed, or beaten.

Parents, you may find yourself cast in one of the stereotypes of parenthood as it relates to schools. If you fall into the Rescue 911 category, you may resent my words. The truth hurts. If you are too busy to be involved, then you're just as guilty as a parent who isn't involved at all. But something in here will strike home, guaranteed.

Fellow educators—gloves off. Enjoy what you can identify with. Look inside these pages. You are not exempt from the criticism—or praise, either—between these paper covers.

If you think you may become a teacher, please read this. There is not a hell of a lot of real reading out there that will take you firsthand into the educational system with no holds barred. Good reading.

—Coach Finesilver

ACKNOWLEDGMENTS

Mr. Mike Peterson: A fine educator who kept me in check as a teen and then advocated for me to teach and coach at GW in 1987.

Mr. Conklin: May he rest peacefully in heaven. He helped me break into coaching and teaching in 1979.

Dr. Sylvia Smith: My first principal at GW who supported me as I worked to change a culture which took time, maybe more than we anticipated. But it worked, because here we are thirty-five years later.

Mr. Larry Blake: GW Athletic Director. Even when you were told from the central admin to fire me as a coach in 1991, you held firm and believed we would have great teams and solid citizens. Both have proven to be true.

Mr. and Mrs. Batey: Mr. Batey was my principal at Montbello. May he be at peace in heaven. Mrs. Batey—I was supposed to show you the ropes as a student advisor, but you actually taught me more than I could have imagined.

Mr. McNeil and Coach Delapp: Both could teach physics to a rock, which is similar to teaching some of the football players and wrestlers over the years.

Coach Marquez and Tim: A father-son duo, Dad was my coach in 1971 and believed in me. Tim has been a wonderful supporter of the Denver Public Schools.

Coach Bancroft: A teacher I admired tremendously. You passed without me telling you how much I looked up to you and admired your dedication to our youth.

Ms. Vivian Johnston: Principal of the year, every year. You put up with stunts and stubbornness and insisted I put my family first, no matter what. So much love to you.

Coach Gurian: My former teacher, coach, mentor, and friend. The consummate professional. So many lessons learned and fond memories.

Ms. Rosen: My colleague, dear friend, and supporter. Though beat up by the system, you have never lost hope. As a wonderful human and caring teacher, my promise to you is that we will change the system.

Wick: Over the years you have become like a fifth son. We have coached together and shared family moments, both sad and happy. You encouraged me to write this through all time periods and emotions. Your advice as an aspiring author years ago have remained in my memory. Thanks.

Ms. Guggenheim: One of the finest educators among our GW family. Always holding true to your beliefs and values. You have been so supportive of what I have tried to accomplish with our students for decades. I truly admire and appreciate you.

Ms. Gosman: Teacher, mentor, and dear friend. We have stayed connected for thirty-five years and will remain so. As a career educator, you imprinted so many in many ways. You have been with me and our family through each step! Love to you and your family.

Coach Clement: Friend, artist, and fellow coach. My hope is that you will be back in Denver working your coaching magic and continuing your devotion to Denver children.

Ms. Midian Holmes: A dear parent and true friend, jumping into the trenches with me to do right for our Denver children. The work is soon to unfold in ways which we have been hoping for. True supporter of equity and transparency.

Coach Blum: What began as a fine friendship has blossomed into connecting as family. You guided much of my coaching and all of the business development of Jobs by George.

Ms. Love: My sister from another mister. You have trusted me with your amazing children and are a bright light illuminating each day at GW.

Ms. Alford: Stubborn as a student and has never changed. Supportive and fiercely convicted. Climbed through the ranks at Colorado Department Of Transportation.

Otis Hamilton: A symbol of resilience, tenacity and an old soul who has never forgotten who he is and his Montbello roots.

Coach Sayyid: Looking down from heaven, you taught me without knowing what "tough love" really means and how essential it is.

Ms. Rodriguez: You have been a pillar for me and our school. Always showing strength, you have been the most important link to our families for a long time. And besides, there is no finer salsa found anywhere than in your own secret recipe.

Coach Fred Harris: With me on the daily, battling a system from the inside to do better for our children. You have changed the course for hundreds of children by what you exemplify.

Pricilla Shaw-Rhan: Not just a teacher, but a dedicated professional who has stayed true to her roots and beliefs. You have never compromised, and you know, at the core, what our children need most in their lives.

Ms. Crawford: Former student, now on staff and providing hope and wisdom for our students. You are a symbol of what every child can become if they embrace a solid work ethic.

Coach Anderson: Working tirelessly with students who really need you. The all-time fitness superstar and supporter of change for our youth.

Ms. Kohan: Possibly the finest coach around. Your speech and debate teams have reached national acclaim, and you quietly guide them with constant love and devotion.

Bright-eyed children: Jazzy, Jazzy J, Lia and her beautiful family, and Sha Nae-Nae and her family. Giving us all hope for a bright future because of your spirit and your daily love of life.

Coach Hall (Uncle Charlie): I'm hoping you'll read this and know that you've touched hundreds of lives and made the kids you worked with feel like Supermen and Superwomen. You've had and still have kids that succeeded and will succeed because of you and only you. You are loved. Thanks for teaching me.

Mrs. Boone: A dear friend who has been a dedicated member of the GW family for over thirty-five years. You have warmed many hearts.

Our uniformed men and women: To those who wear or have worn the uniform for military service, police, fire, and sheriff. Sheriff Diggins, Sheriff Pablo, and many, many others.

Attorneys Mr. Craig Silverman and Ms. Sadie Clement: This does not waive or alter attorney-client privilege. Your guidance and advice are appreciated.

To the most loyal of families: Many of you have sent numerous children through our doors and maintained your loyalty to George Washington High for generations. Despite our faults, you have been steadfast and dedicated to our school. "Our Blood Runs Green"—together!

Coach Ireland: You have never wavered as a teacher and mentor to students. Fiercely loyal and committed to what you know is best for all children.

Curtis Madden: You joined our family and allowed us to have so many memories of great times together and to come.

Mrs. Graver: You have volunteered countless hours to Jobs By George. Your dedication and loyalty to hundreds of children who you have believed in but never met is deeply appreciated.

The Denver Youth Initiative Team: You have committed to impacting not only our children and families, but also the educational system in Denver. The work will soon unfold and blossom and we will leverage our collective connections to become a national model showing how to improve the quality of life for families in major cities. By realizing children are our most cherished entity, we can clarify our focus, providing them with more than they have ever imagined. Time to roll up our sleeves!

Ms. Stephanie Krause: Artist and cover designer. One of the most talented teachers in our school district. So skilled and totally committed to our youth. Much gratitude to you.

Ms. Stein-Shevell: Our school psychologist. Thanks so much for your continued support of all students, staff, and faculty. You have been a breath of fresh air for many.

INTRODUCTION

So what will you read here? You will hear the stories of some amazing former students who are now friends, along with their families, who have chosen to stay connected. You will learn a little about me and a lot about the reality of education from within the trenches. You will read about some amazing educators and some poor ones.

True stories are included about the amazing and inspiring kids I have been with as a teacher and coach. One chapter is very sad because it uncovers subjects rarely exposed in this type of forum. The book contains some school humor in a chapter entitled "Drama." There is a long chapter about myths in education that took years to encapsulate. "Games, Matches, and Jocks" will take you into the mostly wholesome world of high school athletics. At the end of this more than twenty-year endeavor there is a call—a plea—for kids, parents, and hard-working taxpayers to change this system and walk into schools to see if I am lying or telling it straight. This is the one and only way education might change for the better. My hope is that together we become a catalyst for change.

If you are among my six million colleagues, this book will take you through a range of emotions, from hysteria to deep sadness, because no doubt you will have shared similar experiences. The feeling of powerlessness runs rampant through our profession. Teachers have been devalued, disrespected, and beaten up by the system for so long we have become passive. This passivity has made it much worse. The teachers of the '80s and '90s were outspoken and did not or would not tolerate what has now become the norm. "Shut up or else" is the overriding theme. Instead of saying "no longer," "not ok," or "too much," we take it. Our silence is misconstrued as acceptance. We have become too tired and weary to fight what we think we can't change. It's the proverbial double-edged sword—we're damned if we do and damned if we don't. Either way, we lose. If we protest too loud, we could get in trouble, though we know much of what we do is wrong. But we resign ourselves to take the hits. Correct me if I am wrong, but yes, this is happening all over the country, and it is time we admit it. Millions of us are stuck in systems we know are poor and which are cheating millions of children. Where is our conscience?

Parents, be ready. A lot of these words will shock you, but you'll also be encouraged and have hope for your kids. You will learn firsthand that denial ain't gonna work. We have tons of weed, substances, and booze in every school. Now we have vapes, and they too pose a danger. Many schools have problems with violence, sex, and gangs.

If you have a young teen who has been a thorn in your side or a pain in your ass, there's hope. These kids usually figure it out and end up successful unless their support system, which is often their parents or one or more teachers, give up the hope they so dearly need. The delivery, the engagement of the teacher, and the ability to inspire all give hope to challenge and capture the attention of the student and his or her peers. This is everything in teaching. Yet we get caught up in what we teach at the expense of hope and inspiration.

This is not my story. Students from two generations ago, their babies now parents, along with their beloved children, are the characters in this real-life play. Thousands of former students, many of whom have succeeded at life's most challenging tasks, will be put into the spotlight. Despite our inadequacies in this troubled educational system, they have been successful—as providers, moms and dads, and simply *for being good people*. The chapters inside this binding will open the eyes of the public and reveal many heartwarming tales of children who "did good." Four decades of bright flashing eyes. Children with dreams, baggage, happiness, sorrow, and fear. Children who assembled in brick-and-mortar buildings and made them vibrant. *Children who took on life.*

The meaning and purpose to their existence was largely formed inside the walls of classrooms where lessons, both good and bad, were learned.

Values were often cemented by teachers who cared more about the child than their own subject matter.

The most astounding thing? Thousands of families are now living with more meaning, substance, finances, and togetherness because their parents and grandparents embraced what we offered. Where they came from didn't matter as much as where they were going. And the best-kept secret? As a collective group, many started with little or nothing. What they have accomplished as a group of Denver families has been nothing short of monumental.

This could be the story of similar school districts in other large metropolitan areas. Sadly, this storyline is often untold—lost—because nobody from the inside has chronicled and documented what is most important in any flourishing community. The struggles that have been overcome, the barriers, the obstacles, and the failures and successes are what define thousands of you. From the bottom of my heart, I'm proud of you. Thank you.

Chapter One

It's Time

Time to dismantle. To tear it down. Pretty dramatic lead in. But though I've tried, there is no better way to say it. Together we will break down the walls of a public school system that has cheated our children and robbed and stripped them of what could have been. A system in which cultural awareness is almost non-existent and institutional racism and bias run rampant right in front of our eyes. This same system tells untruths and has for decades, and sadly, until now, people—lots of them—believe the lies. We'll start locally, and hopefully a movement will spread across a broader spectrum that will lead to change past our own city limits and state boundaries.

The Denver Public School system, once proud, is now floundering. With fourteen thousand employees, some are part of the problem. But many have been tenderized, beaten down by a layered management system that flipped to a business model many years ago and stayed that way. The treatment of people, our own people, is terrible. But sadly, it is overshadowed by the neglect and deceit that cheats our children on a daily basis. Thousands of people are going about their business, afraid to come forward for fear of reprimand, reprisal, or dismissal.

If the status quo is allowed to remain, our inability to adjust to change and inspire our children and staff will result in an outcome like those in other metropolitan areas. An exodus started long ago and will continue unchecked until we end up with tens of thousands of empty chairs, given up to our private, suburban counterparts. Already, several thousand students are homeschooled, and nobody cares. These are hidden and forgotten children and families.

The arrogance among district leaders and our school board has led to procedures and methods which, when implemented, shut down our schools. Except for school operating hours, the buildings sit empty and unwelcoming, and not just on vacation days. Destinations which could be gathering places are off-limits and often fenced and chained. What happened to the school as the hub? The focal point in the neighborhood? Yet we fund them with tax dollars and throw more mill levy and bond money to enhance, build, and improve them.

Our staff and faculty should be a cross section reflecting the rich diversity of the city population, but we are not even close. Our teaching staff is among the least diverse of any large-city school system. Our students don't have teachers who share common ground. The teachers are not from their countries; they don't know about the students' culture, religion, or foods; and they know little if anything about their lives and daily routines.

Who is at fault? We have a quarter-century-long history of flat test scores and minimal progress, especially among our children of color. Do we step up to the plate and implement actionable methods to change this? Sadly, no. But we do have blame—lots of it. We have all the patented excuses at our fingertips. Our parents are responsible. Our minority children. Our English language learners. Then we are told, like we didn't know, that so much of our population is on free-and-reduced lunch. These reasons and excuses get stated, restated, and verbalized all over our district, and this somehow makes it acceptable.

Excuse me? Being in one of these nicely identified groups presents opportunities, not obstacles. There are hundreds—no, *thousands* of children—who started behind but caught up. Some had nothing but a dream, yet they transcended what we all thought they could become. And still, we let ourselves off the hook constantly by using the same rhetoric that has worked for years while those in the big chairs feel a sense of relief, but they should not.

Now is the perfect time to expose the dysfunction in the system. In our city, it's called reform. This educational catastrophe is labeled as an important change necessary for the children of the 2020s. In reality, it's a nightmare—a system of mediocrity or less and a lack of accountability across the board—which is conducive to non-achievement, hidden agendas, and kids deeply impacted by a system that rarely holds them accountable. Our leaders in the big chairs have ignored entire communities who are historically underserved. Their preparation for college or the brutal real world is non-existent, while we espouse the exact opposite. We are creating a generation that is struggling more than ever and are the least prepared and most failure-prone generation of all time. Yes, dear readers, we own this mess, and it is time you know all our little hidden secrets. After this long, I am shocked it hasn't all been exposed. It is blatant, and the DPS continues the cycle.

The time is past due to let our public know of the coverups, mismanagement, and lack of respect to those who wear (or are supposed to wear) the DPS badge. The reason I write is to let the children, all the parents, and others who support us know what goes on. Our supportive neighbors need to know about our real experiences. We say we are doing a representative job of providing the education we espouse, and it is time to share.

Why? Good question. Am I an author or an educational expert? Am I famous or well known? No, to both questions. I am putting the proverbial pen to paper (which I really do) for many reasons. This is not meant to be an autobiography. The information related to me is background, so you'll know who I am. In a nutshell, I am a career teacher and coach at my alma mater, George Washington High School, in Denver, Colorado. Year forty-three has been a challenge as we have emerged from the pandemic with new obstacles, and needs we never imagined.

This is the story of the families who have joined me and embraced me in many situations as part of their own. I have become intertwined with so many wonderful people who were instrumental in making this journey an unforgettable one. Someone needs to tell the story along with its many subplots.

I could be any teacher in any number of large metropolitan areas. Our city, the mile-high city of Denver, is unique. Nowadays in Denver we have one large newspaper and many media outlets. It was taboo for a long time to slam the schools. From the 1970s through the '90s, the newspapers (there were more at that time) would rip us to shreds. They told it, reported it, and released it. We got no breaks. Daily, ad nauseam, the print media, radio, and television outlets reported on our bad test scores, poor teaching, violence, bad budgeting, and on and on. Running commentaries blasted nearly everything we did as educators and schools. How times have changed. Somewhere in the early- to mid-2000s, there was a shift, as if someone with extreme power began controlling the media. They convinced someone, or a lot of someones, that all the negativity was hurting our fine city, and it was. But rather than continue to seek the truth, the media backed off and allowed the Denver Public Schools to inundate them with public relations fluff. We have had more fluff and positive press in the last decade than ever. The DPS began to tout themselves as the best large-city school district in the country.

A few people believed this, and many who had been quite critical started to back off. Rarely did we then have negative press or coverage blasting our schools. The perception became, by some, that the schools were performing and doing a helluva job. The reports were glowing. Suspensions were down, violence had decreased, and yes, don't worry, we were doing a masterful job of preparing the kids, *all of them*, for college. I wish this were all true, but sadly, it is, as the kids would say, just hype. Except for a few places, our educational system is in the tank.

The pendulum has now swung the other way. People are questioning and using their voices, beginning to wonder what in the hell we are doing. And truly, their voices are what we need. People need to be aware of what is happening in the schools. As people become aware, the movement to better our schools can begin. This complex and tainted system has been substandard for so long that the hill is steep. We have become used to the nightmare we call our public school system. Many people gave up, and those who were vocal were silenced by managers who are experts at stalling and only pretending to listen.

You may be wondering why I have chosen to enter my retirement years this way. As people near retirement, they are either miserable or they're quiet, tired, and subdued. They count the days to the fake gold watch. They can be found cleaning up golf clubs or fishing poles, or they take up a post-retirement hobby and wait to cross the finish line. I am wired a different way. I feel guilt, and I can't sit on it any longer, softly fading away into the sunset like so many in my profession. I am the snitch, the thorn, the whistle-blower, the informant, and the rat. This message won't be popular among our highly paid central admin, our board, and many important leaders. They have an inkling of what is about to be exposed, as we met once. I requested a meeting in 2020 with our then-superintendent, and only after they realized I wasn't going to disappear did they reluctantly schedule a virtual meeting, seventy days after my request. In their collective opinion, I probably know far too much, and they know it is all going to be disclosed. They are no doubt threatened by this, but due to their arrogance and self-importance it won't really matter, at least for a while. If together we demand change, we might have a different storyline with a different outcome. The task is monumental. In this system that is so good at dodging, deflecting, and hitting the pause button, rarely do the people in power get rattled or nervous, but it's time.

Chapter Two

How Did I Get Here?

I was sure. No wavering. I would be a veterinarian. I had a virtual menagerie at the house as a kid, right in the city. My love for animals was so deep that I was able to raise orphaned skunks, raccoons, and deer right in our backyard. We always had dogs as pets, then a kinkajou who is a cousin of the raccoon but more nocturnal. Igor's owner couldn't take care of him. The steady stream of kids from the neighborhood who wanted to see, pet, feed, or play with these creatures was constant. Once the orphaned animals were mature enough, a nice man from the Fish and Game Department would pick them up and transport them to a ranch where they would live in bliss. No hunters, lots of food, and others like themselves would live on a large spread.

I did this for two or three years until I started college, dedicated to the beginning of my pre-veterinary training. College started, and I was living the dream. A little studying, playing ball, lots of friends, and dozens of cute girls living under our roof in the co-ed—yes, the co-ed—dorm. It was time, after a couple of months, to drive from Greeley to Fort Collins, home of the Colorado State School of Veterinary Medicine. I called the school, and they were kind enough to invite me to go on a tour. I was primed. I took the forty-five-minute drive and met with an instructor. He took me on a journey where I observed research animals—dogs, cats, monkeys, and large-hoofed animals.

The professor asked if I wanted to see the surgery center. Pretty cool! In one room there were three dogs, out cold and hooked up to a breathing machine, tongues pulled out and clipped with a clothespin device to ensure that man's best friend would not choke on its own tongue. The incapacitated hounds looked scary with their ten-inch tongues lolling out. One stinky-breathed dog having his teeth cleaned had some serious plaque build-up. Gross! The next was being neutered, and I could feel his pain. The last was having some type of abdominal surgery. The vet student and the veteran teacher were up to their elbows in dog intestines. This was a bad visual, both educational and gory as hell.

Next I was ushered into a large warehouse-looking building. No small mammals here. This was the large animal surgery center. I immediately saw a large bovine, half-standing, hoisted by two large straps with its feet barely off the floor. The master teacher was with two pale-looking vet students who appeared quite nauseated. He explained that the cow had an intestinal obstruction.

The doctor, who was not bashful with the scalpel, made a quick incision. He cut a flap of skin on the side of this milk- and meat-producing creature. The intestines, spleen, and other pink and red visceral parts were exposed, and in about fifteen seconds the blood began to flow. So that's what the large stainless steel tray was for. Within minutes the tray was full of blood. But no worries. A guy in a white trench coat took it and replaced it with another.

I had to sit down quickly. At that moment, my dreams of being an animal doctor were crushed. With each drop of blood my career choice was unraveling. The blood, the guts, the euthanasia, and the precision were not in line with how I was wired. I couldn't do it.

Driving back to Greeley from Fort Collins proved to be the perfect time to change my career choice. I had an epiphany. I would be a social worker. Once back at my dorm I hurriedly looked at the course catalog. I was going to take an "Intro to Social Work" class.

I was eager to get started. How noble was my new chosen profession. I would help people. I would be a saint, a Jewish male, a double extra-large version of Mother Teresa. I sprinted to class on that first January day and walked into a small classroom.

The room held nine of us, and I was the youngest. Interesting. The professor came in, a bit disheveled and quite disorganized, but hey, he didn't need to be organized. This class wasn't like that.

"Call me Jerry," he said.

Damn, this was amazing. I had never called an adult by their first name, but hell, I was game. No doctor or mister when Jerry was around. He had us arrange our chairs into a ten-foot circle, then proclaimed, "We will start our first activity." Unique. I had never been in this situation before. We didn't even do the circle thing in kindergarten.

The professor went deep. He clenched his jaw. "I have been suppressing my feelings, and that's not healthy. My marriage is on the rocks. I am not sure how long I will stay at the university. I'm very depressed." He teared up. "My marriage is on the rocks, and she's going to leave me." He ranted, raved, cried, and pleaded.

Eight other students were mesmerized and sympathized with this dude's inner feelings. After a few more minutes he heaved a sigh of relief and let us know how much better he felt. Wow. He turned to the girl next to him, and asked, quite femininely, that she go next.

Oh damn. My turn, right after her drama. I had no baggage I could think of. I barely heard what she was saying, but judging from the reaction of seven undergrads and a hippie-like prof, she was getting deep. She talked about her relationship with her mom, her Aunt Hilda, her issues in school, and her manic depression. Poor thing was crying and hugging Jerry, who was also shedding tears. I tried to cry but couldn't. I thought of sad things. I squinted my eyes. Nothing worked. The girl finished and all eyes were on me. What could I say?

"Well..." I paused, buying some time, but not enough. They were staring, waiting for me to expose my feelings. I continued to pause, still trying to manufacture some tears, all the while grimacing like someone was choking me. Jerry told me to "let it go, deal with the sadness," except I wasn't sad, and I was not angry. I had not suppressed anything. Yet I knew that wasn't going to cut it with this group. Our way of getting to know each other was to cry, sniffle, and expose our brutal memories. Finally, I closed my eyes for one last time, trying to make sense of this introductory lesson.

I got it! They wanted drama! I was about to give it to them. I whispered, "I am in pain. I am in so much pain that I can't even talk about it. I can't discuss it because it's too raw." I continued. "Please, let me work through this on my own." There it was. I had now laid out the biggest crock of crap I had ever come up with, and they bought it. They went on to the next guy, who was bawling. How I felt wasn't anyone's business. I had a nice childhood and didn't know or want to know any of these touchy-feely folks. Social work was out, done like an overcooked steak.

I had another revelation. I would be a teacher and coach. I was taking science already and could be a science teacher and a physical education teacher. But one last hurdle remained. I had to tell Papa. Papa had pulled himself up by the bootstraps from humble beginnings to the Federal bench. He started with nothing and became quite renowned. His oldest son had already declared that he would be a doctor or lawyer, the younger sister had assured Dad she would hold multiple degrees, and then there was me. I was so steadfast about becoming a veterinarian for so long I was scared to death to tell him, so I didn't update him on my change of plans. I assumed he would insist I stay with the veterinarian thing or go into the study of law, like he did.

I stammered out the words. "Dad...I want to be a teacher and coach."

The pause lasted for about a minute. He looked at me with those deep blue-green eyes, tears forming. I teared up with him, not knowing why. "Good for you, son! Be the best you can be. Help the kids—all the kids—they need you."

I hugged him, not minding the gouging of his thick whiskers or the lingering smell of the Aqua Velva cologne he splashed on every day. It was over; I had told him. What a relief. This major hurdle was cleared. Not only did I have Papa's blessing, I also had his support. His support didn't end there. He watched hundreds of football games and wrestling matches, heard me speak at graduation, and shared laughs and tears, both happy and sad. He asked a couple of times if I might consider being a principal, and when I explained that I didn't want that, he again supported me. That's it, in a nutshell. Now, after four decades, I sit amazed at how this school system and public education has changed so dramatically.

I didn't quite get it when Papa would stare at me and proclaim, what to him, should have been obvious. "Son, loyalty is about as thin as this piece of paper." He would grab a piece of paper, any piece of paper, to emphasize this point. "But when you find it [loyalty], embrace it with all your heart." He meant it. Papa felt that an individual or an organization's success and value was tied directly to their level of loyalty. I get it. It just took a while.

Preparation

After getting my dad's approval and blessing, I was determined to be a double major of sorts.

I took the necessary physical education classes and made sure I also took the required science classes during that defining freshman year. Then spring ball started and here I was. After a redshirt fall developing my skills, I was determined to get on the field, though I was only 220 pounds, trying to be a contributor on the offensive or defensive lines.

I did well (I thought), but I learned later that I was too undersized and lacked the talent to play college football at the Division 2 level.

Spring ball ended and we all had to arrange a meeting with the head coach. I signed up and waited for that day. After a decent high school career where I was named "athlete of the year" as a senior at George Washington High, I was sure I would be considered for a scholarship and retained for the next fall. Back then, George Washington, with nearly three thousand students, was considered a school rich in athletic talent. But this day, I was wrong.

The head coach brought me in and floored me with his cold, calculated words.

"Finesilver, you are awfully small, and God didn't bless you with size or talent. We aren't going to bring you back in the fall."

I felt small and humiliated. With tears in my eyes, I nodded. For years I regretted not saying anything that day. As I left his office, I cried openly that he had cut me from the team and had been quite heartless about it.

I lived to play sports. I had chosen football over wrestling where I had been recruited by several good-sized schools. I didn't drink or smoke, and I lived the way I though a school athlete was supposed to.

I lost purpose. I was embarrassed to tell people I was not allowed or anointed to return to the team because a coach who was deemed an expert decided that the Lord had not blessed me with size, skill, or whatever he thought necessary to compete on the team. For five days I believed him and spent most of my time in my dorm room feeling quite sorry for myself. Then my thinking flipped, and I was angry.

I realized the coach's proclamation was not sacred. After checking, I found nobody had enshrined him or prayed to him. I asked around and learned he had done this with a lot of other Jewish and minority kids—yes, he cut them loose. His team lacked diversity and he had earned a reputation for running kids off in a similar manner.

By then I had told my dad, and he and Mom encouraged me to give up ball or beg to return after working out through the summer. I chose neither and started a regimen. That coach was wrong and I knew it, but proving it was something different.

I worked construction that summer, and between 5:00 and 6:00 p.m. I was in the weight room. After two to three hours of weights each day, I did sprints, ran hills, and finished with two hundred pushups and a hundred fifty sit-ups.

I returned to the University of Northern Colorado the next fall and had reached out to other programs for a chance to join their team. At my expense I visited the University of Nebraska at Omaha, Ball State, and one or two other schools.

A coach who had been a graduate assistant at UNC was in law school at Washburn University. He talked to the staff at Washburn, and they reached out and offered me a scholarship—three hundred dollars—and I took it.

Though it was only September, I called and thanked them for the offer and told them I would be there after the first semester had ended. I continued to work out. At 4:15 p.m. each day I would run from the dorm to the football field and stretch while my previous teammates were drilling. Once they left I did my sprints, and then at six o'clock I would sneak into the weight room and lift, then do my pushups and sit-ups. On their scale I was up to 240 pounds, and my lifting numbers were nearing UNC's strongest lifters.

Washburn University—Topeka, Kansas

Months earlier, I was overjoyed when they committed three hundred dollars, and now they had bumped me up to what was a pretty good package, with only room and board left. Coach Elliott continued to say they had recommended me to be an RA. A resident assistant is on call eight or ten hours a week while living in the dorm. This would take care of the rest of my expenses, and I was trying to do the math in my head.

He beat me to it. He explained they were essentially taking care of all my expenses. I was able to play ball, take 15–18 credit hours, bunk in the dorm, and eat well at no cost to my family. I thanked him, with a sense of relief. My hard work had paid off at getting school covered, but I still hadn't been on the field. I spent the rest of that spring wrapping up finals and taking my training to a new level. I went on a more serious lifting, running, and eating schedule. When I returned for two-a-days, I was nearly 275 pounds and lifting a pretty good amount. More importantly, I had been on the track, the field, and running stairs, sprints, and hills. I made sure to do hundreds of starts and stances each week. This monotonous chore entails simply getting into a stance and running ten-yard sprints, the curse of not being smart enough for a "thinking" position on the field or athletic enough to play a position where you actually touch the ball.

Camp started, my numbers were good on the testing of lifts and runs, and I passed the physical. I began camp as a starter from spring workouts months earlier. I was not about to give up pursuit of what I had only thought about previously. Camp ended and I was officially named a starter, at right guard. In the eyes of the coaches, I had earned it. There was some resentment on the team, but it faded quickly as I made friends with Nando, Keeley, Curly, Danny, CT, Grogan, and the rest of the bunch. I was quiet and reserved and felt I had something to prove. Never able to lose that mentality, I was driven by my previous failure—getting cut from the squad back in Colorado.

Soon we were playing games, and I remember one vividly. Not the game or my performance, but the start of the game. The opponent is now nameless, as many games are, but the moment is unforgettable. My mom and dad were at the game. We had gone through the pregame warmups, and introductions were about to begin. The opponents had chosen to introduce their defensive starters. We were in the tunnel-like area and heard the announcer say "...and the Washburn offensive starters...". They introduced five or six of my teammates and finally, "From Denver, Colorado, at right guard—Steve Finesilver."

As I sprinted from the back of the end zone, I looked up to the third row, just above our bench on the sideline at the 50-yard line. Tears streamed down my face, and I caught a glimpse of my dad with matching tears on his cheeks. We were feeling many of the same emotions. Mostly we shed tears of happiness and a bit of relief. This and many similar moments took place as he was able to see me play many games, even some in other cities where we competed.

I played with anger—and heart. I played with the passion of someone with something to prove on every play. I was fortunate to receive honors and accolades that now make no difference. After a huge dinner with their Uncle Nando, my children asked about my football training and career and, much to my disapproval, Uncle Nando told them of their father's antics and accomplishments.

School was easier, though I was both a science and physical education major. Hell, two majors didn't phase me. I was playing ball! I even made the Dean's list several times, and after my senior year I hit the graduation stage. Mom, Dad, Sis, and Bro came out. I graduated on a Saturday afternoon. I put my belongings in the truck and drove early Sunday morning back to Denver. The goodbyes were tough. I had found a home away from home where I was accepted.

Unfinished Business

A week after graduation I was with Dad back home in Colorado watching the ten o'clock news when the president of the University of Northern Colorado was interviewed. He was asking for residents of Colorado to call or even make an appointment to see him and talk about their experiences with their fine university. Papa and I had the same thought after seeing his plea. We called and set up an appointment with the president, the head football coach, and his assistant, who had gone back to recruit at my high school the year after I had been axed. They told them I wasn't very good and could not make their team. Dad and I didn't even talk about the meeting on the hour-long drive to Greeley.

We arrived and the secretary asked us to wait a moment for the other parties. As we entered the president's office I made sure to sit, a bit strategically, right next to the coach who had belittled me four years earlier. The president, Dr. Bond, was a good dude, and he asked what we had to discuss. He wasn't prepared for what we had to say, nor was the head coach and his trash-talking sidekick.

My dad started. He referred to the coach as "mister," not worthy in either of our eyes to be called a coach.

"Do you remember why you eliminated Steve from the team years ago? What was the problem?"

The shallow man looked over at me. I was 280 pounds, wearing a flannel shirt and muscled out from years in the weight room, much different than the 230-pound eighteen-year-old he had dismissed years earlier.

"Well...back then Steve was pretty small?" he stammered, sounding pretty foolish. All eyes were on him, and that was the best he could muster up? We waited for more while he squirmed.

My dad took over. "Are you aware of what happened after Steve left?"

The president and the two men were on the hot seat. No, they hadn't done their homework, but they did not need to. Papa reached into his briefcase and handed each of them several articles from various news outlets along with several football media guides, with dozens more ready to share. The three looked nervously through the materials Dad gave them and two were speechless, while the president was clearly agitated.

I took my turn. I stood up and pointed down at the head coach. "Last time I saw you I was an eighteen-year-old kid. You told me I was no good and that it was God's fault I was too slow and too small. You spoke down to me like I was worthless, and you were wrong!"

The coach said, "Calm down, you don't need to talk like that."

But I did need to, so I continued, with Dr. Bond's quiet approval. "You tried to break me and make me feel like a failure and you have done that with others, but I succeeded in spite of you. I accomplished more than the guys you kept on the team." After that sunk in I finished with "I should thank you—you have helped me learn that nobody will ever set boundaries or determine what I can or can't do."

As I sat down, I saw an upset university president and two small, verbally beaten men. They had done this before, but now they had to deal with the wrath of the big boss. The president apologized on behalf of the university that they had failed me and essentially forced me to get my education and play ball out of state. He shook our hands and directed the men to stay with him for continued discussion. They barely looked up as we left, exposed and uncomfortable now as they had to clarify their misdeeds.

As Papa and I drove back, there was no review or rejoicing. We had done what needed to be done. We had "manned up" and told a true story, and we both knew without a doubt that we had fought back so truth would be known and would prevail.

The experience imprinted so much of what I know and what I do. After fifty-five collective seasons of coaching, I have never cut or eliminated a kid who was too small or not talented. I have been wise to the fact that children grow and mature at different rates. More importantly, I learned the importance of failure as a road to success. We all fail, all the time. I have even failed at this...until now. Yes, I confess, writing this story and this book has been an endeavor I never thought would come to fruition. Why now? I have a believer—an inspirer who believes in me. My editor and dear friend, Ms. Grabau, a saint—has encouraged me every step of the way. No doubt she could have rejected me as editors often do but she didn't, and I love her for this!

Failure, I have learned, is powerful. Not the failure itself, but what we do with it is our personal essence and what truly defines us—right?

Chapter Three

I Entered the Fray

They were spellbound! I had them in the palm of my hands. These tough, streetwise ninth graders were cringing at the thought of me, Mr. Finesilver! My 280-pound frame, still muscular, was squeezed into a red short-sleeved shirt and a tight pair of slacks. My skin was brown from several summer months of working on the construction crew, my usual summer job, one I'll never forget. I was on rule number seven; my voice was loud. I was the dominant creature in a room full of twenty-five troubled adolescents. I began my tirade about the sins of being late when the back door swung open. In walked a small freckle-faced girl, twenty minutes late the first day of school. Yes! She was to be my example.

"Excuse me, miss!" I bellowed. "You may not be late to my class." The vein in my forehead was pulsing. Surely, I had made an impression.

This pint-sized girl sauntered up to the front of the room and stood before me, her head barely above my beltline. Up came the middle finger, nearly touching my nose. "Mr., just kiss my ass!"

The class went insane. I sat down at my desk. My cheeks flushed and I was unable to speak. My little darlings proceeded to argue—about my ethnicity!

Right on Margaret, way to tell off that Indian! He's not Indian, he's Greek! He isn't Greek, he's Italian! Way to go Margaret, he ain't s——t!

I sat in disbelief. My five years of college readiness and student teaching had left out this scenario. I was unprepared that day as well as that entire school year.

It would be nice to say I made an impact my first year, but that would be a lie. The first day exposed that I was a rookie. I was someone to be tested and to disrespect, someone to dog. I made feeble attempts to teach but was tossed aside in only minutes. I had wasted a lot of my students' time. I did, however, learn a hell of a lot. Thankfully, I gained valuable insight into many issues that year.

Surprise, surprise. These kids were different. I had been raised in a middle-class home, with a dad who worked hard and a mom who worked at home doing household duties. I had a brother, a sister, and a dog. I always had parental direction, someone to keep me in line when needed, and food in the fridge. Sure, I had been a substitute teacher in Topeka, Kansas, but those kids were in awe of me as a football player in town, not as a teacher. They liked me, but they didn't respect me. How could I capture this elusive concept called respect? Hence, lesson number one.

A few teachers, I observed, could hold the class in awe. Those teachers could get kids to recite, to reach, to work, and to sweat. I couldn't break through. The more I tried, the worse it got. Suddenly, it became more important for me to be popular than to be respected. I was clueless. Worse yet, these troubled kids began to occupy my time outside of school.

Sherri, not her real name, came to school crying. Her drama was about a dad who had stabbed her mom repeatedly the night before. Mom survived. How? I don't know. I lost a week of sleep worrying about this girl as I saw her sadness engulf and consume her.

Frank, also not his real name, got thrown in jail. The jail was appropriately named "The Gill," short for the Gilliam Juvenile Detention Center. Frank beat a kid and knocked him down a flight of stairs. To this day, I don't know what happened to the victim. Afterward, I had an insightful discussion with our school social worker. Now when I looked at Bob's hands and arms, I understood the round scars were from years of abuse. He had been burned with cigarettes for even minor indiscretions and would shamefully carry the scars, both physical and mental, for the rest of his life. I had a girl in class who was molested by her father. Another girl had been shot, and she rarely went home. At thirteen, her life was on the streets. She was out of control, living a life that made her look like a twenty-five-year-old woman. Another girl worked the streets. She reported to her man, her pimp, and survived only if she could find enough johns to fuel her and her pimp's drug habit.

Two or three of my kids were into drug use and got high early in the school day. It took me three months to realize that Don, a small kid who sat in the back, didn't suffer from hay fever. His red eyes were from his dad's weed. Sometimes he smoked weed with Dad. I spent thirty minutes one morning describing our upcoming full-day excursion to the Denver Zoo. The kids were excited. I asked if there were any questions. Don raised his hand. That day, his eyes were the color of red delicious apples. I reluctantly called on him.

"Yo, dude, what time's this skurjan begin, man?" The class became hysterical. Once again, I was at a loss. I had no idea what to do. About halfway through this, my first semester, I was fried. I had gained thirty pounds. I wasn't sleeping. I had no one to make me understand how to help; how to break through. Maybe I was in the wrong profession. I was failing! Here, surrounding me, were children who needed help and who, despite all the sadness, poorness, and violence in their lives, still came to school every day. There was nothing I could do for them. I was helpless.

Coming to school every day had few rewards. Mostly, I felt frustrated. I had trained and prepared to be a teacher, but here I was, just a big, frustrated babysitter. I developed some terrible habits. Every day I tried to be organized and really educate these kids. I woke up early each morning, had a huge breakfast, taught several classes, then had lunch. The ladies in the lunchroom loved me. For one dollar they would give me a huge tray of food, and I downed all of it and washed it down with milk or punch. I then went to my afternoon classes. I had a thirty- or forty-minute break at about 1:30 in the afternoon. I would sprint to the nearest donut shop and have a dozen donuts, then return to school for my afternoon duties and then drive to a local high school where I coached wrestling. By Thanksgiving, I was over three hundred pounds, large and very frustrated.

The kids came to like me, but respect was another story. I had a little knowledge in the classroom material but couldn't convey it to them. At times I talked incessantly, often with no one listening. I had no choice. In my shallow way, I thought I was teaching. I wasn't. These kids were very needy. They were put in this class because they were potential dropouts. They needed serious guidance and serious rules. I gave them neither. At night after my usual fast-food raid, I would do my lesson plans, get in bed, and think for a few minutes. If it had been a tough day at school, I wouldn't sleep well, which contributed to my ineffectiveness and frustration. I had started the year and continued it, never insisting that the students pay attention to me.

Each day repeated the same vicious cycle. Each day I left school, knowing what I had done that day didn't matter. My frequent conversations with my parents were not helpful, because neither had been teachers. They supported me and reassured me that at some point I might make a difference. Looking back now, I'm amazed I didn't quit right then and there. I felt like a cheater. I was earning $11,500 per year for doing nothing. I think that's why I didn't quit. Back then, that was a lot of money. I was happy to have it. I even bought a house. Even though I was doing poorly, both the principal and assistant principal thought I was doing fine. I got a great evaluation and lots of compliments, but it didn't matter. I knew I stunk.

As a whole, the kids seemed so sad, but so willing to try. Despite their individual situations, they came to school every day, most with a good attitude. The bosses thought I was doing well because nobody had been beaten or stabbed. I had done a great job of keeping the lid on the chaos. The kids didn't complain because they didn't know any better. The parents didn't complain because they were not involved. The other teachers didn't whine because they were not teaching this population of kids. They were happy to have somebody else doing it. What an eye opener. The years of planning and all the courses in my student teaching had meant nothing. Not until years later did I realize it is common to be terrible as a new teacher.

It took me a full year to realize I had lost control that first day. Yelling and screaming did not work. Real respect is earned, and anyone can earn it. At least I was astute enough to learn about the kids and their lives. Their world was similar to the world many kids live in today, forty-two years later. I had to develop control. I had to establish boundaries. I had to speak truthfully and softly, but I had to get their attention. Who was I kidding? One man or woman can't compete for airtime against twenty-five or thirty rambunctious teenagers. It won't happen. Ever. A teacher who yells has lost the battle and will never regain control. Teaching 101...so simple; so obvious.

My preparation for life in the classroom had been terrible. One college professor, however, told it like it is. He was honest and accurate. Mr. Sarkesian, at Washburn University, spoke the truth, but I was too full of myself at the time to listen. He used to say, in his thick eastern accent, "Teachers, when you're dealing with the public, you're dealing with the masses, and the masses are asses."

He was right. Student teaching doesn't expose you to what you'll do for the next thirty years. As a student teacher, the real teacher is always either in the room or close by and can save your butt. Plus, the kids don't take you seriously; they regard you as a peer. You're someone to lie to, cheat in front of, or be tested. First-year teachers are not much better. In an instant, the kids size you up, display their laziness in front of you, and use you for their fun pranks. Why don't we change the way we teach teachers? Few will argue that our new teachers struggle with control, behavior, and respect. We need to wake up. Teachers need to be prepared, and in the current system, they are not.

What can we do about this? First, the student-teaching process should include classes about multicultural education. Some of this could be learned at a desk. Better yet, these teachers should go into the communities where their kids reside. Our children come from homes, neighborhoods, and communities which help explain their behaviors, habits, abilities, and so forth. Simply, there are reasons why kids act out. The reason kids fight, why they don't do homework, and why they achieve can be found in the homes, the places of worship, and in the neighborhoods. Aspiring teachers need to be out in the community in their junior year, learning and observing. What an eye opener that would be. What a wake-up call to these prospective teachers. This rarely happens, and it should.

Next, the teachers need to learn how to set rules, guidelines, and expectations. They should have to write these expectations out in detail and present them to their peers and supervising teachers. Many new teachers have no expectations and just wing it. It should be mandatory for each new teacher to outline exactly how they will handle twenty or thirty key situations or scenarios. I assure you this is not taking place—not now. We do a terrible job getting our new teachers ready.

We're rolling now. The next step is to pair the teacher with four or five more experienced teachers for observation of their teaching methods on a rotating basis. Allow them to see what works and what doesn't. They will see how and why teachers become powerful and dynamic. Let them see why some veteran teachers are boring and ineffective. They need to observe in the classroom to see how others do it. Let them learn a style that will work for them. They will adopt some methods and toss out others, thus making and owning their own style.

Gove Middle School

So there I was, floundering around teaching at Gove Middle School. I learned about teaching while observing the characteristics of junior high school kids who would soon be high school students. In April that year, I received a call asking me to interview for a position at the new high school named "Montbello." During the interview, they pulled no punches. I was told they needed a white teacher and coach at this predominantly minority school. I would teach physical education and be an assistant football coach. The perk was that I would be the head wrestling coach. I apparently interviewed well because they offered me the job on the spot. I accepted, then winced when they told me they didn't ever expect our wrestlers to win any matches because Montbello was a basketball school.

I didn't get too put off by this. I knew we'd be tougher than an old boot in wrestling. I knew I would be reassigned in the fall, yet I had unfinished business at Gove Junior High. I spent the last several months at Gove taking a new approach. I sat my students down every chance I got. I had a desire to learn from them after they trusted me enough to open up. I became increasingly amazed at how they were able to function at all in the school setting. Now I had vivid details about kids who went home and took care of three or four other children. Mom had to work to pay rent or buy food. In some situations, kids were raised by their grandmother or grandparents. Rearing kids as sixty- and seventy-year-old grandparents is hard. Much harder than keeping up with teenagers in your thirties. Imagine what it's like to raise two generations of kids.

Some kids invited me into their homes and apartments. In about half the situations, the kids functioned better than the parents. I saw firsthand what poverty meant. One girl lived with her mom and siblings in a room scarcely larger than a college dormitory room with no privacy. This bird's-eye view of reality changed my perspective.

I began to look for the good in kids, something I still do today. That first group of kids at Gove Junior High had a couple of singers, a cartoon artist, some gifted athletes, and a little girl who wrote beautiful poetry. Too bad it took me nearly the whole year to realize these talents were there all the time, hidden beneath the rough-and-tough exteriors these kids assumed daily. By June, I had gotten a clue about kids, homes, and families doing life and the importance of earning respect. The school year ended, and almost all my crew went to continuation and made plans to enter high school.

I started working on the transition to Montbello High School. I was going to teach in the physical education department and would be an assistant football coach and head wrestling coach. The summer of 1980 was unforgettable. I was once again doing labor on the construction crews and going out to Montbello High for football workouts a few evenings a week.

Early one evening, I was heading into the school and noticed a group of kids huddled near the parking lot. Before I could tell what was happening, one of the kids clocked another kid in the head with a metal pipe. In a split-second, the kid who had been hit, with his head bleeding profusely, delivered an uppercut that knocked the original hoodlum out cold. It took several minutes for me to revive him. Ultimately, the paramedics took him for more serious attention. The kid who had been smashed in the head was headed home as if nothing had happened.

"Not so fast," I said. I made sure he was okay, and he assured me he was. He again headed for home on foot, but not before I insisted he come out for football and wrestling. He promised to do both and lived up to his promise. That day too was an eye-opener. The positive in it was that we would have at least one tough kid on the team. We ended up with a bunch.

Chapter Four

Getting Respect

Montbello High

What a great place. Kids who had been riding the school bus for an hour-and-a-half or more each day would now have their own neighborhood school in far Northeast Denver. It was built on two levels, with ramps instead of stairs. The sprawling building had pods for different subject areas. The planners, however, designed this structure with thirty-four entrances and sixty-eight doors. What was thought to be cutting-edge design became a supervision nightmare.

With great excitement, including speeches by politicians and school dignitaries, Montbello Junior/Senior High School opened its doors in 1980. With new support staff, teachers, students, and administrators, settling in took some time, as is the case with all new schools.

I loved my new job but started almost as ineffectively as I had my first year. As I look back, I see that some important moments took place. That year put me on the road to teacher worthiness.

First, word had somehow leaked out that I had wrestled Victor the wrestling bear. Legend had it that Victor had beaten thousands of foes until the match with me in Kansas City. Victor was a Canadian black bear. He stood over seven feet tall and tipped the scales at over six hundred pounds. Plus. And he could wrestle! Long story short, some of the kids wanted to see this match on videotape. I obliged, and this started a buzz around the school that a teacher actually wrestled and defeated Victor the wrestling bear. But the bear-wrestling experience didn't help my football coaching a bit. These youngsters didn't care at all who or what I had wrestled. I was invisible as a coach when we started. My requests to get in line or to hit the sled, to block this way or tackle that way, went ignored.

Finally, I'd had enough. It was time to let them know just who I was. In the middle of the drill, which was going really badly, I said, "Get low and block with your knees bent!"

One smart mouth muttered, "Well, why don't you show us?"

I blew my whistle. Enough was enough. I got a hand shield and tossed it to Big Steve. Twenty-three linemen gathered around. I explained that I would get in a stance and Steve would line up, armed with a protective bag also, ten yards away. One kid would give the snap count, and we would meet full force in the middle. There was bedlam!

The kids, now cheerleaders, yelled, "Knock that white man out, Steve!" They screamed, "Kick his ass, Steve! Run him off! Hurt him!"

For a moment, I wondered what in hell I was doing. Here was Steve, all two hundred fifty pounds of him. He was jumping up and down, the artery in his neck pulsating like a giant snake, the earring hanging out of his helmet glistening in the sun. As I assumed my stance, my knees were popping from too damn much football. There was no doubt. Steve was going to try to brutalize me.

"Down...set...hut...hut...hut!" The appointed player–coach was enjoying giving us the snap count. The cheers of the crowd of kids who were mostly bigger than me had grown louder. The sound was deafening. I sprinted forward—so did Steve! We collided fifteen feet from where we started. A moment passed as we slammed loudly into each other, then a split second of eerie silence ensued. In the next blink of an eye, Steve was airborne. He went up and did three-fourths of a back flip. His helmet flew east, his earring south, and the hand shield kind of northwest. Again, it fell silent. There was no doubt now about who was in charge.

Now, with my back turned toward the crew, I said, "Get in a line."

I waited for no more than five seconds to face my charges, and when I turned, they had formed the most perfect line I had ever seen. It was beautiful. In front was Big Steve, with a bruised ego and some very hurt feelings. Behind him was Dennis, who a year later signed with the

University of Arizona. And Arnold, who played at the University of Colorado. Oscar, who played at Northwestern University. They looked like statues, standing in that line. Coaching suddenly became a lot more enjoyable. Big Steve ultimately played for the Nebraska Cornhuskers before transferring and playing for the Iowa Hawkeyes. Quite a résumé, for my first year of coaching.

Again, word traveled throughout the school. Kids in class started to listen, and finally, to respond. I had an identity. People were beginning to know who Coach Fino was! While this opened some eyes, not all were impressed. But that would soon change. Wrestling had started.

Remember the Big Leo story? Leo was that kid who had been hit in the head with a pipe. He was tough and played football. He was feared in the hood and undefeated in wrestling. He had, however, become a huge pain in the butt. I had been partially responsible for the proverbial creation of a monster. Leo's ego was getting too large. He had gotten about four sizes too big for his britches. I had spoken to him repeatedly about humility, about not being a braggart, and about keeping a low profile. He didn't care. He would answer "Yes, Coach," but in truth, he thought he was the toughest dude in the valley. He began challenging me, but I found it laughable. His words didn't faze me until he began to confront me in front of the team.

"Coach, I can even handle you. Coach. When will you wrestle me?"

I chalked his mouth up to attention-getting and ignored him. He was just a kid, young and green. He simmered down for the most part, then he won a couple more matches. His conceit reignited.

As practice ended one day, the challenge came. "Coach, you must be a sissy!" he said.

I looked at him.

"You're afraid to wrestle me," he said.

I dismissed practice. He'd hit a nerve. As the team was leaving the practice room, I called him back, along with his buddy Reggie. Reggie was allowed to be the lone spectator. We closed the doors to the wrestling room. The room was still smelly and musty from a brutal practice. Wrestlers and wrestling coaches love and appreciate this smell.

Leo was elated. "Okay Leo. Here's the deal," I explained. "We are going to do takedowns. When you take me down, I have to put my hands down to my sides. And you get to slap me as hard as you want, across the face."

"Cool!" Leo said.

"Now if by some chance I get lucky and take you down—"

He interrupted. "That won't happen."

I repeated myself. "Now if by some chance I get lucky and take you down, then I get to slap you!"

He agreed.

Reggie sat on the stool, his eyes as big as saucers.

Leo was pretty strong. We tussled for about ten seconds, and I executed a duck-under and got behind him for the takedown.

He was angry. "That was luck!"

"I know, Leo, but a deal is a deal." I reared back and smacked him with a sharp slap. Not too hard, but I had cracked him right across the face. Reggie's eyes got bigger. Leo began to hyperventilate. He wanted another turn! *Okay, cool,* I thought. *Let's get ready for round two.*

This time, I chose again to tie up with him. I waltzed around with him for about thirty seconds and then quickly, BOOM...*Boom!* I had caught him with a fireman's carry. He hit the mat—hard—but jumped right back up.

"No, no!" he screamed.

I said quietly. "Leo, first the slap." This time, he quickly glued his hands and arms to his sides. I decided it wasn't fair to neglect my backhand. *Crack!* The back of my hand went across his face a bit harder, but still not hard enough to hurt anything except his stubborn pride. He was just plain pissed. He ran back to the center of the mat. He growled.

"You're mine now!" he said.

Round three. This round was shorter than the other two. He was surprised when I didn't tie up with him. I faked like I was going to catch him with another duck under, then grabbed his wrist with my left hand

and caught him under his armpit with my right and arm-dragged him. As his body was extended, and he was going by me, at a high rate of speed. I reared back and gave him a swift kick right in the derrière and pounced on him to solidify the takedown for round three.

He stood up with tears in his eyes. I began to ham it up. I went to my best Bruce Lee martial arts imitation. I warmed up. I faked kicks. I did some chops and stood in front of him. As I was about to deliver a backhand and forehand simultaneously across both cheeks, I realized he had learned a lesson he would not forget anytime soon. I hugged Leo, who was then ushered out of the room by our witness, Reggie.

Word of this traveled quickly. I saw kids I didn't even know look at me in a different way. Big Leo adopted a new approach. He had been humbled. He became more of a gentleman, studied harder, and kept on winning his matches. Ultimately, he went to the state wrestling tournament and represented our school in a way that would've made any coach or team proud.

I saw Leo some years ago. He hand-delivered a wedding invitation directly to me at school. I was touched. He had driven out to Denver from Colorado Springs to personally give me the invitation. He wanted to reconnect and fill me in on his successes in life. I was unable to make it to his wedding, but no doubt we will meet up again sometime before too long.

I began to settle into my role at Montbello High School. Our football team won some games. The wrestling team was winning most of their matches and teaching in the gym was going well. I was spending twelve, thirteen, even fourteen hours a day at work and enjoying every minute of it. I bought a house in East Denver on my colossal $11,500-per-year teaching salary. I was as happy as a pig at a buffet. I had developed good rapport with the kids.

A few bumps in the road did occur. I went outside for duty one day to see three or four hoodlums, seventeen- and eighteen-year-old dropouts, starting trouble at our school. I told them to beat it, and they all jumped me. Now, kids who saw the scuffle would tell you I tossed a couple of kids projectile-style through the air. I wasn't hurt, they went to jail, and I was well supported by the school administrators and parents. Even though I was considered a real hard-butt, I felt a certain level of respect and admiration from my kids in class, as well as in athletics. I had also developed a strong relationship with the man who became my mentor, Coach Charles Hall.

Chapter Five

Coaches

Coach Hall

The man's impact on me was profound. When we met, he had already been teaching for eleven years at Smiley Junior High School. Some of my buddies from George Washington had told me stories about him. He ran his gym classes in the classic dictator style. If kids came in late, they would get the paddle. If kids chose to scuffle, he would grab them by the back of the neck and chew their butts out. He commanded respect. He was legendary to me, even before we met. He too was selected to teach physical education at Montbello High School and then became a football assistant with me. Here I was with this man who had struck fear into the hearts of my rowdy buddies who had gone to Smiley Junior High. *I'll be damned*, I thought.

When we met, this man weighed only a hundred fifty pounds. I watched him teach. He was firm, fair, and tough; he was a veteran. After a few weeks, I asked him to work with me and be my right-hand man, my assistant coach, in wrestling. He hesitated. I knew where that came from. He had wanted to coach early in his career but couldn't seem to break into what he described as "the good old boys" network. I knew what he meant, but I didn't care. He was my guy. I was not going to take no for an answer.

We became inseparable and even rode to work together. What a sight. A big, heavyset white dude and a small, wiry black guy. We were together for days at a time and sometimes weekends. On his days to drive, we rode in a small, beat-up Toyota. On my days to drive, we rumbled around in my old Dodge pickup truck.

We've always had the perfect understanding, except that what he learned from me could be put into a thimble. What I've gained from him has been priceless. I taught him the basics of wrestling. He taught me about kids, professionalism, teaching style, and discipline. I could write a book exclusively about the things I learned from him. When we took walks to the office to get our mail, I would occasionally see kids cutting class or smoking weed, and I was out the door sprinting as fast as I could to catch them. Most of the time I couldn't. He'd crack up and say, with his trademark stutter, "There will come a time when you won't do that." I didn't believe him. I was the crusader of the do-gooders. He wouldn't ignore that behavior, he'd write down their names and then call the discipline office and report them. Same result, except he didn't sweat trying to do the right thing. He was correct, and I don't chase them anymore. I make them come to me. Or I report them immediately for the wrongdoings.

Once a kid picked up a chair in gym class and hit Coach Hall with it. In an instant, Coach Hall reacted by picking up the chair to hit the kid back, no doubt harder than he had been hit. I jumped in, grabbed the kid, and threw him on top of the six-foot-high set of bleachers. Coach broke his wrist, and the kid went to jail, sadly, where he spent significant time.

Coach was organized and had the highest standards for his students and athletes. He too fell in love with coaching, so much that when I left Montbello High School in 1987 he became the head wrestling coach in addition to coaching football and baseball. He did a total of twenty-three years, many of them coaching three sports a year. If he hadn't retired, I'd have made sure he coached my sons. It wouldn't take him long to channel the Finesilver rowdiness in the right direction.

He was and still is loyal as hell. So am I. How lucky I am to have a cherished lifelong friend like him. To our children, he is Uncle Charlie. He even stood out in our wedding and, looking sharp as a tack, gave a toast that made many people teary-eyed.

Our relationship was not always centered around work. We got into plenty of mischief together. It amazes me we didn't end up going to jail together. A couple of times, we almost made it.

The first was when he called me at four o'clock on a lovely spring day. He had just dropped me off about thirty minutes prior. He said he was on his way to pick me up to get a seat latch for his old Toyota. I still don't understand why he chose to replace the latch at that time. The bucket seat held up my weight, nearly three hundred pounds at that time, just fine with a cardboard box he had propped behind the seat. Maybe he had a wild hair, but I was game. We drove to Commerce City, just north of town, a locale famous for its junkyards. Our junkyard of choice was huge. Nearly a full square block, it was full of old-fashioned foreign cars, mostly Toyotas and Datsuns.

We decided to check in at the trailer. The attendant had lots of muscle, a shortage of teeth, scraggly hair, and about fifty tattoos. He was a scary individual. He pointed to the back and scowled, then said something about not loaning out any tools. As we headed out back, Coach Hall froze, spellbound. The chain link fence before us certainly secured some serious type of beast. The links rose higher and higher, up three, four, and finally five wooden pallets. On top of the pallets lay a huge dog, still as a statue. We surmised he would mean business, judging by the size of his gonads. The testicular formations owned by this junkyard dog had surely made him the envy of every canine and human alike. No doubt he had sired twenty other junkyard dogs. He was asleep, oblivious to the two humans marveling at his genitalia.

Consumed by being in such close proximity to this animal, I could not help myself. I reached into my pocket and pulled out two dollars and thirty-eight cents. With one hand I grabbed a handful of rocks. I whispered, "This is all the money I have. It's yours if you'll hit that hound right in the nuts with one of these rocks."

He took the rocks. He knew that change would buy a sixpack of cold beer, which he craved back then. He was thinking, doing geometry in his head. I, not as gifted, was counting the links of chain to determine if, with one second of reaction time, we could run far enough and fast enough to not get shredded by this canine. Coach was doing the same math, but geometrically. He reared his arm back, and this is where we got into trouble. The dog, probably hearing the loud thumping that our hearts were making in our chests, lifted his massive head, and I almost fainted. The growl that followed nearly stopped our hearts, but what happened next was worse. The creature reared his head. He was missing one ear, and the other was sewn shut with gruesome stitch marks surrounding it. We froze! Our plan had hit the wall. If anyone had timed me right then, the NFL would have drafted me.

He dropped the rocks, and I dropped the money. As we sprinted, the brute jumped off his perch and opened his massive jaws. *Snap!* His teeth narrowly missed the fleshy lard of my rear end. In an instant, we were in the car speeding away, making a screen of dust from our rear wheels. The dude in the trailer came outside, yelling words not appropriate for this book—or any other.

We sped down the highway in silence for five miles, unaware of direction. Finally, we pulled over, both sweating from our near-death experience, muttering silent prayers to our own individual Lords or any that would listen. As wicked as that dog looked and sounded, I've often wondered what kind of creature could have inflicted such damage upon that junkyard dog. That individual was the real junkyard dog.

In his domain, Coach was masterful. During my free periods, I got to watch him in action. He would walk into the gym, look around, and *boom*! The kids would fall into place, awaiting his instructions. Any youngster deviating from the daily routine would get put back in his place with a word or a whisper. Coach didn't yell or raise his voice. He was in charge and rarely challenged. He would laugh and enjoy his classes. In no way a friend to his students, he was Mr. Hall or Coach Hall. He maintained separation and the kids admired him and knew he would put up with no horse crap from them. His presence and demeanor reflected a true professionalism.

Besides coaching, he taught social studies for a few years. In the classroom he wore slacks, had lesson plans, and insisted on homework, recitation, and high standards. His classes were quiet, and it was clear the students were actively involved in learning. If any kid in physical education or social studies fell short of his standards, he would call home. He knew how to deal with a parent who was confrontational. While speaking to a parent, he did not get rattled, but he told them what the problem was and then asked for their support. Almost always, the parents supported him. If they didn't support him, nothing changed, but the kid was still expected to perform, no ifs, ands, or buts. He didn't socialize much with teachers during school time, but he had friends. Coach never went into the teacher's lounge, at least not that I remember.

During wrestling, we would meet for hours. I showed him the moves we needed to teach. We'd walk into the practice room together, and in an instant, he would have the team lined up in eight perfect rows. Some years we had sixty, seventy, even eighty wrestlers. It didn't matter. Within ten seconds of his appearance in the room, every kid had jumped into position.

Coach would take the moves I had just shown him and break each one down so the kids could learn them. He made them practice each move hundreds—no, thousands—of times, insisting that everyone got it right. We would do live wrestling for twelve to fifteen minutes, with seventy bodies flying around in a single wrestling room. He would circulate like a bantam rooster, making sure that everyone was doing their level best to tear their opponents a new one. He would stutter commands and give directions, sounding like a broken record, until they got it right. Under his tutelage, the room would jump to about ninety percent humidity and ninety-five degrees. We measured our success in training the kids by the amount of sweat on the walls. Yes, you could touch the walls and find a salty moisture. Every kid, coach, and visitor in the room would sweat. Coach Hall would be drenched. Even our managers or random visitors would sweat. He was a marvel!

I used to love him during the final sixty or seventy seconds of a close match. It got to where I felt sorry for a kid's opponent, and sometimes, their coach. Our guys—yes, the good guys—won every time. We were not going to get beat at the buzzer, ever.

First, Coach would make eye contact. Then he would give instructions, which only our kids could understand. Then he would stomp and storm, contorting himself relentlessly until our kid scored on the other kid with either an escape or having executed a takedown. I looked into the stands in both our gym and our opponent's and found that most spectators were watching Coach, not the match. Our kids weren't afraid to lose, they wanted to win—for him. They knew he believed in them. They knew they mattered, and they knew he cared. He was the ultimate motivator. Every match he coached, whether his kid won or lost, the latter being seldom, he gave a hug and some encouraging words. He was "Dad" to every kid. Even to the kids in advance, and all my years as a teacher and a coach, the person who could get the most out of kids in class or in sports was Coach Hall. Kids went way beyond their potential and surpassed their ability to succeed. He gave them drive. He gave them heart. He gave them pride.

Coach Stahl

I shouldn't have judged. Yet I did. When she chose to enter our department two decades ago, I met her and decided instantly she was too young, too blonde, too cute, and too quiet. She was going to get eaten up and swallowed by our population of over 1700 students, 150 of whom she would mold daily. How in the world would she jump into this role when she, standing on her tippy toes, barely came up to my collarbone? I was sure I would have to intervene while she cowered to the much larger students, many twice her weight. She hailed from our heartland, South Dakota. Now I love Mount Rushmore and both of the Dakotas, but South Dakota has neighborhoods, not "the hood," where many of our youngsters come from. I grew worried for my new bright-eyed, blue-eyed colleague. I confess. I am sorry. I was wrong, and now, years later, embarrassed by my doubt.

She is, was, and will always be the G.O.A.T. (greatest of all time). Never has there been an educator who could connect like Coach. Her approach was the complete opposite of mine and maybe more effective. She spoke softly or not at all. On some days her instructions were given to her students on the overhead projector, other times, on a half sheet of paper. Like soldiers, the children were compliant. She captured the group the instant they entered the gym or classroom and within a split second engaged them. No matter what the lesson was for that day, they knew from the moment they met her what was most important. Was it that she cared? No, not strong enough. They knew they were safe and that she loved them. She had love for them like a mom and a teacher, meshed and blended, and much of their efforts were to make her proud and happy. How powerful is that? A teacher? Not in their eyes. She was a mentor, guide, hope-giver, protector, and coach. After many years as a successful soccer coach, she left the sport but still coaches in a more important way. Her coaching will never end because the daily lessons she gave in life were far more important than the momentary decisions of coaches on a soccer field. During her tenure she created a lasting legacy. Hundreds of former "all-stars," now "Stahl-stars," have been impacted by her message of resilience, self-care, and an "I can do anything" attitude. Her impact on our school can't be measured.

Narissa Stahl has been a champion to our students with disabilities. This group, often underserved, has been her focus and her passion for over a decade. Her tireless work with these beautiful children is inspirational. She hosted her own version of the adapted physical education games, involving several hundred students who were under the spotlight, as they should be. Students from the entire Denver school district were transported to our school and competed like gladiators in many athletic events. This was precedent-setting.

Uncle Dickey

When Coach Nye (Uncle Dickey) interviewed for a coaching job with me, it was so important to him that he wore a light blue suit, but he was uncomfortable in it. I was more so, knowing he would rather be in his coaching regalia.

He gave me a notebook as his resume. It contained a little about football, but what caught me off guard were four or five letters of recommendation from some big-time coaches. Yet I didn't need them. Two minutes in I was ready to ask that he join our staff but had no idea how deep the relationship would become. Being on a team, or leading one, creates bonds that rarely occur elsewhere on the opposing team.

The man could coach and was loyal beyond measure. We scouted together, hundreds of games in all, and he took copious notes and dissected each facet of the other team's game. Then he spent eight or nine hours preparing a scouting report. It detailed information on special teams, offense, defense, tendencies, and was, like everything else, done in the most professional way. He had been a college coach and it showed. Coach Nye was the master of counter, trap, misdirection, and other football nuances few understood on his level. More importantly, the players loved him dearly. They played their hearts out for him, and the largest part of our success was a result of his dedicated coaching. The league titles and playoff appearances were possible because of his commitment and grind.

Uncle Dickie became more than I ever expected from a coach, teacher, mentor, friend, bromance, and my daughter Mary's godfather. In my estimation, he is the finest, the standard, the golden one—in each of those roles. There has never been and will never be anyone like him, and he has been with me as my rock and pillar for more than thirty years. He is the eternal optimist, the wise older gentleman who aligned morally and philosophically with my daddy, the finest human ever.

Chapter Six

Denver

This is the Mile High City. Denver. The Big D. The name "Mile High City" was coined many years ago for our thin air and our true, legit mile-high elevation. The dual meaning is also tied to our notoriety as one of the first major cities to legalize weed. We are the mile-high city with thousands, on a daily basis, a mile high.

Our school district is much like others in our nation's big cities. Despite what you hear or read, we are smack-dab in the middle of an educational crisis. We left the traditional school model we were part of until the mid-2000s and in fifteen years, plus or minus, we have sold out to a very different school model. We now boast—or are cursed with, depending on which side of the fence you are on—more than sixty charter schools.

We claim to be a lot of things. Our boasting has caught the attention of some, but we are another struggling urban school district among many. Our rhetoric doesn't align with what many know as our reality. In a district driven by data, we don't speak about what the public should be aware of. It is hush-hush to talk about empty chairs. It is taboo to speak of our longstanding business model that has failed and keeps failing our families. We don't have the uncomfortable conversations about our underserved (and unserved) communities or our huge achievement gap, which should be renamed an "opportunity gap." Our students are further affected by our outdated curriculum and the lack of teacher diversity, resulting in children who feel like outsiders in their schools. This system, which claims to be financially strapped, throws away millions of dollars with no oversight. At the end of the day, the public has every right to be aware of the truth, the whole truth, and nothing but the truth. Read on.

George Washington High School. The envy of many other schools and districts for three-quarters of our existence. The Mighty Patriots have been a crown jewel in our city for more than four decades in our sixty-year history. But now we are a struggling mess. We have another principal, and our revolving door pattern reveals that we will have had eight principals in eleven years. Our enrollment is declining, and only fourteen percent of our neighborhood high school-aged students attend our school. Not long ago, educators were visiting from all over to find out why we were the best at nearly everything. Our academics, athletics, speech, drama, debate, music, clubs, faculty, students, and staff were the envy of other schools. Teachers who were fortunate enough to get placed at George Washington were in educational heaven. The school was safe, and parents were proud to send their sons and daughters through our doors and into our classrooms. We would go months without fisticuffs or incidents, behaviors that erode the very soul of any institution. We saw highly motivated students who cared deeply about what they were doing in class and in the community. Check us out now.

We've been in a decade-and-a-half demise, even though important people have thrown money—big money—to change us back to what we were, but the money is not working. The "One George" initiative was introduced about eight years ago. This touchy-feely gather-round-the-campfire quest was designed to unite our school. We wanted so badly for our black and brown children to have lunch with our white students. We formed committees and had meetings, then more meetings, then more. We came out of them with a plan to wave a wand and have the genie fix it! Many of the well-intentioned outsiders, loosely connected with our school or neighborhoods, grew tearful with their testimonials and their dreams for our school. Finally, a long, drawn-out, written plan came out, like a public relations campaign, anointing that One George was now ready for its birth. But the stork didn't deliver. I have been told that someone kicked in several hundred thousand dollars for this creation. And now, many years later, nothing has changed. If anything, the relationships among our students is worse. They are more separated, segregated, and tense.

How did we respond? Did we own up to our failed efforts? No. But take heart, here's a new plan. What is the new vision? One George 2.0! My colleagues accept this, nod, and follow like sheep. As newbies, they have no history. They can't understand that we have done this before. Will it work this time? Not a chance. Why would it or should it work to bring people from the outside to hypothesize, theorize, and talk about unity and inclusion? The secret is not from the outside, but from the inside. Children gather with those who are like themselves, who share something in common. So let them do this naturally. Don't force it. Let these children interact naturally, and guess what? It happens automatically. Friendships form when it runs a natural course.

Look at the football teams, wrestlers, and fitness students. They have, for decades, formed lifelong friendships with their workout buddies or teammates. Through clubs, activities, and common interests, kids will come together. It is so simple and obvious, and yet there's not a chance we will do that. It's too simple; too plain. And trust me, education is neither. We feel compelled to flower it up using experts, doing mission statements, listing objectives, and spending inordinate hours dissecting something that doesn't work anyway. Because of this, education is a hot mess. This model exists throughout our schools and is part of the reason we keep failing. The sickness is insidious, and like many of our sins, under the radar. No doubt the One George theme will continue with One George 3.0 and then 4.0. When will it stop?

Flavor of the Day

Merchants use flashy advertising techniques, and this can become great marketing. Fast food and ice cream parlors use this kind of advertising daily. They post their specials or their flavor of the day, and this attracts people. Education is no different. Our public schools love the flavor-of-the-day concept. We recently changed the daily schedule for all our high schools in Denver. Instead of a 7:30 a.m. start time, we will start at 8:30 or later at all the high schools. Why?

Because the board read a study showing that our darlings need extra sleep. So we knee-jerked and changed it. We did this in 2007, and some schools in 2008 also. Yes, the high schools went to a late start because the fourteen- to eighteen-year-olds would achieve more when they got the extra well-needed and well-deserved sleep. And the research, we were told, backed this up. It said, with the backing of doctors and psychologists, that the darlings needed eight or nine hours of sleep daily. These were the same people who did studies on school lighting, or the colors of the walls in the classrooms, or the seating arrangements. People love to weigh in on all these wonderful innovations that will make this group learn more and do better. So we went to an 8:15 start time. Activities got delayed, children got home later, they started their homework and chores later, but it was well worth it because our children were achieving more now. Right?

Wrong. Our tracking showed that 280 of our then 1500 students failed their first two classes. What? They stayed up late doing what kids did, both then and now, but more. Gaming and social media and that damn device. The experiment was a total disaster.

So we had the all-important data, and all the high schools had similar results. The idea went bye-bye, but at our school and JFK (Kennedy) we stayed in for another year because we are *all that*. We were going to do it better next time.

The following year we had well over three hundred students with similar results of class failure. We pulled the plug. And we did it without telling the public we had failed again with yet another experiment. We don't want to talk about this disaster, but we should.

It's 2021, and guess what? We are doing the cyclical pattern again. Except that we are starting even later. The gurus forgot that we did this before. Not one person, except me, will stomp and storm and say, "We tried this, and it failed. It was a disaster. Now quit experimenting with our children."

Our children may as well be in a laboratory the way we experiment, taste the flavor of the day, and change and adjust, and we do it *just because*. We have no real proof that this is what the kids need. It is just accepted. Why do people trust us so much? We use and exploit our children and fail with our methods and techniques and then the educators have the nerve to complain and blame. I confess. That is what education has become, most often in our big cities. A chain of failures, all serving special interest groups at the expense of our children. When will we have had enough as a public and say, "No more"? How much more can we tolerate? Parents have accepted our standardized tests, our outdated and non-inclusive curriculum, and our ever-changing calendar and scheduling. They have listened to false promises and flowery verbiage as our children continue to struggle. If we don't teach job skills or a multicultural education in our schools or prepare our youth well for college, what are we doing with your millions? What are we doing with your children's time? The voice of the people, families, and children need to take over and demand change. This is our only hope.

At the risk of ruffling some feathers, I need to say that you politicians can stop the verbiage and save the rhetoric because you don't know diddly squat about our schools. In more than forty years in education, I haven't seen one legislator or politician in the schools I've been in. How can you make a decision, appropriate funds, or have even a clue about my world, the kids' reality, when you don't know the population you serve? If you haven't seen what really takes place in the school, how can you make a decision that affects thousands of lives? The educational system is dysfunctional, but it works. It works because of kids, because of persistent parents, and because some educators challenge themselves to improve this screwed-up system.

Instead of finding out, you pass judgment. You take the money and mandate tests to gauge how kids are achieving. You take data from your tests, give a school a grade on performance, and let people draw their own conclusions. In some locales, a threat exists that if the school doesn't perform, it will be taken over by the state, the city, or the county. How phony. I invite you to come into my world with your wingtip shoes on my floor and rub shoulders with my kids.

Thousands of kids have played ball under our tutelage and over three hundred went to college and played a year or more of college football. Among those, nearly fifty played Division 1 football and well more than a dozen played in major college bowl games. They go to college all over the country, and some continue their careers in athletics, but almost all of them graduated and many went on to graduate school. But what is more important is that more than four hundred young men and women who played ball earned college degrees, and many were the first in their families to do so. Many others chose the military and served valiantly, and some became officers. Those who chose the trades became highly successful as a result of the work ethic they gained from their homes and our school family.

These kids from the inner city have gone to MIT, Yale, Harvard, The Air Force Academy, and hundreds of other schools. Yet nobody has ever asked why or how. Was this destiny? No. Was it luck? Hell, no! What's worse, no one over the last quarter century has ever called, asked, written, or even wanted to know how so many children of color—poor kids, homeless kids, kids from single-parent homes—have pulled themselves up to graduate with honors. These kids have traveled abroad and are leaders in our community, and this was never supposed to happen. Yet it did.

My legacy is not championships in football, although I've coached several. People don't remember the 1986 wrestling title, won by kids who were not supposed to win. The legacy I've left is the kids who graduated from their high school, went to college, got degrees, and did so against all odds. These kids, some without fathers and with moms who worked two or three jobs to pay bills, are my inspiration. My students have earned degrees, become military officers, and are proud and wonderful parents, many without having parents of their own who did any of those things. Yet I see none of our high-ranking officials. They don't ask, and until now, I haven't told. I've been too busy doing my job to toot my own horn or brag about my students.

Still, you would think that at some point, some politico would wander into my domain and ask, "Coach, how the hell do you do it? Why are your kids going to college when kids at other schools are dropping out?" Kids are doing drugs and joining gangs, and nobody has ever asked, *How can you have complete control over your classes? You don't yell or threaten, and you rarely write a disciplinary referral, yet your classes are orderly, respectful, and hard-working. What are you doing that others aren't?*

Now it's time. Either put up or shut up. Our leaders talk about educational reform but don't leave their offices to see what reform is all about. Calling all mayors, governors, and state representatives. City councilmen and women and congressional leaders. Leave the office. Go out into the schools and talk with students, teachers, and parents. Do your homework before you bash the system. And make sure to do so before you try to change it. The statewide tests you require are taken by kids who would rather not take them. The results are skewed because kids prepped for the test and teachers taught to the test to avoid public criticism and state sanctions. Education has largely involved proficiency testing. Our kids become expert test takers at the expense of deep knowledge, free thinking, and being creative leaders. If you mandate something, mandate something worthwhile. I invite you to visit and take a close look at our schools and our kids.

Chapter Seven

The Last Decade

2012–2022

It's a new year with shiny floors. We've had a facelift with fancy industrial tile in the school lobby. We have twenty new teachers and lots of excitement. Same schedule.

Uh-oh. Four days of incessant meetings. We're into another year with more of the same. Meetings on emergency preparedness and procedure and protocol. We spent a day or more talking about our new teacher evaluation system because we got more money. Bill and Melinda Gates gave us another ten million dollars. They must have thought we were doing a masterful job and that our teachers were getting better. After two years and the misspending of the previous millions of dollars, we are nearly the same. Obedient teachers jump through our district's hoops. They nod and kiss up and we call it good. Did Bill and Melinda put an asterisk on the requirements before they anted up? I think not. Did they insist that our instructional classrooms be innovative, respectful places that are conducive to in-depth learning? Are our instructional practices, marveled at by our students, better now because of their well-intentioned money? I think not.

2013

Ready to celebrate surviving again. Oops, I mean, ready to start year thirty-five. Anxiously awaiting the arrival of our students, all thirteen hundred of them (used to be two thousand or more). I get the once-a-year mailing giving us our pre-student schedule. In the '8os, pre-student meetings were a half day of planning, rules, and regs, and off we went. We would all show up to kick off each year. Fast forward to 2013, and it was a week—yes—a flippin' week! What do we do for a week? We have meetings about our exciting, innovative, cutting-edge evaluation system, a two-day dog-and-pony show. Then two days of other meetings that could have been condensed into a three- or four-page email or paper document. In reality, after our fifth day, Friday (our own planning day), we have done absolutely nothing to support, benefit, enrich, or prepare who we are supposed to be here for—the kids. The rub? This week of foolishness costs, in teacher payroll alone, about ten million dollars. Ten million dollars paid out to the four thousand teachers, and no contact with kids. The administrative gurus would disagree, of course, to justify their intense knowledge, arguing that teachers need this all-important training. Truth be told, our kids could benefit from teacher contact to start the week, and most teachers would rather have the time with the students.

The teachers of this decade are much different than their colleagues with twenty years of experience. This group of teachers is incredibly bright, and they know it. They are highly social and, much like the kids, they love the electronic media that surrounds those age thirty and under. But they are ill-equipped to deal with this generation of millennials and their complex, entitled behavior. This unique generation is the most emotionally deprived of all time and is the product of a questionable phase of education. Teachers today need to be much more than someone who stands in front of the class. Many teachers never realize that kids don't need their teachers' friendship. The inexperienced teachers foster a friendly relationship that usually comes back to haunt them. They begin teaching and learn very quickly to stay under the radar and keep the lid on the chaos. The kids then struggle with the emptiness of their existence and disconnect from reality.

To most of our kids, the real world is quite small and consists of their house, their hood, their phone, maybe a computer, a gaming system, their school, and some neighbors. Those of us who hold power and influence do little to change that. We could expand their world and open up its narrow scope, but we don't. That's not in our job description and is not deemed important by our school leaders.

Leadership touts statistics that justify their decisions, and central leadership follows the money, jumping through the hoops to get it. If someone offers the dinero, the admins jump on it and somehow justify and then spin it so it has to show up as a success. What happened to late starts we implemented because kids needed more sleep? Where did double-periods go, where kids could have deeper immersion into content areas? How about all these models, initiatives, programs, and innovations? Where are they now? If they worked, we would still be doing them.

According to high-salaried consultants and administrators, we are in the middle of educational reform. Reality check. We conduct repeated million-dollar educational experiments at the expense of the students we serve. Why should we care? Because people still buy homes and pick neighborhoods based on the quality of the schools.

The Finesilvers are but one example. I admit we moved our village two miles south to be in a better school district. It's painful that we moved, as we are both proud DPS grads and I'm a DPS veteran employee. We did this to give our kids a better education. Now, more than twenty years later, we see it as the best decision we ever made. The schools are amazing and are everything a kid or parent would want. The high school has more than a hundred clubs, a fully funded business program, DECA, and more. Our baby girl flourished with a tough but honest teacher in the AVID (Advancement Via Individual Determination) program. They've got it going on. The kids compete in academics, speech, music, debate, sports, and clubs.

The school I attended and at which I teach are in the tank. We've had seven principals in eight years, and now, in 2022, we have yet another. More than a dozen assistant principals went through the revolving door during that time. Our once proud and high-achieving school, like many big city school districts, is in the middle of an educational identity crisis. And we are not alone.

2019

Seven years later not much has changed except that we had six days without the kids this year. Six days of meetings, planning, games, discussion, and music. Finally, for about an hour-and-a-half, we got deep with some significant and meaningful content about educating our kids. Twenty new staff members were introduced. We had a new chant where the principal or another person who gets the mic says, "Shout Out" and the rest of our staff mimics those words, "Shout Out." Kinda cute the first three or four times, but after the sixty-second time the repetitive phrase had long become mundane and puppet-like. I won't play this copycat game, but no doubt it will be fun and folly for at least a year for teachers who love the entertainment value of these meetings.

Long lacking substance and anything meaningful, the most compelling takeaway from the pre-schoolyear meetings for me was that we can be encouraged that our freshman class is the biggest it has been in about a decade. That's great news, but our enrollment is still the same. Nobody said so, but I did the math that showed a hundred of our previous students left us. There was no exit interview; they just disappeared. They either chose other schools, no school, or we don't know and act like we don't care. While introducing this large freshman class, we were told, accurately, that the success of the students as freshmen would determine the overall success of their high school journey. If we start a kid out and provide a meaningful freshman year, they are usually on track for success and graduate on time, except that our record at doing this is miserable. Up to a hundred freshmen a year fall behind and have to take credit recovery or end up with a graduation delay and one of our numerous rescue services. We were shown a slide show with the pictures of eighty-three kids returning to our school who were not proficient in any of the tested subject areas. This was presented with an emotional plea compelling us to do better, but we were left by our presenters, as always, with no plan.

Nobody suggested, explained, or portrayed a path by which we could assist the kids who were so far behind or the numerous freshmen coming from more than twenty middle schools. Their freshman year is very important, we were told, and now "you figure it out" is the agenda. Of course, we'll get it done with fifty percent of our staff having less than seven years teaching experience and little direction or guidance. We can sort this out and do a bang-up job. We'd been set up for failure once again. The message, which was no message at all, was delivered and the teachers accepted it as they often do. A few of us knew better, and once again felt empty and powerless.

How about this approach? Our eighty-three kids who are struggling will meet once a week on Thursday mornings with a faculty member and a volunteer (usually a parent). We will work with them for ninety minutes, with two adults supporting each of the students. One will look over the work from the last week and contact the student's parents to keep them in the loop. The other will work directly with the student on any subject in which they are struggling, whether it is reading or math or a specific subject or class. More importantly, the student will know that two people are deeply invested in leaving no stone unturned to help them improve and gain confidence.

To our thirteen- and fourteen-year-old freshmen we say, "If you show a pattern of something that will derail you, as soon as you have unexcused absences, a tardy, (yes, even one incident), the proverbial sirens will go off. If you blow gas, belch too loud, be a jerk, or do no homework—busted. Several infractions of this nature are met with our disapproval, your parent or guardian being notified, and a lunch detention. Continued incidents and you are on surveillance with a parent meeting to get you on track, as well as after-school detention.

Now, let's say that you are doing a great job as a freshman. We feel you. A group of teachers will call you once a week for a few minutes to thank you for your fine effort and yes, we will make a complimentary call to your family. We will build the strongest support system for the kids who need us most, and then work like crazy to get every other student—yes, each one—to improve. Use your tracking methods and all the resources available to improve achievement, across the board. Get rid of anything that does not promote the improvement of the kids. This includes the class assemblies, the meetings, and the foolishness and fluff we have been calling education for too long. Make everybody sweat, every day, to give the students a chance to actually immerse themselves in the education that they could get for seven-and-a-half hours each day. Then, on some Thursday morning at 7:30 when the teachers are doing their "shout out," have the faculty celebrate with some donated food. At eight o'clock, bring the students in for a celebration, an assembly, a concert, a movie, something to let them know that we notice their hard work and their improvement, together. Then do it again and again. And finally, instead of *saying* we'll move the bar, we actually do move it.

How hard is this? We have the resources, the volunteers, and the systems in place to do this, but we are scared. We walk around in our shells afraid to actually teach something away from the sovereign curriculum, because that would negatively impact our evaluation. This is not the only way to accomplish this, it just a plan, damn it. Finally. Without a plan, we spin in a circle but never gain momentum.

The Pandemic

We were blindsided. Yes, we were all watching the news and following the story. But none of us thought we would actually shut down our schools, the anchor for millions of children's lives. We now know, without question, that our schools fix us, give us support, and keep us in place. In March 2020 the news came in an email and then the public knew. Covid-19 had arrived. They called it a worldwide event, though kids rarely took ill. It became a worldwide crisis. People would get sick, and many would die. The unknown created fear and indecision among those who decide how to operate our schools and do right for our children.

We were clueless and didn't know what this really meant. So the students went home and educators all over the country got to try education on the computer. I say this because all we did was try. The leaders who make the decisions that reverberate the loudest were the most clueless. We had little direction, even though the leaders had their roles and were paid quite nicely to make those decisions. There are lots of these people and they fail all the time; failure has become the norm. Sadly, this time will be the most long-lasting and impactful on our children.

Most tragic was our response as we returned to school. We had every chance to reset and make this system better, or at least different. And...it got worse. After many months of being back, our children are more wounded and fragile than ever, with little hope and direction. They are proving to be resilient as usual, but we should be ashamed.

We had every opportunity to reset, to rebuild, and to start over with new vigor and a sense of purpose. The chance to bring the children back and hear their stories and their all-important voices has been lost. We could have been ready to hit them with support and excitement, and instead we gave them the same they had before. As I walk by our classrooms, they no doubt resemble the classrooms all over our country. Kids on cell phones, on their computers, engaged in their own worlds, which are rarely the same as the world of education. Our district had no plan except to grind and mandate more testing and micromanage even more than before.

We all hoped to see a plan. In August 2021, the rhetoric was huge. *Education can't be the same as before*, we were told. The theme was to restart, jumpstart, and make it new and exciting...and now the children are bored, starved for attention, and right back in front of their damn screens. Even our teachers are resolved to accept this as normal, and many are behind their own screens. Talk about wasted potential. We came back tired, unable to cope with the new mentality of our children.

During their so-called education in their own homes, they were disengaged and knew quite well how to play the game. For their entire last school year, they would turn on their computers, log in to class, and then turn off their cameras and fake it. Yes, millions of kids all over the country were getting credit and earning A's and B's while doing nothing. We were told directly not to push too hard. At our school the underlying tone was to play the game and not make the children turn on their cameras. The reasoning was that so many children had it so tough that they would be embarrassed to show their homes, or where or how they lived. What a shame. We shut it down when the children needed us the most. At a time where there was illness, death, despair, loss of income, and loss of housing, we ignored our kids. We deserted them and said as a group *we don't want to see you.* My colleagues all over the country complied and did as they were told. Like good soldiers, they followed the script.

I made it a requirement of virtual teaching to turn on cameras, not wanting to play the "cameras off" charade. At times I was chastised and ridiculed over it. But I insisted each child turn on their camera and promised not to judge. I grew from this. I saw firsthand the living rooms, kitchens, bedrooms, garages, and in some instances, the inside of a car or van. My eyes were opened to the reality of how our children lived. I got to meet parents, reconnect with some, see siblings and cousins, and see and meet grandparents. The students could sometimes be found living in communal situations, and these could often be very heartwarming.

This is where my children lived, and I needed to see that. And guess what? Not only did the children appreciate it, but the families did too. After a short time there was no pushback, and the norm was that you got on the call and turned on your camera. I learned more than I taught, for sure, but after forty-some years, I needed to see this. Some teachers were following the script, but I was connecting in a different way. This real view of the students has made me better—as a teacher and as a person. Student and family voices moved quickly to the forefront for me.

I asked questions not tied to my subject matter or my class. *What do you need? How can I support you?* The answers were revealing. Most of the time I was told, *I need you to be patient,* or *I need you to understand what I am going through.* My peers never heard those things and were not directed to ask. The longstanding talk about building relationships with students does not include that type of conversation.

Abril came to my class as a brave sixteen-year-old. Brave, because she had not attended for weeks since she promised to come to class and participate. My stubborn side kicked in and I asked in a not-so-tender way where she had been.

"Mister...I have been taking care of my mom. She has had doctor's appointments almost every day." I shut my mouth and listened. "Mom had Covid about a month ago and has never fully recovered."

As we talked, I realized this little girl was her mother's caregiver and was doing exactly what she was supposed to do. Take care of her family. Yes, this was a helluva lot more important than my class or any other.

The conversation got deeper. I took the risk and asked, "Where is Dad?"

She paused for an uncomfortable amount of time, and then said, "He died when I was twelve."

Now my pause became uncomfortable. I said all I could say and thankfully, it was enough. "Dear...I am so sorry. I lost my daddy when I was fifty and was torn apart. I am so sorry." She and I both needed that moment, and tears flowed freely from both of our eyes, and we hugged. Yes, we hugged right in front of the class. We needed that connection. Two grieving children, separated by generations.

We have become increasingly detached from our students as time has gone on. The children have become so entrenched in their world of cyber-connecting that the meaningful teacher-student relationships have disappeared. Young people have suffered and will suffer more. Those with whom the child can connect the most, who are the most present and visible, have become the most detached. Our "systems" program us to do other things—to test repeatedly, to cover the required information, and to go by the script written by those who don't know or really care. Why aren't we ashamed? The testing gurus, the politicians, the special interest groups, and many others have been allowed to define what education should be as our children are victimized by years of failed methods.

Chapter Eight

How We Teach is More Important Than What We Teach

We are creatures of habit. Consequently, we teach kids the same antiquated thoughts and theories and offer classes identical to those we have taught for decades. Our society has evolved in many ways, yet education hasn't. I spend much of my time wondering why. Worse, our public has accepted this and bought into it without a whimper. We then wonder why so many of our students are ill-prepared to face the challenges of college, the military, or the real world. Our curriculum has barely changed over the years, and we don't demand enough. We are told way too often that today's learners are different.

They are different. Our millennials and Gen Xers are entitled and bright, and they spend between four and ten hours of their waking time every day occupied by their screens. They are looking at phones, computers, notebooks, tablets, or game systems for much of their waking hours. This, in and of itself, throws a wrench in our ability to teach. Our schools perpetuate this style and do not have confidence in our ability to change this poor habit or the courage to do so. We resign ourselves, throw our collective hands up, and give in. In class we allow more electronics, including the incessant chatter on social media, which has become commonplace for a large part of our population, both young and old. English class is not called English anymore; it is now Language Arts. That sounds good, but we have moved away from grammar, comprehension, real writing, and research. Because it is watered down, the kids never get what they need to know. In a single high school class we can have kids at every educational level. A kid who has the skills of a third grader in reading or math may be sitting next to the kid who is at the college level. Often, we are teaching our LEAP (Leading Effective Academic Practices) methods to the state or district-mandated tests, or to a curriculum given to us, after assurance it was the Holy Grail.

The standardized tests given all over our country measure and allow us to place our children into identifiable groups. This is supposed to paint a clear picture to the parents or guardians, as well as to higher education, as we put these "valuable" statistics on the students' transcripts. The labels run the spectrum. Johnny may be unsatisfactory, below average, partially proficient, emerging, proficient, or "the second coming." In our state there are tens of millions spent on these tests, which kids abhor and parents find meaningless. I am a father of seven kids. The first time the tests came in the mail, I opened them up, anxious to see how the Finesilvers were doing, as students and as our world's next great scholars. But once I waded through the verbiage and looked at the graphs, comparisons, and explanations, I was convinced. The scores were meaningless.

After that drill I knew better. The next year and for more than a decade they went straight to the trash, often unopened. You see, Tommy or Tina, who get labeled as early underachievers, may not have ever heard of math facts, Dr. Seuss, Mother Goose, or Shakespeare. Likely their parent or both parents were busy trying to provide basics such as food, shelter, transportation, and other necessities, but who cares. Let's test them anyway because they need that label. Once we have this valuable information, of course, we do wonders bridging the achievement gap. The testing gurus—there are many—are highly paid and don't know or care that these differences exist. Their livelihood depends on the public supporting, endorsing, and analyzing these meaningless tests.

What about the kid that ends up partially proficient? What the hell does that mean? How cool. You know only part of this meaningless bull feces, but we want you to know more...got it? Then we get to label you as proficient. Kids dig this. Study a lot, work your butts off on these tests, and someone you don't know, or a computer, will determine that you get the prize and whatever comes with it.

I encourage you to check it out. Ask our teachers, our college professors, our military recruiting officers, or better yet, ask some parents these questions. Do these tests matter? Do they have any correlation to what happens later in life after the K-12 experience?

What can we do differently? We can start each class with a review at the start of the school year. Going back to basics in any educational setting is never bad. Some schools start with basics and then move their students on a journey, often together. Unfortunately, maybe twenty percent of our public schools have this back-to-basics attitude that values the educational foundation piece and has the important mentality of building upon a stable foundation.

In some elementary schools, kids who have little more than an educational glitch are caught early by the system. All but one of our children, six out of seven, were identified by third grade as having some educational deficiency. One had a learning disability; two needed speech therapy; two were behind in early reading; and one could not pick up math in the normal way. We signed permission forms for the school to remediate and educate according to what they, as experts, believed should be done. Right on. But we got lucky. The public school system our kids attended used their resources to detect these problems, early and often.

Our district, though having the money and the personnel to do the same, gets away with not doing it—once again part of the "have nots." What a travesty. This happens each year to more than ninety-thousand students and families, and it's accepted without question. This needs to stop.

Let's track the path of a typical kid at a typical school in my district. This could be any of millions of kids across our country. Let's call this typical kid Mark. Mark lives with mom and has two or three siblings. Mom works hard and is a supportive person who trusts her kid and the school. Dad may not be around and never has been. Mom works days, plus three or four evenings a week to provide her best for her family. Mark begins elementary school after spending a lot of his early time watching television and playing on the gaming system, and through no one's error or omission, did not grow up learning math, reading, or being read to. In kindergarten and first grade, it becomes clear he is behind.

A number of kids have been more fortunate than Mark. They have been read to, learned basic math, and had a parent to jumpstart them on their formative educational journey. They flourish and continue to excel based on their situation. Mark's situation is different. The school makes some feeble attempts to remediate Mark, but he is distracted and not used to the structure he needs but won't get. Mark is labeled as an underachiever, and we explain that we have tried but don't have the resources to bring him up to speed. We throw him back out to a mother who loves him and wants the best for him but can't offer any more than she has been giving. Mark stays behind through his whole educational journey and then he's out the door, lacking skills that he could have learned. He is yet another kid cheated by our system. This could have been prevented but has instead been perpetuated. Mark has been told, along with his peers, that every kid goes to college. During his senior year, pushed and prodded by the school, he applies to college. Despite a terrible foundation and twelve lost years in the system, he gets accepted somewhere. He may even get some financial aid, and he should.

So he enrolls, picks classes, and starts college. As part of the admissions process, he does a couple of tests, including the famed Accuplacer, a math test that indicates the student has basic math skills. Uh-oh, he scores too low. The college requires students reach a baseline to do college math, so he begins to take remedial classes in math and English, because his reading, writing, and verbal skills have stayed low for too long. Someone has to pay for these classes that should have been taken in high school. The family, financial aid, or a combination of people foot the bill, and Mark is off and running. Mark begins to get swallowed up and can't compete, largely because he has never been taught how to study or take notes, and certainly has not had to "grind" as we moved him through our system.

After a couple of semesters with some average grades in a few classes and a handful of dropped or failed courses, Mark gets frustrated and leaves higher education. All he has to show for it is an incomplete transcript and some debt which haunts and follows him for years, affecting his credit and his ability to get employment, transportation, and housing. Multiply this story hundreds or thousands of times each year for the seventeen- to nineteen-year-olds. Look at the fallout—the damage. We have wasted the potential of a whole generation of youth who we promised to educate, protect, and provide hope. We have stolen from these kids, families, and communities. This is our biggest sin, and I along with the other perpetrators and puppets, own it. What will we all do with this knowledge?

Competition

Our world is full of competition. We compete for jobs, housing, credit, and hundreds of other necessities. Certain pockets of education are fiercely competitive. Students in my kids' classes compete for grades while athletes compete for starting spots. Everywhere you look, a competitive spirit exists among young people. But do we find this same competitive drive in our school? No. Most kids will not compete in this way. Apathy and lack of drive is evident in classes and sports. You can either play or sit in class and exist. Why compete? Here's the rationale. Why should I bust my chops to get an A when I can slack off and get a B or C? I can show up to play sports, but there is no guarantee I'll be a starter. We have few, if any, real competitive athletics anyway.

Our city has been hit hard by this prevailing commitment to mediocrity. Why should the district change? We recently got another financial vote of confidence, another four hundred and some million, by our too-trusting taxpayers. We really needed the money, right? We are doing so well with the more than one-and-a-half billion dollars per year we operate on that we need more.

The city itself is suffering as well. People who care don't know what to think. The district officials point to all their amazing data, but trust me, it's fluff. Let's have a candid talk about graduation rates, college preparation, and fiscal responsibility. Let's find out how we are suddenly graduating more kids. Where is the pie chart? Wouldn't we like to see where the money is really going? Let's ask questions about cronyism, nepotism, the treatment of staff and teachers, and more important than both, the treatment of our kids. We don't get to the "real truth" ever! The board and upper management are experts at deflecting, dodging, and covering it up, protected by public relation experts who are always available to spin it any way they want. We have a deeply layered system and a top-down business model, and the "squeeze" persists.

Where are the watchdogs that monitor and audit us? Who holds us accountable? It looks like no one. Do the taxpayers want us to stay out of their hair, or are they giving us unlimited trust? It's deceitful and dishonest to say we need these millions and then waste them with more consultants, administrators, directors, managers, and failing initiatives. What is amazing is that the public doesn't question us. They assume we are educating our kids and are providing a quality education. Quite the contrary. We are playing games with numbers when it comes to graduation, college readiness, suspension rates, and enrollment, and we tell the world that Denver is a leader in school reform. We talk about core values and reaching out to each student. If you ask our dozens of high-ranking, highly paid administrators, they will parrot the company line that we are among the nation's leaders in many areas, but you would be a fool to believe it. Ask anyone who buys or rents a house in Denver. They rarely choose housing because of quality schools. They obtain housing in the city because Denver *is* a great city. They take their chances and roll the dice. If the schools are substandard, they homeschool, go private, or go out of district. This has happened for years, and we hide it with fluff and smoke.

Our Dirty Laundry

Lately a few news pieces have suggested all is not what it seems. According to a recent report, some schools cover up violent acts and don't report them to the State Department of Education. Despite the recent proclamation by our last superintendent anointing our schools as safe, the reality is the opposite. Our schools are not safe. They are, in fact, violent. Teachers and students are both scared, and we are masters at covering it up. We can play the semantics game or play dumb by saying we did not know which category to report it under, but believe me, where I and many of my colleagues work are places where lawlessness prevails. Almost daily, acts of violence, defiance, and crime are committed. Weed is running rampant, as is alcohol. And now, the new high is the vapes.

This is nothing new. These choices have been around since the sixties. When I leave for a meeting or drive around our campus, kids get high openly and defiantly. They know nothing will happen. When they beat the hell out of each other, they know nothing will happen. Cussing out a teacher is no longer considered a real offense. Stealing repeatedly from the tip jar at a barbeque restaurant next to our school will not get you suspended. A hate crime against our neighboring Jewish merchants is brushed under the rug as is a weapon pulled on the clerk at the gas station one block away. If we reported each act we would have a hundred documented incidents during any given year, at our school alone. We probably reported none. If we were honest, in our district we would report a thousand or more. It's time we all insist on the truth and demand the transparency we say we are providing. Allow a citizen group of taxpayers to have open access to the campus and let them look around. Anyone with a shred of common sense will see and be appalled.

When?

When will we get a clue? Let's do some math. There are 180 days in the typical school year. The kids attend class for about seven hours a day. One hundred eighty times seven is 1,260 hours our kids are in the school per year. Now multiply that by twelve years of formative education, and the grand total is 15,120 hours. Deep! We as public schools, as educators, spend fifteen thousand hours with our students, not including kindergarten or pre-k, which our district has in full force. We get millions for having this early childhood education program. Given these facts, I think everyone— parents, educators, and administration—would agree that more than fifteen thousand hours is a huge amount of time to educate a child. With these facts and figures, how are we doing?

We are sucking money from our taxpayers. We have more access to quality education than ever before, and we still give excuse after excuse. The kids are from poverty; the kids have language barriers; the kids have no educational foundation. Then, we love to blame the parents and proclaim that some kids have broken homes and no discipline, or that the parents just don't care. Let me admit something that sadly, you may never hear again. Our excuses are cop-outs. They are lies. There is no excuse for what we do. Even if a kid comes to our doors with no skills, no foundation for problem solving, and a language barrier, we can certainly teach them a helluva lot more than we are. Our current system cheats kids, rips off taxpayers, and sucks the energy and creativity out of teachers. Students have had the collective stuffing tested out of them. We have the finest technology ever available to our students and teachers and schools. In four decades, I have never seen this much support from volunteers who give hours and money to our schools. We have more money than ever, despite our constant whining. Where does one-and-a-half billion dollars go? We need to demand some public fiscal accountability.

How many pre-k through twelfth-grade kids live in the city of Denver, and what percentage of them go to schools within the city? Another guaranteed eye-opener. Many of them go to private or public schools outside the city. Digging deeper, we know that graduation rates have improved. Take a bow, but not so fast. How have they improved? Are teachers told to pass the kids? Are kids being given higher grades? And what about this credit-recovery program? Is it legit? A whole lot of kids are suddenly promoted where they previously had to come back for an extra semester or year until they got it right. We give the numbers and pat ourselves on the back, but in reality, we should all know that many kids are allowed to graduate far less qualified than they were even five short years ago. Why do so many of our kids need remediation after they graduate?

We have layers to uncover, and it is hard to know where to start. What do 14,000 people do? Yes, we have many departments, and we know there are 4,500 to 5,100 teachers in our schools, depending on what you believe. How many superintendents do we have or need? What roles do the 700 to 800 administrators have? We give the public information that is completely inaccurate and untrue, but who checks us? Are we really working toward equity? My visits to dozens of neighborhoods a year ago would rebut this, but my view is different because I went out and asked the tough questions. Has anyone else done that? It is possible our highly paid staff has never been given or cared to get this global view? We are a hot mess right now and the problems are so vast they have become deeply entrenched. We have everything at our fingertips to make a tremendous difference, yet we stagnate more and more. Those closest to us are aware of our flaws but have given up out of frustration. Even former politicians, school board members, and central administrators are wondering what in the heck has happened and why, how, or if it will ever change.

We will also tell you about our success preparing our graduates for college, but the percentage of students who earn college degrees after graduation is abysmal. I have been told attendance is between ten and fifteen percent each year and has been since the early 2000s. If true, the compelling question is this. What happens to the existing eighty-five to ninety percent? We tout the college prep theme and then after four, five, six, or ten years we have validated the fact that our preparation stinks. Worse, most schools cut the vocational ed programs long ago. We stink at preparing kids for college and we no longer attempt to teach skills in the trades, even though we have huge shortages in most industries. Our high schools have college readiness centers, fully staffed with capable people. Yet who gives advice to those who want to go into the military or into trades? In summary, we are bombing out. Our college preparation stinks, and we quit exposing our high schoolers to the trades long ago. If we aren't doing either of those things, what *are* we doing? Will we ask? Do we care? We better.

Whistleblowing

Once again, time to snitch. We have a problem. We throw things away, sometimes sneakily, discarding items that are perfectly good. Not long ago, I was in the gym in our Covid-deserted school. Our custodial staff was hard at work with tools and socket sets, disassembling tables. The laboratory tables were quite similar to those I ordered not too long ago that were worth about five hundred dollars each. These were lightly used, and I was informed they had been directed to take them apart and toss them. I personally have seen, with my own eyes, tens of thousands of dollars—everything from books, carts, furniture, electronics, you name it—go right into the trash. Multiply that by more than two hundred schools. Year after year, DPS's assets are thrown away after trusting taxpayers bought most or all of them. I promise this is the absolute truth. We have discarded scoreboards worth thousands of dollars, as well as many other small, medium, and large items. It seems to be a mandate to not have "junk" lying around. Our leaders call it junk, and the discarding happens constantly.

I spent a year setting up a state-of-the-art exercise physiology lab. We needed two quality, industrial-sized treadmills, not the cheap ones. I finally got two donated to the school at around six- or seven-thousand-dollars each. We used them in the class I had worked for years for the students to have, and when the class got dropped, I was told the treadmills were being thrown away. They were fully functional though not brand new, but someone didn't like them. They were pulled out for the trash. No doubt someone came and rescued them, knowing their value. Hell, I'll take a free treadmill, how about you? But this is the way of our district.

And then we spew out sickening stories about how broke and destitute we are.

Ask around and check my facts. If we open our collective eyes, we will view this firsthand. But we are lazy. It would require work to repurpose what we discard. We could donate plenty of things to help schools who are really underserved and have nothing. Or we could auction it off, selling it for pennies on the dollar. Yes, trusting taxpayers, we waste your money in this and other ways, and you have every right to know.

Voice

We don't have one. The parents don't have one, nor the children, and for sure not the teachers, yet we are all told we have one and that our thoughts, ideas, concerns, and suggestions actually matter.

Essentially, we have no say, and it has been like that for a while. The rhetoric of the school board and school website gets old. I personally reached out to the board and the superintendent recently and was ignored. My mission has always been to improve lives *and* education for the children in Denver. So I sent a direct letter to the Denver Public School leadership on July 10. This letter requested a sit-down, eyeball-to-eyeball meeting to make improvements across five areas with an actual action plan. Now these good people who are supposed to be looking after the children finally set up a meeting on the last day of September, nearly seventy days after I had requested one. Am I, in their eyes, not worthy to be heard after forty-one years? They responded because they became aware I had assembled a team to do the work they should be doing. The pressure from important people became too great, so they pacified me and gave me fifty minutes of their important time.

The meeting was interesting. I had spent ten weeks in most of the Denver neighborhoods. I met people—good, hard-working moms and dads, grandparents, and lots of children. As I introduced myself as a career teacher, I was met with both gratitude and distrust as people wondered what my angle was, my reason for being at the park, the grocery store, or the playground. I simply had to know how we were doing as an educational entity.

These folks on the board don't have a global view of what goes on in our neighborhoods, homes, schools, and communities. They were clueless when I spoke of hidden and forgotten underserved families and entire neighborhoods. Not one of the assistant supervisors had, by their own admission, walked these neighborhoods. They are clueless about the plight and daily lives of most of their students' families while making decisions that impact them.

They winced as they became exposed. I told them they had contributed to the hopelessness many of our families experience daily. This is not a welcome message. Our upper management—the superintendent and fifteen- to twenty-five assistants—have not been out in the neighborhoods with the families. They don't know what challenges exist for so many of our parents and children. I did ask whether any of our assistant supers, their direct subordinates, or our board president had been out and present in our city's neighborhoods. Their silent response was telling. They serve in their lofty roles, yet don't know or care who they serve. If you haven't been in the community and don't know the landmarks, restaurants, safe or unsafe areas, or where the playgrounds are, then you are a phony. If our highly paid assistant superintendents haven't spoken to the parents, children, taxpayers, faculty, and staff members about our mission and heard from them what we could do better, then they are color-changing chameleons and should be ashamed. Their disconnect from the families they are supposed to serve is sickening. It has been this way far too long. These titled people are among the least connected and invested in our entire system. What should be a requirement, knowing our families and their challenges, is not even mentioned when these people are placed in their jobs.

Chapter Nine

Inspirations

When people find out I've been a teacher for forty-three years, I get hammered with questions. *How can you do it? Kids today are so different, so disrespectful.* Or someone will say. *I'll bet you just can't wait to retire.* Actually, it's just the opposite. The kids are great, have been great, and will always be great. The kids who are pains in the neck don't stay that way very long. I wonder why?

I constantly draw inspiration from kids who do amazing things; the greatness and uniqueness of the children I deal with every day. You see, I never know which of the youngsters will become that inspiring force to keep me refreshed and invigorated. Success in high school does not always mean the same in college or in the real world. Often the little pains are the most surprising. Each day of teaching is different. Each child in each class has a distinct and unique personality.

Big A and Family

Big A, Adrian Mendoza-Green, is named first because we met first. We connected back in 1987. He came out for wrestling and proved to be hard-working, loyal, and serious about school. I met his mom and dad and other family members shortly after meeting him. His family had ties to the San Luis Valley, and he was a good young man with bits of southern Colorado, North Denver, and assorted locales bred into his persona. His people came from all over.

The Mendoza-Green crew ran deep, and now runs deeper with his better half, Rene, and her family. Now, cousins, grandparents, brother Joe,

Dave, and family all came en masse to wrestling matches and other events, highlighted by Mom and Dad, who supported anything that A did back in the day. Whether a school event or athletics, they were all in. Always quietly in his corner, Dad was clearly supportive of the coaches and teachers.

It was no surprise Adrian studied hard, came to every practice, and was a true pillar in school and a mainstay on the wrestling team. It is true he was surrounded by a cast of other high-quality students and athletes, but he stood out because he tried to not stand out. But he was intense, outworking and outlasting others his age. The coaches and teachers all knew his drive would set him up for success in whatever he chose.

He chose college and college wrestling. As I recall he was a kinesiology major, matching the grind that he established as a sixteen-year-old. We stayed in touch after he graduated, and he chose a circuitous route to become a teacher. Eventually, he ended up right back with me at George Washington. Soon we were hanging out as colleagues, and he ultimately became our head wrestling coach. He was very technical in his approach but also a reserved tyrant of sorts who would not hesitate to crawl down your throat and box, figuratively, with your tonsils. No. Coach Green was not by any stretch reserved in the classroom or on the mat. He soon became the consummate educator and coach, having success with students and athletes.

To date, he has inspired scholars, military men and women, and coached many of the top wrestlers in Colorado. As crazy as it seems, I believe he is in his second generation of students. While completely committed to the young people he serves, he never flinched. He and I spent hours at a time, for many years, aligned in our philosophy. He has never compromised, and I am quite proud that he has remained true to his belief that children must be motivated and nudged, albeit firmly, to reach their potential. He sees each child as an individual with a bright future. Coach Green's success is immeasurable as a coach and teacher.

His finest accomplishment, though, lies not in the schoolhouse. It lies among those in his family. As a family, the Greens are what every family aspires to be. They are warm, nurturing and highly successful, and this radiates when you are around them, individually or together. Rene is an acclaimed mother, wife, daughter, and teacher. She is fierce in her belief that each child has a place in class and is a voice of the future. Mariah, now coaching and a college graduate, is establishing her place in our community. Darren is working on his college degree and wrestling at the University of Wyoming. They have been a fixture at our family events, and no doubt we are part of each other's families. We have shared a few sad moments, but far more happy events, and will share more.

Little did I know when we met over thirty years ago that our families would intertwine and become so close. We love them and feel the love back. I'm so proud to have shared our journeys together. Love always to this very special family.

Swifty, P'nutt, and Reggie

From teenagers to colleagues, men who make a difference. Two Swifts, Big Swifty and little brother P'nutt were not the wildest children back in the day, but certainly not subdued. Big Bro was the recipient of gassers and up-downs. Nutt was boisterous, often enjoying class too much, especially when provoked by one of his boys. He sinned once by laughing uncontrollably when his teacher, Ms. Ostrum, was talking about the dangers of venereal disease. The teacher was heated because syphilis is not a funny disease. Yet Stevie and Nutt were enjoying another anonymous male's unfortunate plight way too much. By the time Mrs. Ostrum told the story, I knew what I had to do. I suggested that she put him on the "EL" list. That meant that he had to go through "Blue Tuesday." Blue Tuesday is what happens when children, usually males, end up with a "D" or "F" on eligibility.

The list usually comes out on Monday or Tuesday mornings and is (fortunately) a printable document. The sinners who have been slacking in their classes line up and are told what class they are doing poorly in. Imagine Nutt, an honor roll student, called to the line and told that he's got to be with the eight or nine others who were legitimate slackers. His shock turned to anger as he dutifully followed the others as they began step one of this infamous drill. Like soldiers, they were on all fours doing their dutiful bear crawl for one entire lap, a quarter of a mile. One of the larger kids usually made them start over. A big fella would touch a knee to the ground, requiring them all to start over. Nutt was livid about the whole thing, and now, decades later, I admit I was the motivating factor for this.

On the second attempt they all made the lap in bear-crawl mode. Then they lined up for their hundred up-downs, a well-known torturous drill where they hit the turf after pumping hands and feet, chest first, and bounce back up. These went well. They only had to repeat maybe twenty. If one of the large fellas once again did it wrong, they lined up for step three. Yes, in full uniform, they had to do forward rolls across the field and back, twice. Nausea always hit them and was often followed by vomiting. When they finished this routine, they were released back to their drills with the students who had done school the right way. Nutt was mad and yet helpless in this situation. Big Swift and Nutt both knew the drill.

Lori, their lovely mother, was always on my side one hundred percent. She ruled the roost and kept these two under her thumb, and school was what they were expected to do. Nutt knew I would tell Mom he thought STDs were funny and that she would follow up with home consequences. Maybe he could complain to Dad? No, Dad, in Oklahoma, was a boxer, and a boxing coach wouldn't play that either, so Nutt was stuck and had to take the hit. He didn't belch, blow gas, look at Stevie, or do anything but immerse himself in the content of Mrs. Osrum's class. She marveled at this dramatic change. Nutt is now our head football coach, doing amazing things with our very competitive team. He traveled this road and is a testament, through his journey, that success follows hard work. As a competitor, he is one of the finest athletes we have had in the last quarter-century. He coaches the same way he played back in the day. Full throttle, pedal to the floor.

Reggie, our head basketball coach, has a different story. Though a bit wild, he was rarely in trouble. A great athlete at our school, he was now likely the finest "roundball" coach in the state. He is on a great run and has led the team to the championship game three times in the last several years. Coach walks softly but makes a huge impression. He teaches technique and gets kids to play hard, an amazing accomplishment in this day and age. Coach Hammons is also an amazing dad. He has three sons, and the two eldest are quiet and respectful. They have adopted his work ethic and soft demeanor unless confronted with a competitive situation. The evolution from student to educator and colleague is fascinating. Seeing them as men who are fine dads and true professionals in the place where they grew up is heartwarming.

Tommy

Tommy was a different sort. As a fifteen-year-old, he was raw, tall, had a good frame, and was serious in class, with a strong motivation to get good grades. He ended up in my fitness class as a sophomore at mid-year. I knew of him but did not know him, same on his end. He had heard that there is only one way in the old coach's class, yet like others didn't believe it was actually true. On day one he showed up to class in the appropriate uniform and the second we started stretching he turned to talk to his homeboy. Boom!

"Tommy, get out. Go sit on the third step of the stairway and think about it!" He looked at me like I was on both edibles and concentrates. I gestured and he went and parked it on the third step as he had been asked. He was fuming, and I didn't care. On day two, to his credit, Tommy made it through stretching, but during jumping jacks he got caught talking again. He was really pissed now, sitting again on the third step for the thirty-eight minutes until class was over, clenching his jaw the whole time and staring at me. *Damn,* he must have been thinking, *this old man isn't like my other teachers. He actually will jump my case and make me do what he wants!*

Day three. Tom comes in and goes to an area by himself, isolated by several feet from the nearest student who could possibly distract him. Hallelujah! Tommy made it through stretching and the workout. Tommy started about average, with a 21-inch vertical jump, a 135-pound bench, and a 165-pound squat. Right in the middle. But he had tremendous drive and a competitive spirit. Fast forward four-and-a-half semesters. He was now a big man at 6'5", had improved his vertical by ten inches, benched 250, squatted in the 3s and had gained about twenty pounds of muscle. Hell, I went to the games and focused on my student. He wasn't poetry. He wasn't graceful and he didn't have the best handles. Yet he played with a passion and a grind that made him the best player on the court, every game. He dove for the ball, he banged the boards, had bad breath on defense (just kidding), he scored, he did it all and there were none better, at least in Colorado. He played angry and with a love of the game that I will probably never see again. Tommy ended up at Boise State, and now many years later is playing in Spain. In the summer he plays on the Nuggets developmental squad and then goes back overseas for the remainder of the foreign season.

I am proud as hell of Tommy. But my love of how he plays basketball is second, by a long shot, to my love of this stellar young man as a person and family man. Between elementary and middle school, Tommy was a hellion by his own admission, almost out of control. He was so bad he got bounced out of traditional school and ended up at an alternative setting for the most raw, incorrigible students. Youth in this situation often get worse and the system cheats them out of their "formative education." The kid falls through the cracks and ends up even worse off and sometimes completely out of school, yet another ugly statistic.

According to Tom, his peers at the new building got in his ear. They told him he was bright, that he had a future, that he could actually do something, and that he should change, and the words were so powerful he believed them. Through their words and a mother who would not give up, he changed his attitude. He shut his mouth in class, addressed his teachers respectfully, and became obsessed with getting out of Denver. He maintained his grades in high school and took challenging classes. At Boise State he played in the NCAA tournament and played well enough to make a good living overseas and stateside during the summers.

We spoke not long ago when I asked if I could write his story. I asked how long he planned on playing. Tommy explained that he would play for several more years, as long as he stayed healthy, and would leave the competitive game after first his mother and then he were financially secure. Damn!

What drives him is his desire to take care of his mother. He still plays with the same intensity that he embraced in high school. He feeds off of his hunger to be great, and no doubt keeps his mother at the forefront of his journey to pay her back for being the pillar throughout his life. Tom is a symbol, a model of what can happen when a person decides who they really are and that their own potential is unlimited.

York

I could take no more. York was in trouble again. For the third time that week, Sean had been given a referral for general disrespect. He never was in big trouble in the school's eyes. Mostly because he never got caught. Now he was in my office again, and frankly, I was tired of seeing him. I honestly can't remember the details of the referral, but I do remember our conversation. I mostly vented on him.

York was a good-looking kid. With large eyes, he was about 5' 11" and 170 pounds. He didn't walk, he swaggered; his walk was half pimp and half cool. York was well known throughout the hood for smoking, drinking, and the ability to put up the dukes. He left the Big Apple, though the Big Apple had never left him. His accent was replete with slaying profanity and York-isms that he and his homies understood. Most teachers were afraid of him, due largely to the persona with which he carried himself. He could change the mood of a class in an instant with a joke, a cuss word, or a wisecrack too often made to the teacher who was already pissed off that he was in class that day, or that entire semester. Sean was a piece of work. He was rowdy, even by New York standards. Imagine what he was like in Denver.

I read the referral, jumped up, and closed the door to my office. He sat up in his chair, shocked! Usually, he slumped to remain cool. His eyes grew large.

"I'm tired of your disrespect. You are acting like a punk and a hoodlum. I am not impressed. These little kids may be buffaloed by your bullcrap, but I'm not. I have half a mind to knock you across the room." I paused, or you might say, I came up for air, then continued. "Why don't you quit acting like a thug and do something with your life? You come in with another referral, and I will send you home, maybe for the rest of the school year."

I was done. The bell rang and he stood up, expressionless. I ended with a "Get your butt out of here and get to your next class." As he laughed, I detected a slight quiver from his left eye, which may or may not have been a teardrop. In any event, I was pretty sure that his I-don't-give-a-damn attitude would prevail, and he would be back to his old tricks. For the rest of the year he was mostly out of sight, out of mind.

Many years later our paths crossed when a relative was in the local hospital requiring surgery. I went to visit. I heard a familiar voice from the past yell, "Coach." The accent was unforgettable. It was Sean. He looked great. He filled me in on his life and pulled me to the side.

"Coach?" he said, "Could you please call me Sean? What you're saying is not what I want to be known as around here."

I agreed. He said he started as an orderly and was hoping to move up in the hospital hierarchy. Two or three years later, I bumped into him again. The hospital had sent him to school for additional training. He began in radiology setting up the operating room schedule, and he began to develop a career. His goal was to become an operating room nurse. He moved up the rank and is now well known to all in the hospital.

We once lost touch for about eighteen months. During that time, I decided to have surgery for an umbilical hernia that I had delayed for almost a year. Part of his job was to schedule operations in the hospital. He called me, sounding worried as hell. I knew he was at work.

"You okay, Coach?" he said. "What's going on?"

"I'm great, why?"

"I saw your name on the surgery board," he explained. I told him I was fine. Just having a quick surgery to fix my hernia. He said he wanted to talk to me before the surgery, so I happily invited him for dinner the next night. He came over and asked if I was scared. I told him I was scared to death about being put under and not seeing my family again. I was fearful that I would go to sleep and never wake up. We ate quite well, I might add. He told me not to worry, because he had me all hooked up. I wasn't sure what he meant, but out of complete trust dropped the subject.

On the day of the surgery, I was told to show up at 6:15 a.m. Once I was there, I was counting on the usual waiting delays and general aggravation that all hospital visits and surgeries entail. I was shocked to see the nurse so ready, so prepared, as she said quite professionally, "Coach, we have been waiting for you." And they were prepared for Brenda too and offered water or coffee along with her choice of breakfast.

Not five minutes later my nurse, quite pretty and shapely, was taking my vitals. Then the anesthesiologist, a cool, middle-aged man, walked in. He said, "Coach, I'm going to get you intravenous sedation, which means you won't have to go to sleep."

I got the picture. Sean had taken care of every detail. I had the finest staff to take good care of me. My surgery, which was scheduled for 7:30 a.m., began at 7:20. They got me on the table, and after about twenty-five minutes of "slice me and dice me," I was in recovery. I was fully conscious, listening to two nurses gossip.

"Sir, are you okay?" one said.

"Yes, I'm fine, can I go home?" They looked at each other and then at me like I was nuts.

"You will need to hold down some ice chips. Then you'll need to hold down some juice. Then you'll need to move your bladder," they explained.

I was ready. I ordered my ice chips. They came in a cup the size of a thimble. Down the hatch they went, and I was ready for part two. They looked worried.

"Mr. Finesilver, don't rush this. It usually takes several hours or half a day."

I persisted. "Ma'am, may I please have the juice?" They gave in. Not five minutes later, I asked them to allow me to unload some liquid. They then called Sean.

"Coach...rest, you can't rush this," Sean said when he came in. I told them to walk with me to take a leak or to leave one in the bathroom. He watched without embarrassment as I did my best to pass test number three, and I succeeded. He was surprised. We walked out of the lab, and he nodded to the nurses as they were preparing my discharge papers. I threw on my sweats, grabbed Brenda, and laughed. In and out in about ninety minutes total. A millionaire, celebrity, or dignitary would not have been treated any better.

Sean has continued to prosper. He is now several degrees deep and has been through the traditional nursing school training. His work at various hospitals has been vast. I'm sure there have been some bumps in the road for him, but Sean got married and is a wonderful husband. We still talk to each other frequently and see each other at times, just not often enough. I'm proud as hell of him. He inspires me. How honored I am that he was nearby for the birth of my sons, all four of them. He sat with me and cried with me as I lost my father. No one would have predicted that he would be doing what he is now, working a job that requires patience, compassion, and love. He has already had a long career and now is a lead operating room nurse. When we do connect, it is truly a breath of fresh air. He has the same passion and zest for life that he had as a juvenile. "York" has been a champion of the patient in his chosen work.

Mo

Mo was a lanky seventh grader, a "yes sir, no sir" kid to everyone, every day. I had no doubt he would be a smashing success because of his drive and work ethic. He respected his parents. His real name is Maurice, but he much preferred Mo. Thick-necked, wide-shouldered, and strong as a bull, he was getting beefy by the time he hit his sophomore year in high school. By this time he had also established his academic prowess. Almost every course he took had "A.P." or "accelerated" as part of its title. His parents required him to take the toughest, most demanding courses offered at his school. Mom and Dad were quiet, intense parents with high expectations who kept their kids in line. Except for once. In addition to his smarts, his strength, his athleticism, and his work ethic, he had depth. The kid was maxed out on integrity, respect, loyalty, and leadership. Maurice was loved by his peers and revered by the faculty.

In contrast to his normal demeanor, Mo was full of the devil. He knew precisely what was okay and what would get him busted by Dad, a former Olympic boxer. Or worse, by his mom, a strict disciplinarian. He was as rowdy as they came. He had an arsenal of locker-room pranks, stunts, and jokes that were more than comical.

One day he came to school with thick, black-framed glasses with a wide strip of athletic tape on the bridge. He wore a dress shirt about four sizes too tight and the most butt-ugly tie with the worst paisley pattern imaginable, the kind many school administrators wore in the '80s. He was a colossal nerd that day, and people who saw him didn't know whether to laugh or cry. In football drills he would cut up at times by grabbing a butt in a pile or by giving a teammate the proverbial wedgy.

One day he crossed the line. After an early November practice, we headed into the locker room. It was snowing, and about ten degrees outside with a hefty wind chill. As we entered the locker room, a freshman said, "Coach, Maurice fainted." The informant was a freshman, and because of how well I knew Maurice, I didn't give it a second thought. Maurice was strong, and too tough to faint. Our coaches began our meeting to debrief after practice. About five minutes later, another kid, a more credible sophomore, interrupted.

"Excuse me, but Maurice passed out in the snow." I gradually became more concerned and went outside to look.

"He's just screwing around. Just ignore him," I said. I returned to the important meeting. Ten minutes later, I finally took notice when two juniors interrupted with the same info. Time for me to take action. I instructed the two juniors to recruit seven or eight others to bring Maurice into the locker room. In uniform, he was three hundred ten pounds of solid muscle. They carefully brought him in and laid him down smack dab in the middle of the locker room. We continued our meeting. About six minutes later, the next interruption came. Maurice was still in the middle of the locker room, lying on the floor, still motionless. By now the snow had melted, forming big puddles around him. The older kids were nervous, wondering what was wrong with their big teammate. The freshmen, typical to their squirreliness, were playful. They were bravely tickling his chin, armpits, and sides. A couple had even gone to the ice machine and shoved ice down his pants inside his jock strap. I now was worried. Ice on the genitalia will wake anyone up. He didn't stir. I grabbed eight other kids and brought him into the coach's office where we kind of propped him up at a ninety-degree angle on the chair. I hurriedly got mom on the phone.

"I'm sorry to bother you, but Maurice has passed out. He would never joke like this, would he? He's now in our office, and it seems like he's out cold."

She thought for a few minutes and said no. He would not do that ever.

I made the call. I dialed 9-1-1 and spoke to the poor dispatcher about my dilemma. She asked me to repeat myself. I started to see the edge of Big Mo's lip quiver. Looking a bit like his devilish grin, I asked the 9-1-1 operator to hold on. By then, he had the full low grin going and I politely excused myself and hung up the phone. I was livid. He had pranked me, his teammates, his mom, and almost a group of paramedics. I screamed, ranted, and raved, and I instantly called Mom. With his butt humbled and true to his upbringing, he was full of apologies.

Mo was recruited his senior year by the finest schools in the nation and ultimately went to Harvard University in Boston. After an agonizing spring waiting for the news, he was given the highest honor accorded to any student football player, a prestigious Golden Helmet award. Once we found out I called them into my office and said, "Congratulations. You've won the Golden Helmet award." We both cried tears of joy. He hoisted me up in the air and carried me into the hallway of the school. I'm not small, and back then I weighed probably 270 pounds. To Mo, it made no difference. He had to express his joy by lifting me like a sack of potatoes.

Some rookie security guard thought I was being kidnapped. Before long, the whole security staff was involved. Teachers and students wondered what in tarnation was going on. We raised such a ruckus that a couple of the administrators even came out from the cozy confines of their offices. Finally, we simmered down.

Big Mo's career at Harvard was outstanding. He received national honors in academics and football and earned his bachelor's degree in four years. We were in contact in college, and every chance he got he would call to visit, keeping me up to date on his many successes and very few failures. After Harvard, he studied and coached at the duo universities, University of the Pacific and Tulane University. While at Tulane, he met his beautiful future bride.

I can't forget to mention his seven-year professional football career in Spain. He was a player and a coach who made himself a running back. A damn good one, I might add. Big Mo has now relocated back in Denver. I see him on occasion, but again, not nearly often enough. He is a gem. He is vice president of a large savings and loan corporation. More important, he is an extraordinary husband and daddy. Maurice has been a constant source of inspiration for me. Every coach should be lucky enough to interact with an individual with his qualities. Loyalty, pride, a bust-your-fanny work ethic, and humility, all packaged into one lovable devilish brute with a brain. It's sad that many coaches never have a Big Mo to inspire them. I'm touched beyond words to have shared such special moments with him. He has and will always be not only one of the finest players I've coached, but the epitome of what a young man should be. I hope and pray that my sons will grow up to have the passion and compassion that Mo has.

Steel Will

Every time I crossed the courtyard for a rare journey to the main office, I saw him. Each time I saw him, I got angry. He wore a retro-looking Chicago Bears jersey most days and hung out with his fellow crips. Some wannabes, they were usually up to no good. They would shoot craps, talk, and ditch class, which was the norm for Big Willie each time I saw him. I deviated from my pattern and confronted him to go to class.

"What a waste," I said. "You should grow up. Leave those guys alone. They don't care about you."

He usually issued a defiant comment back to me, but he never crossed the line of disrespect. He had apparently chosen to hang out rather than do anything positive in school. He was well on his way to a life of misery. I was sure my words didn't matter and did nothing more than piss him off. He was sadly, I thought, just another kid sucked up in the gang life. Will back then was a freshman, 5'11" and about 210 pounds. He was barrel-chested and stocky, with a toughness about him that got him noticed with his homies, his friends, and made teachers wary of him. He was no one to mess with.

Imagine my shock when, as a sophomore, he showed up for football one day. I sent our manager to pull a copy of his report card. He was barely eligible. I knew we could help him bring up his grades. I would get him locked into the team concept.

Two or three days of conditioning nearly ruined him. Two or three years of tar and nicotine were flying through his respiratory system, circulatory system, and maybe even his excretory system. We kicked the conditioning up a few notches. He would not quit.

We knew he was strong and tough, but what surprised the coaches and players alike was how quick he was. He could anticipate the snap and rarely could anybody block him. As a sophomore, he played defensive tackle, where he made fourteen or fifteen tackles a game, even though he was often double-teamed. His grades improved dramatically, and we were able to change his mindset and activities. He only got a few referrals to the office his sophomore year, coincidentally after football season had ended. He was ready to start his junior year. He had lifted weights, he was in good shape, he weighed about 212 pounds by then and could bench press about 290 pounds.

One minor problem arose. A running-back coach wanted to make him a doggone fullback. I explained, not very patiently, that Will was a damned defensive tackle. He kicked everyone's butt last year, and this year he is still a defensive tackle. Coach Nye persisted for many months, and finally I gave in. We kept him on the defensive line, but also gave him a shot at fullback. His junior year, he had about ninety tackles on the defensive line and gained about 600 yards as a fullback. He could run and block and was turning into a hell of a football player. During one of our summer workouts before his senior year, he came to see me. "Coach, I need to talk to you."

"Will, tell me what's on your mind."

"Coach, as you know, my mom has been ill. Dad hasn't had a job for a while. I need your help. I want to go to college. Really."

"I would love to help you, but you have to listen to everything I say," I said.

"Coach, I'm game."

I looked at his transcript and, with the help of a college buddy, determined he really needed to double up on his academic classes. Yes, two math classes, two science classes, and two English classes. Both semesters his senior year, Will had a full schedule. On occasion, as he would get lazy during the fall semester, I would remind him of his dreams and goals and his desire to go to college, and he would conform. That year, Will was a beast on the football field. He gained a thousand yards at fullback. He had over a hundred tackles, and he made the "All Colorado" team. That team won their first nine games and was rated number one in the state. His teammates loved him. He had made a dramatic turnaround from the young kid he used to be. He was recruited by Wyoming, Colorado State, and Arizona, and he chose Colorado State. I vividly remember sitting in the principal's office with Willie, his mom, and his dad on the day he signed his full-ride scholarship. All of us, including our principal, had tears of joy over what this young man had accomplished. He went on to play for Colorado State and even played in two or three bowl games. I haven't talked to Willie for a few years, but I'm sure he's doing well. I plan to look him up soon. No doubt he's a great father, and he's doing positive things for himself. He has remarkable toughness and tenacity.

Sammy

He lives in the hood. Actually, he lived in the hood. By the time this is published he'll be "adultish" and out chasing life. But for now, he lives in the hood near the "points" and near downtown. He has eleven siblings and is the baby. He showed up years ago, went out for ball, and has beefed up, a tyrant in the weight room, and he has busted his tail in school. He isn't the best player I have ever coached, but he might be the best kid. He's one of my all-time favorites. I used to see him several times every day. Sam is at the top of the list when it comes to toughness. With three games left in his sophomore year, he took a hard hit against a salty Lincoln High team. Unfortunately, his knee went one way and the rest of the leg stayed in place. It was gruesome. Right away the doc on the sideline said he had torn all the ligaments you could tear. He tore the ACL, the MCL, and the PCL, and he was devastated.

We were more devastated. He was our quarterback and our spiritual leader, even though he was fifteen years old. We were well on our way to win the city title, and the quarterback behind him was real young, and very much a free thinker, which in our system spells trouble.

Sammy was unable to get adequate medical care because of insurance issues in his family. He toughed it out for a month, still coming to practice, where he hobbled around and kept the team in check. Finally, we got a discount MRI that told us what we already knew. He had torn everything. His career was in jeopardy. By the time January hit we were still waiting for his insurance to kick in. The positive is that Sammy was able to see his football brothers capture the city title. The negative was that Sammy didn't get approved for surgery until close to March. We got tired of waiting and went out and found a "mensch." This mensch happened to be Dr. K, who ran a rehab clinic in an upscale fitness club. Doc had been seeing Sammy for free to get him ready for the knife. Sammy would go several times a week to get the quads, hams, and glutes stronger so when he had the surgery, the rehab would be minimal. Once Doc got word that Sam was clear for surgery, it was too late. Sam had trained so much the doctor felt he could wait until after the next season. He hooked Sammy up with a brace and Sammy worked his tail off to get prepped for his junior year. He played well, and even completed thirty or so passes to lead us to another city championship.

We planned to have the surgery after his junior year, but the doctor that Doc K had recommended could not get the insurance lined up. Sammy worked his tail off, even with a knee held by one ligament out of four, and he played linebacker and fullback his senior year. He missed one game because he tweaked the knee a bit, but he did a great job. The surgeon of choice finally said that even though the insurance might not pay, he would do the surgery anyway. Sure enough, the good doctor repaired the damage, and after two weeks of immobilization, sent Sammy back to rehab. I still wonder how in hell this kid did it. He played for two full seasons with a knee that wasn't totally hooked together. He didn't complain once and showed toughness rarely found in any kid. What an inspiration, and what a rowdy kid. He could come up with a "your momma" joke any time with anybody. He would hang around with the sophomores, frequently referring to them as his cute little *daughters*. What a hard-nosed fantastic person.

Billy Lyle

Billy could play a bunch of positions in football. Tall, strong, and fast, he could play D-end, tight end, and linebacker. He was raw-bone tough, and on one occasion punched a kid who was a bit selfish and not nearly as tough. He took discipline for his transgression, running and push-ups and football up-downs, even though the other kid deserved it. Billy ran his gassers (training sprints the width of the field), did more up-downs, and took his punishment obediently. He would repent after he sinned and would learn lessons—the hard way. He also ran track and ended up a good trackman as well as being a starter on the basketball team. Lyle stood about 6'3" and weighed 180 pounds. He punched another kid out on the upper ramp, visible to most of the school, during a passing period. This kid deserved it, too. A few days later he had the nerve to be tardy to a class. That time I yanked him from basketball practice and sentenced him to two full days practicing with the wrestlers. He hung tough even when tossed in with the eight or nine wrestling monsters, who were all pretty good at whipping their opponent's tails.

Billy is, to say the least, a bit of a pugilist, a lot of stubborn, and hugely hung up on the principle of the matter. He had opportunities to go immediately to college, yet he decided to become a marine. He did this with the same gusto he did everything, and before long was in D.C. as part of a unit that helped secure the White House and protect the presidential party during their travels. He was a company guy, fiercely loyal and willing to give up his life in the line of duty.

Last year I got a call.

"Hey Coach, this is William Lyle."

"Billy, how in the world are you?" I said. He was in town from back east to see some family members who were ill and was near the school and wanted to see me. I couldn't wait. He walked in and I noticed a bit of a limp, but I didn't ask. He finally told a story that made me tear up, validating what I had always known about him. If I were in a dark alley, I would choose to be with him.

Turns out Billy was, as a cop in Alexandria, in a dark alley looking for a drug dealer, most likely a criminal who was armed and dangerous. He and other officers gave chase, the criminal took off, and they ended up in a foot race. Knowing Billy, he no doubt gave chase very fast. A long chain blocked the end of the alley from vehicle traffic. The perp knew the area better than Billy and avoided the chain.

William never knew what hit him. He was on his back and drew his gun, ready to shoot as he saw this menacing figure swinging on the chain. In the stone-cold darkness, he realized that the figure teetering on the chain was not the bad guy. It was his leg, which had nearly been severed by this unlikely collision. Then and only then did Billy realize that he was in deep trouble.

Days later he woke up in the hospital where a team of doctors had tried valiantly to save his limb. They couldn't, and informed him of the inevitable. After much medical deliberation, the decision was made to amputate his leg. Bill Lyle was in the hospital on the highest doses of morphine, recovering from surgery and fighting infection. But once weaned from the morphine, he got antsy. We common men and women will have a hard time understanding this attitude.

Billy Lyle just isn't wired like the rest of us. His drive comes from the depths of his gut, his stomach, his bowels, his heart, and his brain. A representative from the police union came to inform him that his new cop duty would be at a desk and not with the men, his men, on the streets. Right before this suit came in, Billy had decided to try walking. He knew he was missing his leg, but he had to give it a try. He fell quickly and hard but was undaunted. Now weaning himself from the narcotics, Billy jumped into the bed, latched onto the triangular traction bar, and began doing some sort of inverted pull-ups.

The police official came into the room expecting a morose and somber William Lyle, but he came to an abrupt halt, unable to speak. William was a bit perturbed that he had to stop exercising, and even more pissed off when he heard the messenger's words. He was not going to be placed on active duty; he would sit at a desk for the rest of his career. Billy called it a bullcrap decision and meant it, and then said he would return to the streets with his fellow officers. The man left and Billy fumed. Shortly he started therapy and was finally discharged, largely due to his anger at the possibility of finishing a storied career behind a desk.

Billy appealed the department's decision and ultimately was told that the only way he could return to the streets was if he could pass the physical training required of all cops. He did indeed surpass the physical requirements and ultimately went back to the streets. He worked the streets after passing all the police department's tests, which no one except Billy thought he could pass. Billy Lyle did several more impressive years of active duty. When he retired, he was active with the church and spent his time coaching football and basketball. He speaks with great pride of his family and the young people he coached.

As I listened, I was in awe. Most people who have been through this type of situation would relax and slow down. It would have been easy in his situation to hit the canvas and stay down. The routine, which he followed after the surgery, was brutal at best. Hours spent daily learning not only to walk and balance, but also to run and dodge, to lift and carry, and to serve and protect. His story has been written in some of our nation's finest publications. Billy Lyle, the teenager who I knew in my early twenties, has now become William Lyle the man, the role model, the teacher, the, coach, the symbol, the inspiration. They don't come any finer and there are none better. He has received honors and accolades. He is a hero among us.

Shakib and Shuaib

They were a dynamic duo. The brothers had a slight difference in age, but they were in the same grade. Early in their freshman year they flew under the radar and I didn't know them, but eventually I met one and then the other. They were good kids, and I was sure they were good students. They passed the first two tests, so I encouraged them to play ball. They began lifting weights and I saw they were a bit athletic. When I asked them to attend a workout, they came early and stayed late, showing nice dedication for kids who had never played organized sports.

The brothers were born in Afghanistan and came to our soil in the early nineties. Shakib was taller and outgoing. He was obedient, as was Shuaib, but like all others, certainly not an angel. They were in our school's International Baccalaureate program, which back then spoke volumes. I finally got them to take my fitness class and they worked hard and followed instructions. They were living with Mom, who put in long hours to provide all she could for the two boys. Shuaib was handsome. He was on the heavier side, so we made him a lineman. He was a bit reserved, except when alone with his brother or his other misfit teammates. I encouraged them to work for our summer work–study program. They became supervisors and as they got older, they helped administer the program. They were natural leaders. In his youth, Shakib was undependable. When it was required that he be in the lunchroom at 6:20 a.m., he either cut it close or sometimes had the audacity to come late. Though it happened rarely, I became annoyed that he wasn't early enough. This started a series of phone calls that would last for months at a time. I would give him a wakeup call between 4:30 and 5:15 a.m. to make sure he was developing good work habits. On some of those mornings he wasn't working, but nonetheless still got the call. Then I would lay off for a couple of weeks and then resume the calls because I was compelled to help with that skill. This pattern went on for about eighteen months, but I eventually stopped, as the young man hadn't learned to manage time.

Like his brother, Shuaib got into Colorado College and after earning his degree went to work and then earned an MBA. He has proven to be a good man, husband, and father. The values his mom instilled are no doubt etched in his psyche as he emulates her work ethic and moral compass and is committed to doing right for his family. Life has prevented us from seeing each other as much as we would like, but I get updates from his brother.

Shakib and I have been more connected. I have his picture on my bulletin board with his infant son, and he has brought his dear wife and family over to the house to spend time. Years ago, he opened up to me as former students often do. The horrors of his early life had caught up with him. Seeing relatives live in exile and die while they are hiding imprints even the strongest of children. The atrocities he was exposed to never left his complicated memory. He shared that he became reclusive and depressed, classic in the sense that he could still parent and perform at work.

Shakib's educational and career journey took him into medicine. A hospitalist at a large hospital, he was respected, but he needed to take care of himself and rid himself of his own demons. He got to the point where he was distant, and he cried out for help. After a painful intervention by those he was and is closest to, he checked himself into rehab. He came to see me to confess what few of us knew. He had a sense that those who loved him would support his need to clear his mind and understand how to manage the violent memories from his past. Once he shared this news, he seemed relieved, and deep down he knew I wouldn't judge.

After this difficult and painful journey through counseling, he emerged back into the lives of his beloved family and closest friends. He seemed to now understand why he had the continued images, nightmares, and psychological baggage. Shakib had lived with PTSD for far too long. What a huge step he made to admit how he felt and what led up to it. As he allowed others to understand bits and pieces of his other world, he felt a degree of comfort. His journey into healing will continue, yet he is committed to the daily battle of the healing process, and he will continue to win. What an incredible path Shakib and Shuaib have traveled. They came from the humblest of beginnings into a life that is happy and enriching. But my pride in them boils down to this. They overcame so much and endured. Their mom deserves so much credit, which is documented later in these pages. What inspires me the most is the incredible life they have built for their families and beloved children. Through Mom's strength and their grind and resilience, they will earn well-deserved happiness. Let's pray for their continued good health, both physical and mental.

Brock

"Bernard" just didn't fit, so he was quickly anointed "Brock." He was a tall, rangy wild child. Full of words and bravado at first, as he got tougher, he became humble and soft spoken, but it took a while. He gave clues at sixteen that he had a tough upbringing, included being ridiculed at times by his own people for being a mixed child. He endured and decided to play football his junior year. Saying that he was gifted, talented, or even average when he started would be an untruth. He struggled. His desire to be a free safety and punt returner required football savvy and good hands. He was quickly exposed because he was new to the game and just couldn't catch. This was related to his eyesight. A ball in the air with Brock giving chase was scary! On occasion he would actually touch the pigskin, but more often, it would hit him on the head or the shoulder pads, and he often misgauged the ball entirely. His dream of being a skill player quickly got crushed. Frustration set in and he played on special teams and as a backup. By season's end we had decided that his senior year would be spent as a defensive end. He was all in.

Senior year started and by July he was 6'3" and 185 pounds. He spent ten months in the weight room and was able to put that motor and the suppressed anger to good use. Brock was a one-man wrecking crew and could often singlehandedly shut down half the field. He did not get knocked down, and he played at the best speed—full out! Even on the rare occasion (not that rare) that he got flagged for a late hit, we could survive, give him a quick chit-chat, and turn him loose again. He played on a great team with a supporting cast that nearly won a state championship. Big Brock went to a local college and, through a multi-year endeavor, earned his degree. He became less thuggish and more aware of his great potential. His best decision ever was to marry a GW girl, Jodi, who gave him balance and support. He is father to three, and in addition to his high-level computer business, as a coach he has become a surrogate dad to hundreds.

For long periods of time during his youth he did not really get it. I knew he questioned why I insisted he be early, work hard, and study in every class. Fast forward twenty-five years. His journey is gut-wrenching. You see, he was yet another child who wasn't supposed to make it. Thank heaven he was resilient enough to take life's punches and dropkicks and fight back. Brock's and Jodi's oldest daughter has earned a degree, with honors, and has a great job. Elijah is at the Air Force Academy and chasing his college football dream as well. Kyante, who graduated with the class of 2018, attended South Dakota School of Mines and Technology and will also play ball.

Cenea

My girl Cenea, pronounced "Sa-nay," is the picture of persistence and resilience, as tough as any I have known or taught. It took a while for her to become a legend, as it doesn't happen overnight. She sat in the lunchroom at 6:00 a.m. on a late May morning in 2005. She was there because her parents had both been former students and insisted she work. They did not play. Their baby was going to study, play sports, and work each summer to start a college fund. She was intent on absorbing all she could. Mom and Dad had planned that she would be in the program for several years. She was going to work and work hard. Did not matter that she weighed only a hundred pounds, her work ethic had been ingrained in her early. She handled Jobs by George (JBG) that year and many others.

Now Jobs by George is an untamable beast. Started in 1993, JBG has launched hundreds of kids into the real world of work. Cenea steadily worked through the ranks for five years and then decided on or accepted the curse of running the program. Talk about stepping up to the plate.

She almost fired me. I will not forget her tirade, done respectfully no less. *Coach, you need to be more organized! Coach, don't ask me to do five things at once. That's not realistic. Coach, slow down!* She laid down the law and had me on my toes. She was organized and thorough. We met each day at five a.m., and she had her plans for the day which included directions and paperwork for fourteen or fifteen crews of four-to-six people, a supervisor with a team, ready to go out at 7:00 a.m. and work across a fifty- or sixty-mile radius. She would start each morning meeting at 6:30 sharp. In a quiet voice she would say, "Good morning, everyone." In unison, the puppet-like crew would return "Good morning, Cenae." Let one little joker not move his lips enough, and he would catch "the stare." A pretty young woman with eyes like daggers would pierce to the very existence of the culprit, then she would repeat again. "Good morning, everyone." This time everyone greeted her properly and she moved on. Now on occasion a kid would be late. He too got the "daggers" and did his obligatory pushups until my girl gave him a nod that he could join his crew. Here she was, at the age of twenty or twenty-one, running a business and managing a work crew of eighty-five of her young peers as they did nearly five hundred manual labor jobs over a six- or seven-week time period.

After graduating from Colorado State University with honors in only three years, Cenea applied to medical school at well over a dozen schools across the land. She was rejected by each one. The next year she applied to two or three and got into Mehari, in the southern part of the country. Though not her first choice, she accepted and informed me that she would leave her post of running the program after three weeks in order to begin her study. A week before her departure she got a letter from the University of Colorado medical school. She was asked to be in a program with a handful of other students who had applied and been rejected from their schools. The school was willing to pick up the costs of a year of study, with each student taking seven or eight three- to four-week blocks of classes. She would have to achieve a ninety percent or above in each class, and after doing so would be admitted to the med school the following year. What a challenge! Few could have done this, and several from this small group did not qualify. This resilient young lady exceeded the ninety-percent ceiling and after all the obstacles and challenges, she started her career path the next year.

Her end goal was to be a cardiothoracic surgeon, one of the most intense and grueling of all surgical fields. She went through the three required years of medical school, the internship and residency requirements, and applied for a surgical residency at many schools, including The University of Colorado. After more roadblocks and challenges, she was accepted again and is currently on the downside of her training.

Then, another punch in the face. Her dad, Rod, passed unexpectedly in his sleep. He died a young man, with no warning of pre-existing conditions. The news hit her like a ton of bricks. Yet another devastating blow, to lose her daddy, a fine man, at a young age. I have no doubt Cenea will bounce back from this as she has her other setbacks and end up more resilient and certainly loyal to the memory of her daddy.

Cenea is legend. She is the unquestionable G.O.A.T. as far as her resilience and ongoing quest to chase dreams and succeed at everything. I could teach for another couple of generations and not be blessed with another like Cenea.

Lillian

This amazing lady deserves a celebration. My Lord, she is the most resilient and toughest of them all, at about a hundred pounds. She has waged an epic battle with cancer and has been through treatments few of us could handle. Our school treated her horribly, and she endured the insulting and demeaning attitude and behavior by adults, some who were in leadership roles.

I knew Lillian as a fourteen-year-old. She came to gym the first day, a tiny young lady sitting toward the back. Her eyes never left me. In ten seconds, it was clear she had some serious physical education anxiety. She was a wreck as I covered the five or six ways you could actually fail physical education. Her nervousness that first day was all but forgotten by the time we hit the second week. She came prepared each day, did her exercises, and participated with the rest of the class. It was clear she didn't love PE but was prepared to "gut it out" for a semester or two. Within a month, she had made up her mind she would handle this, get her credit, and earn an "A," and she did. Lillian even enjoyed some of the games and became friends with several other students in the class. Her apprehension subsided and she fit in well, as I suspected she would.

Fast forward a year to the first day of my honors science class. As the students came in, leaving their backpacks as requested, Lillian entered, complete with an illuminating smile and quite comfortable. She knew the drill and grinned as I covered the basics, which she had heard a year earlier. By then she was well aware that my bark was worse than my bite. She liked science and knew that the class was a hands-on experience with anatomical models, recitation, and a few well-organized presentations. I'm sure she knew she would end up with yet another A on the transcript, but at the weighted honors scale. She was right. Lillian could recite and present, and she was at home sitting toward the back of the room with her science cronies. She was great at a lot of things, and science was one of them.

As I got to know her, I heard she was a talented equestrian. Heck, this was the first student I'd known who could even ride a horse. I asked her about it, and she brought in a picture. Not only did she ride, but she also competed. One of the best, she was celebrated among other riders and owned a horse or two. I still have the picture of Lillian and her horse. Accomplished as a rider, she rode daily or close to it. Here is this tiny, delicate-looking young lady who was not delicate at heart, riding massive animals very fast and jumping, too. I don't know to this day who else knew of her special skill set. I was awfully proud that she was so good and had shared it with me.

In February of her senior year, I got an email that Lillian was sick. I got her phone number to find out what was going on and reached Mom who, in an emotional conversation, explained that her daughter was very sick and going through treatment. I was floored. It's hard to know what to say in this situation. I offered my support and prayers. Other teachers who had Lillian in class were largely unaware of what was going on. Only one teacher shared that she was quite sick from the treatment and could rarely come to school. I hoped, at that time, that our staff and admin were supportive. Later I found out she'd had little support. Shame on us. This young lady was at the top of her class and on everyone's list to be a top ten senior and receive awards while she walked the graduation stage.

Lillian was so ill her last semester she was fighting for her life. For months, justifiably so, her grades were not nearly as important as her health and her need to survive the cancer, the repeated treatments, and the devastation that accompanies these grueling episodes. She was clinging to life. To this day, I am convinced I was the only adult in the building who knew or cared. She graduated without even a mention, though she was a top senior, a most courageous young lady, and a well-rounded student. Her family was there to support her, but her battle to remain on earth and the courage which she displayed remained, until now, a secret. What a travesty, and we call ourselves educators. It came to my attention that after her treatment started and she lost her hair, we mistreated her with our no-hat policy. Back then, a doctor's note was required, and Lillian had a note on her person, approved by the school nurse, to be allowed to wear a hat. Plus, it was damn cold, and she, in her most fragile state, needed to protect herself. Each day when she entered the building she was confronted by a female member of the administrative team. This self-centered adult insisted that Lillian take her hat off. I am still angry to this day about that. How dare she and all of us be so damn insensitive when a child needed us the most. Yet Lillian endured. This beautiful, bright, talented, humorous little girl, now a woman, proved to be better and more resilient than all of us combined. Through three surgeries, numerous radiation treatments and continual chemotherapy treatments, she remains undaunted.

Dear Lillian and family,

I apologize on behalf of the faculty at George Washington High School for the poor treatment as you concluded your high school career. Lillian, we collectively treated you as if you had done something wrong, and you haven't. We should have celebrated your many accomplishments before and after you became ill, but we did neither, and there is no excuse we could possibly offer. I personally want you to know how much you have impacted my life and my career as an educator. Thank you for being, more than anything, a fighter in a world where our youth often just give up when life gets tough.

Your resolve, your courage, and your ability to walk around life with that beautiful smile, with all that you have overcome, makes you my hero. Yes, at only a hundred pounds, you are my true hero. Now and for eternity you stand in front of me and many others as a symbol of what true strength really looks like. Keep on living, my dear, and keep on smiling. Thank you.

Big Fred

As a freshman, he was tall and very athletic. Word from the elders was that he liked basketball better, yet I didn't care. Big Fred was out for ball and was a rarity. A big, tough kid who was smart. No, that was an understatement. The fellas said Dad was strict, but Mom was the toughest in the house. The message was crystal clear—there would be no slacking in the classroom. This was a bit of a mystery because Dad, affectionately nicknamed "Steak" or "Steakhouse," was always around but never around. So, Dad was at practice but far different than the other dads. He let the coaches coach and supported them when they did. He would never second-guess, demand, or question. Dad would be on the sidelines or back a bit, and the aroma of his presence preceded him. The stench from his stogies arrived several ticks sooner than he did. Nobody has ever enjoyed a cigar more than Mr. Harris. It was that simple. He would eyeball it, admire it, inhale it, and revel in the manliness of it all. Even when it went out— yes, when it was not lit, he may have enjoyed it more. He would chew, salivate on it, chew some more, and after another glance of admiration, light it again. What he did with a cigar was obscene, and he didn't even know it.

Big man plays right away in both basketball and football. By his sophomore year Fred was becoming a nightmare. He was putting on weight and getting stronger, and by then he really understood football. He played defensive end and a bit of tight end. As he hit his junior year, he was a fixture on everyone's recruiting list. The mail came to his house in bundles. He was the top prospect at fifty or sixty major colleges—some for basketball, others for football. Midway through his junior year darn near every school in the nation was recruiting him for one sport or the other. He remained low-key. Mom and dad had raised a level-headed kid, and their priority from an early age was to develop a great young man and a top-tier student. The sports were just icing on the cake. He was able to choose the sport and his own dream school and surprised many when he chose football and the University of Southern California.

His career went well. He played in two Rose Bowls and became part of the USC mystique and tradition. Had it not been for shoulder surgeries (one may have been from poor taping of his shoulder by yours truly), he would have been a star player and no doubt an NFL prospect.

Fred graduated from college and spent time in Las Vegas working in management for a chain selling athletic gear. He did well and was a natural at guiding his team and interacting with the public. After a while he came back to Denver and worked for the same chain in management. Fred then worked for Hertz, again in management, at the busy Denver Airport location. They flourished under his leadership, and he was able to help when he could as a volunteer football coach. He was darn good right away, a young man from Denver who had earned a degree and had a fine career as a player. Naturally, the young men and a few young women respected what he had accomplished. He then entered the corporate world of the early phone companies. Nextel team hired him in management where he again was a great leader and manager. Plus, as he gained more job flexibility, he was able to come out and coach on a more regular basis. Coach was right at home coaching, teaching football and important life lessons to a group seeking an adult to inspire them. He became a very important fixture on the practice field and on the sideline during game time. One day after a particularly grueling practice, he hung around a bit longer than usual. We went into the coach's office, and he shocked me with his words. "I want to be a teacher and coach, full time," he said. "I want to make a difference."

I took a moment to make sure I had processed correctly, then said, "You will be taking a huge pay cut." He thought he could make it work financially. I was so excited he was serious about this. The next day I informed our principal, who was always looking for talented teachers. In a short while Coach was teaching in our building and getting certified through the state Department of Education. This required that he go to class once or twice a week to be able to pass the state's now nationally mandated test showing proficiency in a content area. He fulfilled these obligations without a hitch. Class was a breeze for him.

Fast forward to 2011. We had now logged many years of coaching brotherhood, and I had a desire to see my own youngest four villagers chase their dreams. My boys, two sets of twins, were then fourteen and twelve. Their dream was to go to a good college and wrestle on the same college team. It was August, during our first week of a two week minicamp. As had been the case for many years, the team had met on the outside stairs for attendance. Lots of bright faces just before 7:00 a.m., ready to practice for two hours. After attendance, I took a few deep ones and began.

"Listen, get your eyeballs up. I have been doing this for a long time. I have missed out on a lot of family time doing right by my family." This grabbed their attention. "Coach Harris and I have decided to switch duties. He is going to keep me on as an assistant. I am not ill and no one in my family is sick. I need time to be there and support my children as they chase their dreams."

Now imagine the reaction. People used to joke that I would coach so long that upon my death they would bury me under the turf below the 50-yard line! I assured them I would be around, and that Coach would be great in his new role.

Next, I called our principal and our athletic director. I informed them that after twenty-nine years as head coach I was stepping down and Fred Harris would be the new head coach.

I had to protect him. He had more than earned the chance to run the show. So, for three years I helped the team and did whatever he asked. He coached tough, hard-hitting teams. I got to leave much earlier than usual and was able to roll into my son's practices and wait in the car to pick them up. The time supporting them and the family was so refreshing.

Fred did an admirable job with the team for three years. During a time when our enrollment was dropping and our school losing status, he was able to put tough and competitive teams on the field every week. The lessons he taught beyond football are immeasurable. Fred Harris chose to leave the corporate world and enter teaching. Many who, like him, get into education later in their work career, jump out after a few years when they realize the harsh reality of it all. Not Coach. He is now on his way to hitting two decades in our field. He went back and got his master's degree and is currently an assistant principal at our school. Yes, he is my boss. And I love it. He hasn't been cursed with doing my evaluation yet, but I relish that opportunity. Spending time with him and learning from him would be amazing. He actually was in the classroom long enough to accurately assess what effective teaching looks like.

Lauren

She was blonde and stubborn. I knew her before she knew me. Her interaction with her peers at the pep rallies and in the hallways said a lot about her. She was social and walked with an air of confidence. My close colleague, our soccer coach, told me Lauren was good enough to play in college. If you say that about a kid in Denver and you've been around the game, it usually rings true. Yet, attending a Division 1 school to play soccer only happens to about three out of every hundred high school players. Her coach was explicit—it was Lauren's dream, and she was good enough. I knew what lay ahead for this highly spirited female. I waited, and then waited for another year, and by then my girl was cordial and respectful but hadn't taken the plunge. Word gets out at our school pretty quick. If you want to live the college dream as a jock or jockette, hit the dungeon.

The dungeon arose after our old weight room. It was dark, musty, and in the basement. It had no windows, poor ventilation, and was the spot where many bright-eyed students carved themselves and their path. In 1998, we moved the dungeon upstairs to a deserted auxiliary gym.

Time goes by quickly, and after encouragement from her coach, Lauren called me. Now it has been a while ago, so forgive me for not remembering every detail. Lauren had first period free, so she came to tell me she may not be able to go to her dream school, West Point. Her explanation was that she had not been recruited, even though she had been in their summer camp for two years. According to Lauren, the head coach had been cordial but not committed to her being a candidate for entrance as a student and athlete. Lauren asked if she could voluntarily join my first hour class and train with this advanced group. She also wanted to come several days a week on her own so she could master the military fitness test and maybe have a chance.

I told her that would be fine. I was skeptical, as many athletes say they want to have the college athletic experience, but in the end, very few can survive the grind and accept the lifestyle of school and the various training components. But this seventeen-year-old was wired with a different degree of intensity. She was there every day and returned many times a week doing everything the class did and much more. She trained on her own for hours on end, knowing she may never have the chance to wear the military uniform, attend her dream institution, and play her beloved soccer. The odds were stacked against her.

I learned later that she had internal stress well beyond what any child should have. Her parents had extreme issues with anger, alcohol, and substance abuse, and she lived in a world where Mom's and Dad's issues became hers. When she was finally in the place where her dreams were coming to fruition, she lost her mother.

Lauren began to progress. After several weeks of pain, agony, and the discomfort of incessant advanced training, her numbers took off. She was able to do a dozen chin-ups instead of two or three. She was able to ascend to the top of the class as well in sit-ups and push-ups. I called the coach at

West Point. I had to see for myself and asked for her thoughts about Lauren McGovern. This very important-sounding coach told me that Lauren was good, but in the scheme of things, pretty average.

She may have been average when compared nationally, but she was nowhere near average in my book, and I have been fortunate to coach many All-American athletes, so, as they say, this isn't my first rodeo. I asked the coach what Lauren would need to do to be a viable recruit. Coach explained that she would have to be in the highest percentiles on the fitness tests. I explained that based on what I had seen, and the gallons of sweat Lauren was generating in the weight room, the young woman would surpass expectations on the fitness test.

After many months, I tested her. She did thirteen chin-ups, and her push-ups and sit-ups would have rated in the 80th percentile among male candidates. Her mile was near elite and her basketball throw was the best I have ever seen from any female, as well as from most males. I called the college coach with the numbers. The coach was quiet at first, and then said that if indeed the test scores were sent in as official, Lauren would be slotted. "Slotted" means she would be given a spot for admission. I sent it in, and a few days later the coach called with the good news. She was going to offer Lauren a nomination for admission. I decided to wait and let the process play out. Sure enough, Lauren came to see me a few days later in the middle of the day, and those pretty blue eyes welled with tears. I got the good news, officially, from my most amazing student. She could hardly contain herself. After a hug and some mutual tears, she informed her high school coach and her family members.

Lauren's career was amazing. It took her a while to crack the lineup due to changing positions and a knee injury, but ultimately, she was in the mix and no doubt flying around at her only speed of 110 percent. She competed at that velocity and lives life the same way. Her picture hangs in our weight room, the place where she carved her tremendous work ethic. My hero— Lauren McGovern—will always stand as a symbol of persistence, resilience, loyalty, and devotion. As time goes on, she will no doubt become a hero and inspiration for many others. What she accomplished to go to her dream school and live her dream career has been amazing. Yet these accomplishments pale in comparison to what she overcame within her own family and personal life. Go, Lauren! Chase the next dream!

Ray

I don't know a lot about Ray's early years, except that they were rough. He shared with me that food was scarce at times and clothes were secondhand. He was a slender, bright-eyed elementary school student hanging out on the football field. He halfway asked to hang out, and I liked having him around. He would stay for hours, going to watch the older fellas on what would ultimately become his "field of dreams." Ray was content just being there, a small part of something that to him was huge.

Little did I know what would become of Ray as he grew and made choices. Ray came by the house selling magazines or candy when I lived in East Denver. He was somewhere around eleven years old, and he had his grind going even then.

As a kid, he was a lot like he is now. He went to Colorado State after an incredible high school football career. As a college baller, he was one of the best in the country and had a six- or seven-year career in the NFL. Then he became the Director of Player Development for the Pittsburg Steelers. After a number of years with their organization it was time to return home.

As Ray returned to Denver, we ended up on the same plane. He was coming back to the Denver as the Denver Broncos' Director of Player Development. Now he is their vice president.

Ray Jackson is a classic, the model of what can become of a kid with a dream. The seeds of hope for Ray were likely planted as a young child hanging out with the team. Those boys embraced and accepted him even though he was younger. He was the little brother to a family of high school athletes who grew used to having him around. They needed him and he needed them, as is so often the case. We are all so proud of Ray, and he has never forgotten his roots and ties to the community. He is a hero in the purest sense.

Emmy

It was early November. The wrestling room was electric. We were having a preseason workout with about thirty wrestlers, and the smell, which only wrestling rooms have, was pungent. She came in with a friend and walked to the edge of the mat.

"I'm Emmy. I don't wrestle, but I want to join the team." She whispered this, and I got it and instantly said fine. How could I refuse? This demure young lady with chains on her neck and hoops bigger than her delicate cheeks had set me straight in about ten seconds. Heck, she belonged more than me or anyone else. She chose to make this her new family, and instantly the others embraced her. There was no fancy introduction, no hype, just a beautiful child who was the final link in a big chain that has become a family of brothers and sisters.

At that moment she jumped a bit into my heart. Now three years later she has become my youngest and most recent hero and is deeply embedded in my brain and heart. To say that she is a manager is an understatement. To refer to her as a trainer or scorekeeper is not accurate either. She is our backbone, the heart and soul of our team, and has never wrestled a match for us.

Emmy runs the show. She coaches, scores, washes uniforms, translates, organizes, teaches, and motivates. She does this better than me, and I have done this for over forty years. My baby is a natural, if there ever was one, at all of it. With no weaknesses, she is at home with parents and other coaches and can sit in the corner and manage a match better than any coach I've seen. How does she do it?

There is no answer to that mystery, except...Emmy. She "is" the answer. Mother Nature made her from a mold of one and then likely destroyed that mold.

Her eyes don't hide a hint of pain. Yes, she has seen her share of loss, grief, depression, drugs, and illness. And yet those soft eyes look back at you with hope and love. She doesn't try to hide that either. Two minutes spent with her, and you are a fan, instantly, of Emmy, but she doesn't seek or even want that. She is true and loyal to a fault. I am sure that somebody gave her that insight or taught her lessons of loyalty which many parents choose to discuss.

Yet in the previous description, I have barely touched the surface. Emmy is nearly a straight-A student. She works and takes care of her family. She is bilingual. And she volunteers many hours to feed others who have little or no food. Her "grind" is unmatched and unsurpassed. I realized a long time ago that I would never figure out how she became so worldly wise at such a young age. Instead, I embraced all she stands for and tried to make myself better because of her.

Emmy has that effect on everyone. When around her, one tries to improve oneself as a person. Without trying, she makes a person feel the need to be good and simply be like her, even though it's not possible. Heroes come in all shapes and sizes, and Emmy proves heroes come at all ages as well. Though just a baby, inspiring others by who she is and what she stands for is what she does. There is no doubt Emmy is destined for greatness, but more importantly, she will make others better as she widens her circle. The pain in her eyes will diminish and never leave, but it will be replaced by her dreams of hope and happiness. *To life*, dear Emmy, and to all who you have touched.

Dre

He didn't look like a wrestler. As soon as he reported on that first day, some of the guys who were a bit more primeval smirked. André Holiday? I could read their minds.

He was handsome in a delicate way, his skin smooth, with no acne or scars like his teammates and a well-done Jheri curl, also different than the others. Some of the guys didn't care, they just put their gel on and it looked like it, so right away he was targeted. Coach Hall and I knew he would have to earn his spot, and he would have it hard and take a whole bunch of beatings. I had a strong hunch that he would survive the conditioning, the discipline, and the grind. His grind was Teddy, Terry, Glen, and Anton, all aggressive beasts who would tear each other up and wanted to be "alphas." The alpha always changed. A coach's expression "metal sharpens metal" defined this group. Let up for one moment and you would be brutalized and shown the light—yes, the bright ceiling lights. If one of these cats put you on your back, you stayed there and got no mercy.

So Dre started as a marked man...or kid. He would have to man-up and endure the nickname "pretty Dre" and either man-the-hell-up or quit. It is that simple in that rancid, sweaty wrestling room. True survival of the fittest. You get better and tougher, or they run your tail out, right outta that room, and you get ready for track season. So, André got thrown to the dogs early in the process. He got ripped a new one the first time we went live. He was new to our room and further behind technically than the older savages. After eight or nine minutes he had a welt on his cheek, his shirt was torn, and we were just getting started. He looked around and saw by the demeanor of his group partners that we had a whole lot more of live wrestling to go. He didn't back off, not even a bit. He made a statement that day, without saying a word. What he said to the crew was, *I ain't a punk or sissy, and I will not back down. In time I plan to wear your ass out.*

Practice ended that day, and Dre, like his teammates, was exhausted. But resolve and determination were written all over his face. He was hooked. I knew then, on day one, that he would survive, and he would be great. Greatness was ingrained in him, I could tell. Fast forward. He was not good, he was great, earning a varsity spot and competing with the best of the best. With time, he could compete with anyone...in the state. We traveled to tournaments all over, and Dre and his posse earned respect at each stop.

André dressed. André didn't care, either. The dudes on the team, both football and wrestling, had fun clowning, mocking, and teasing their friend because he didn't wear the shorts and tees, or jeans and tees, or the baggy sweats and tees that they practically lived in. Every day, Dre dressed.

Dre didn't care what others though. Even as a barely post-adolescent, he dressed with style and in clothes that he had made or were made by a family member. This didn't stop there. As he hit his twenties, he was making clothes and working in retail in this ever-changing industry. He knew the business and was connected with all phases. He could design the clothes, pick the right material, and recommend to men and women what looked best to develop their own personal "style."

After spending time as an assistant manager for many years, Andre was intent on venturing out and starting his own brand, if you will. He was reluctant, apparently because so many people try this and fail, often miserably, with wasted time and money. But not Dre. Though it took him a while to take the plunge, he finally ventured out on his own. He made clothes and incredible suits for some professional athletes.

Word among those early customers traveled far and wide. Within a short period of time, Dre was commissioned to design and make custom clothes for many high-profile customers. Professional athletes, their significant others, people in the business community, and successful men and women from all over the country and beyond were soon hiring Andre for their clothing needs. He created a market that propelled him to the top of his field, one that is very selective and at times unforgiving. Over time, Dre has had hundreds of clients and a huge network of successful men and women who sport his brand.

Andre has never forgotten who he is, or his roots and ties. He is the first to admit that the resilience he learned through facing adverse times made him better and tougher. The 98-pound fourteen-year-old wrestler was destined to succeed, though he didn't know it at the time. Why? He succeeded because he had no fear or quit in him. The way he competed while getting respect among some really tough young teens, was second nature. He simply would not be denied once he set his mind to a goal or task.

Through his immense success in business, he has placed people first. Andre is a family man in the purest sense. He is a devoted father, partner, and friend. He recently spent many days, for hours at a time, connecting with me and my family at a kid's wrestling camp. He is invested in our initiatives to better the lives of the youth in Denver because he is, was, and will always be "Denver Proud." Kudos to Dre and all he stands for.

Chapter Ten

Myth Busting

MYTH # 1

Our schools are safe spaces, and we work hard to create learning situations which are conducive to a quality education.

The Truth:

Our schools are dangerous. Most are only an incident away from becoming front-page news. We spend countless hours in buildings where any sense of decorum can unravel in an instant. We have fights, drugs, and an atmosphere of disrespect and entitlement that results in a lack of civility and a culture of violence.

In recent years we have had a "fight page" on social media which has shown and allowed students to brag about the number of fights at our school. Once the school officials use the content as evidence, though there are rarely consequences, the page is disabled for a while and then reappears. A few years ago, a fight video showed a melee in which our principal was knocked down, as well as fights between students, parents, and random unidentified individuals. We have a school resource officer, a cop, who on occasion issues a citation, but his hands are basically tied. Our school and most others contain dangerous, highly troubled kids. Often, a handful have violent pasts and the school either doesn't know, or they become aware and don't share that information. In the 1990s and 2000s, the dangerous kids were identified and were most definitely on the radar. They were put on behavior contracts, and the teachers who had these individuals in class were privy to the complicated needs of these youngsters. When our enrollment was over two thousand students, we had around twelve or thirteen kids who needed vigilant monitoring. They were well aware they would be sent to another educational facility if they did not comply with reasonable requests. But that is not the case now.

Students today fly under the radar. Some weed? No biggie. A fight, even on school grounds, rarely results in a consequence, nor does vandalism or destruction of school property. Threatening a teacher or even knocking the principal down results in nothing but a slap on the wrist. Each state, including ours, has laws and/or statutes regarding the "habitually disruptive student." These laws are in place to keep our schools safe and to allow the local schools to deal fairly yet firmly with our most incorrigible students. With proper documentation, schools can remove students based on documented acts clearly spelled out by the law itself. This gives us the ability to maintain civility within the school or district. Do we use this tool? Hell no. If we used it, we would have to report it to the state of Colorado which would in turn lower our state or district report card which in turn would further tarnish our extremely poor public perception. The cycle continues until our parents, taxpayers, or lawmakers—someone—questions the ongoing violent acts and takes a deep, first-hand look at how we can create safe schools, or we will spin further out of control. Don't take my word for it. Go into the school, get a visitor's pass, and observe. You will likely be sickened by what you see and hear in our hallways, lunchrooms, and playgrounds.

To Change This:

This can't and won't change from within. It is not enough for me to cry foul. Teachers have little say and even less clout. Our hard-working taxpayers and parents of students (past, present, and future) need to insist, demand, rant, rave, stomp, and storm to get this to change. Start at the local school and look around. If you don't like what you see, inform the school at the highest levels of leadership. You may find the rhetoric unacceptable. You may see something on campus that doesn't "look right." This could be a fight, a group of students smoking weed, or others involved in committing a crime or harassing another student. Take it to the district level, and finally, write, call, email, or text the school board member or the school board representative from your neighborhood. Demand that we follow school board policy. Then, get in touch with your city council member. Tell them what is up in the school or schools that serve your neighborhood. Be as persistent as if you were in the middle of an epidemic, because you are. Demand that the status quo change. Lawmakers need to know, from someone other than me, that schools are freelancing. We do not report. We are not being accountable. We don't place unsafe students with violent tendencies in situations to remediate their behavior. We allow intolerable acts and look the other way, sweeping way too much under the rug.

There are systems and supports in place to identify these troubled children and help them change and manage the anger they have, no matter where it comes from. We don't follow the laws we have regarding chronically violent students who have weapons or drugs or who harass and bully. Require the lawmakers and the school board to put up or shut up. Have both entities clarify in writing what the laws and policies are about drugs, weapons, threats, gang activities, vandalism, and theft. Make sure the consequences for these infractions are clarified and insist, with hundreds or thousands of others, that they follow their own policies. Take them to task when they don't. Pull up the carpet and get rid of it so they can't hide their dirt under it any longer. Don't allow these games of non-reporting to continue. How much longer are we adults, who support education and value the safety of kids, going to tolerate the continued violence where we end up with hurt kids and families ruined by untimely deaths?

Myth #2

We are financially underserved and under-resourced. This affects our ability to offer a quality education for all of our children.

The truth:

We plead poverty and use it as an excuse right after we blame the parents. Why not? It's convenient! Let's do the basic math. Public schools in our state are funded according to the Public School Finance Act of 1994. In a nutshell, for each student enrolled in a Colorado public school district (with a minimum of fifty kids up to ninety thousand, the census of the Denver Public Schools), the district receives around $7500 of state money earmarked for education. The number may be as low as $6500 or as high as $8500 per student depending on the student's educational setting. This money comes from the local tax base and then the state of Colorado supplements the local districts. Additional funding comes from numerous sources. Ultimately, each kid brings in anywhere from $9,500 to $10,200 of combined resources. Districts with large populations of at-risk students, English-language learners, special needs students (including the gifted and talented), and those who meet the family income guidelines for free and reduced lunch are given federal dollars as well. We also receive millions of dollars from grants and free support in the form of programs, including a nice chunk of change from the Gates Foundation, which amounts to many millions. The district employs grant writers who keep the grant money coming in, but not well. What's more, we have yet to be turned down when we ask for tax help in the form of mill-levy money or voter-approved funding. This includes more than twenty-five million a year for teacher pay. This also includes recent money appropriated for enrichment in the Arts and Physical Education. Our district likely operates on a 1.3 to 1.8 billion dollar a year budget. Yes, I said a *billion* plus. The real number lies somewhere in this hidden and secret mess.

Suffice it to say, the district has plenty of money to take good care of the educational needs of the kids. But look around, and please listen. We cut teaching positions all the time. This is called an RIB, or "reduction in building." We have gone through many of these RIBs and have reduced our teaching force to bare bones at a time when kids need us the most. Walk into most schools in our district and you will see outdated, second-rate facilities and materials. We used to offer programs where you could make jewelry and metal and wood projects. We had fully funded clubs and activities. We had a class where you didn't just use the computer, you learned how to fix it as well as the rest of the network. We often can't go on excursions because we are told there is no money. When we as faculty meet several times a year, the atmosphere is doom and gloom, from the lips of the school leaders and administration and up the chain. We want everyone to believe we are destitute.

The students in neighboring school districts want for nothing. We see a night-and-day difference. The "haves" and the "have nots." This is sinful. Unacceptable. Not okay. These schools provide tutors, sessions with the speech pathologist, assistance to raise your college test score, all provided right in your building with professionals who support the teachers and students and provide total access and opportunities for the neediest children.

Try this in Denver. A freshman in the DPS reads or does math at the third-grade level. Tough luck. The kid stays behind because we don't have the specialists that are commonplace in a few neighboring districts. We end up with a huge achievement gap that has plagued our school district for decades.

The physical space is also different. The most up-to-date classrooms abound in certain public school districts, while classrooms in Denver haven't changed since the '90s. When I was assigned to George Washington in 1987, we had fifty-four elective teachers, who taught a multitude of classes and sponsored school-funded clubs and activities. Now we are down to about fifteen elective teachers and have cut back on most electives. How sad and phony. We plead poverty and have an overall budget that may well be double that of our next largest school districts. What's worse, the public accepts this second-rate education and does not question the obvious. Where in the hell is the money going? The funds are there, no question. As a public school district we are subject to public scrutiny, and yet people don't ask, and we certainly don't tell.

Prove Me Wrong

Check my facts. Our constituents, residents, neighbors, alumni, and taxpayers should get nosy, en masse, and ask questions. As a collective body, ask the district to show their yearly budget and how much money they started with in this given year, including all city, state, and local funds; federal grants; donations; voter-approved funding; and endowments. Ask for transparency, leaving nothing out, including the millions any number of foundations kick in. These numbers may add between fifteen and fifty million dollars in any fiscal year. I am confident this information will look much different than what is sent to the taxpayers.

Let's look at the numbers in line items; better yet, let us look at the books which we can request legally, as The Denver Public Schools is a public school district and claims to be transparent.

Compare what you receive (request this through the legal system if necessary) and see how different this is from the yearly report sent out to the taxpayers—I've seen those. Bet the numbers are staggering, but you still won't have much of a picture, because there will be group expenses, not line items. Dig in. Now request the salaries of the top one thousand highest-paid employees, including attorneys, consultants, admin, and anyone who receives income from any source. Don't ask for names, it will delay the process. Ask for titles and where these people are located and take a long look at what you get. A thousand may seem excessive, but according to the data, we have over fifteen thousand employees. What this first layer gets in pay and fringe benefits will be an eye-opener. Wade through the first layer of stench and prepare to uncover the next.

Do we prioritize the group who should be our number one priority? Ask for a complete accounting—a ledger, a document, something tangible—that clearly shows how much money from each kid's approximately ten-thousand-dollar allotment goes back to his or her school. Make them prove the number is accurate by looking at the annual budget at several schools. The math will paint a picture.

There will surely be a major sticking point. The district will claim that its budget is about a billion dollars a year. I don't believe this and have stated why. Keep asking to see all the numbers, including grants, donations, gifts, bond and mill-levy money, and all else that is part of the budget. When you see the discrepancy, that a billion dollars is not the accurate or honest number, ask that moving forward, the general public be allowed to see all the funds in the big picture, not just bits and pieces.

How many teachers are employed in the Denver Public Schools? I've read that there are about 5700 teachers in our district. A recent article came out that the DPS has one administrator for every 7.5 teachers. Basic math indicates that we may have 750 to 800 administrators. If this is the case and it likely is, what in the world do they all do? How many of them made that list of the top thousand highest-paid employees in our district? Do we need this much administrative support? Are they really supportive? Our school, with about 1100 students, has five administrators, one principal, and four assistants. We also have six or seven pseudo-administrators who help with teacher training and evaluations, whose roles provide support for our teachers. These teacher-leaders teach two or three classes and then do what they do. They are usually nice kids, low on the experience scale, good at rhetoric, self-promoting, and walking around with a sense of importance. Almost all are rookies who have barely gotten their feet wet yet now are the liaison, the link to working with teachers to bridge the achievement gap. They are funded through a grant and our district calls it—the title is catchy—*shared leadership*. They share it! I think Bill and Melinda Gates endow a grant for this truly meaningful group. If they have been effective since the program's inception, why do we still have a huge teacher turnover rate? Why has achievement gone down or stayed flat? Why is the achievement gap growing greater between our highest achieving and our neediest kids, currently one of the largest of any school district in our nation? Are we going to accept this? For how much longer?

Why has our enrollment stayed half of what we had enrolled for more than forty-five of our nearly sixty years in existence? And the most compelling question is, are we really broke, poor, and strapped for resources? Make the dollars come back to the schools and to the students who need it most. Are we effectively using our dollars?

To Change This:

We need a movement and a demand from the public for an accounting of all dollars that come into our district. Services rendered or salaries paid by other entities need to be noted and documented.

We need to give a description of each and every department and their salaries. This includes the layered management system, public relations departments, consultants, and everyone on the DPS payroll as well as those who work in our buildings and get paid from other sources.

We need a document or flow chart listing the multitude of assistant superintendents, their staff members, and their support personnel along with budgets and salaries. A recent chart on the DPS website shows the salaries of the school-based administrators. Does an assistant principal deserve more than double the salary of our beginning teachers? What about the DPS central administrator, who makes three or three and a half times the salary of beginning teachers? Some of our highest-paid administrators rarely meet with or interact with a child or family yet are paid this large amount. Is this acceptable?

This will bring about change in teacher pay. Teachers should start at much more than they currently make. The union negotiates with the DPS powers and still ends up with a wage that requires a second or third job by many of our thousands of teachers. This is sinful. Unless we demand this information, the DPS will not voluntarily provide what we have suspected for years. More than a hundred positions could likely be eliminated, which would result in competitive pay for our staff and teachers who work in the trenches. This includes the weary support personnel who create meals, clean and maintain our buildings, and help run and manage the schools.

Myth #3

We prepare our learners well and provide a quality education as they enter college, trade schools, the military, or the working world.

The truth:

In the public school system, we swear we are masters, gurus, experts, anointed, and sovereign, and the best all-around at college readiness and skills for the twenty-first century. As teachers, we are told to provide rigor and set high standards and that every kid can go to college. They actually can, but they don't. We then have the fluff to make it look like we are including college readiness centers in our high schools. We say our curriculum is full of coursework to take them on this educational journey right to the university doors where they will no doubt succeed, because we are "all that."

In higher education in Colorado, millions of dollars are spent on...drum roll please...*remediation.* Our high school graduates need remediation in the basics for college success. When the colleges test the kids in math and sometimes English, they discover many of our Denver students are so behind that unless they get some foundations taught, *in college,* they will never succeed and earn a degree. The college professors scratch their heads and wonder what the heck we and the kids have been doing for the last twelve years. The millions we spent providing this "high-quality" education meant nothing. The colleges have to pay (either the college or the parents) millions for the kids to have any chance of earning a degree. The dropout rate at the college level must be staggering. Many kids who now realize they are under-prepared throw in the towel and begin, at age nineteen, to enter the real-life work force.

Here is how they struggle. "You mean I have to take midterms and then a final which are real tests without do-overs?" Or "What? In Freshman Composition and Grammar I have to write a whole bunch of both short and long essays?" Or this. "When the prof or teacher's assistant in front of the lecture hall says I have to read pages 37 through 104, I really should do it? What happened? I got A's and B's in high school."

Reality sets in quick. Tammy gets her first-semester grades, and Mom or Pops are told or find out she is failing, and the doo-doo hits the fan. All that time and money wasted by a whole bunch of folks. At this point someone, or several someones, begin to hemorrhage money. Lots of it. But rarely does Tammy dig in and, with the insistence of a support system, struggle and make it out with a degree. Most often, Tammy and her peers end their college experience and join the workforce where they are tremendously underprepared for that as well.

Let's identify the problem. First, in our district, we overuse the phrase "We must provide rigor." Stop right there. We say it ad nauseum and then get in trouble for providing it. How can you say to provide rigor and then, when teachers do, you chastise them? Three years ago, my evaluator, who was a nice kid, began my final year-end evaluation with "Coach, do you know that twelve kids failed your class?"

I hit him with this. "Yes, and how many kids earned A's and B's?" He didn't know.

I continued. "Are you suggesting I give kids who ditch class twenty-five or more times a semester a passing grade? Tell me what you are doing with the kids who don't attend class and walk the halls every day."

Guess what? That ended our discussion. He thanked me for another good year and took his inexperienced tailbone back to his office.

The truth was that about eighty percent or more of my students earned A's and B's. Despite overwhelming pressure to give a good grade that is unearned, and most teachers do just that, I won't play that game.

The other buzz word around our district was and still is "relevance." It is supposed to mean that what we teach is relevant to the needs of society, business, technology, and our world as we know it today. We want relevance, but we teach to the standardized tests and to the curriculum dictated to us, which changes every couple of years. We do this to keep our ratings high while shoving kids into accelerated or honors classes because it helps the school rating system. The kids are lost, and the kids that are capable stay in the same place they've been because we have watered it all down. We are in a vicious cycle that is far from providing a relevant curriculum. We say we want relevance, but to have it we have to do the things that will achieve it.

A neighboring district just finished a seventy-million-dollar facility to teach technical skills and the trades. It is cutting edge and designed to allow kids to log apprentice hours, gain employment, and learn one of the many trades and specialties whose jobs are now high paying with a high rate of employment in our state. Kids can go through this program and have careers, if they choose, right out of high school—as welders, framers, culinary experts, and numerous other professions. They get it and are actually serving their students with true post-secondary options. How novel. We have two facilities which are supposed to do the same, but ours are outdated and poorly publicized. I can assure you we haven't spent seventy million, even though we know it's available if it were a priority. Once again, our kids are back seat and second fiddle, cheated once again.

To change this:

Let's change our attitude. Time to put up or shut up; to move away from teaching to the test or to get a good evaluation. We need a real guide, and we need to teach what the kids need to know to be productive, helping them choose their post-high school options. It is our responsibility to make sure they are capable and have sweated and toiled enough to be good at taking notes, doing research, and interacting, with respect and civility. Allow them to learn trades in their high schools and to get two-year degrees in several fields prior to their high school graduation. Career training should be available instead of saying every kid has to go to college.

Let's educate our college-bound kids with the same intensity. Have them leave the high school with a foundation and a pre-college curriculum that includes public speaking, research, and the ability to enter college on an even plane with kids from the highest-rated districts, even if it means mimicking what they do. Let's get off of our arrogant asses and see what we can copy and emulate to give our kids the best. Let's not make or accept excuses for perpetuating this substandard experience any longer.

Myth #4

Our teachers are well prepared to enter the profession and then supported and encouraged to improve their craft as they stay in teaching for a number of years.

The truth:

Teacher education programs are abundant, as teaching shortages have dictated that colleges must train thousands of teachers. The imminent retirement of the baby boomer educators has created job openings in school districts all over the United States. In truth, today's student-teaching experience is very similar to what it was a quarter century ago. The college student declares education as a major and then logs hours of field work, depending on the institution, observing classes for a semester or two, for several hours a week.

Next up is student teaching. The student is paired with a teacher and after a short period of time the teacher hands over the reins to the rookie and stays connected, either at the hip or rather loosely, depending on what the veteran teacher feels like. In theory, this experience is meant to get the new teacher's feet wet and then receive constructive feedback from the veteran teacher and the college advisor who comes to visit once or twice during this six- or seven-week ordeal. Then the student teacher will go to another assignment to get a different experience in another setting. The programs are well-intentioned but too short, and they lack true experiences the new teacher will encounter.

Teaching doesn't duplicate the training methods used in other professions. In medicine and law, the still-wet-behind-the-ears rookie has an arduous path. First, they get their feet wet, and after many hours of on-the-job training, they get to take over. By this time, they are ready to assume control and deal with most situations. In truth, it takes years to be truly effective.

Don't get me wrong. At the front end you can be a bit inspirational. You can reach some of the kids, and you may even be able to get a bit of validation for the crazy, ever-changing profession you've chosen, but supported and encouraged? Try again. You will stand alone, very alone.

Life is peachy keen when the status quo exists. The suits are cordial as long as you don't rock the boat or get a complaint from a kid—or worse, a parent. Life is good if the roof in your classroom doesn't come down, or the children are not beating the stuffing out of each other. Our new teachers are thrown in the deep end and are told to survive. Some do, but not many. Way too green, naïve, friendly, and soft, they are too scared to do much of anything but hold on.

Here is the usual scenario. My much younger colleagues start the profession idealistic and wide-eyed. You are going to get the kids smarter; you are going to be powerful in your profession; and you will in turn save the world by educating the masses. Right? The derailment begins when Johnny comes to class high every day. Lisa and Tina won't shut up while you are trying to speak. When you address the issue, they curse at you and call you a bitch, punk, or some other nicety which is part of their vocab. When you are finally fed up or tired of competing with their devices, screen time, or blasting music, you tell one or more little darlings how you feel.

Johnny, Tina, and Lisa are butt-hurt, even though they need to be put in check. They go to admin or cry to mommy or dad and then the doo-doo hits the fan. Uh-oh! The manure's about to get deep up in here! The rent (a.k.a. "parent")—follow me now—the parent finally gets to the principal, who has a few buffers and layers before they actually make time to talk by phone or in person. The parent issues the complaint, and a quick decision is rendered. The principal usually caves and agrees to make sure this doesn't happen again. The trial is short and quick, with a guilty verdict. Yes, to the teacher.

The teacher, depending on the nastiness displayed by the parent, is deemed wrong and will get an email or a paper reprimand, with no one even asking what happened. Consulting the teacher would be the proper response in a rational, normal situation. But we are long past normal in our schools. The teacher gets ripped and/or reamed and is unsupported. It doesn't matter that the kid or kids were beyond control and that the learning process was decimated by some brats. Nobody asks why Johnny or Evelynn were chastised. It doesn't matter. Principals no longer say, "Let me look into this and get the other side"; or better, "I support our teacher." If only they would say, "Let's sit down and see what we can do to support the professional to be able to manage the class and help Johnny and Evelyn learn."

Our new teachers just wing it. In Denver, they learn both under fire and by trial and error. There used to be new-teacher meetings not so many years ago to lend a bit of support to the newbies. Now we put them in a room with a bunch of Gen-X teens and expect great results. If a veteran teacher had eyes on their room several times a day, the new teachers would improve faster. The new teacher is friendly and becomes pals, then gives in to the ways and methods of our dysfunctional system. They receive no guidance. No suggestions or tips to get the kids off their stinkin' electronics. The kids are loving this, as they have yet another class—fifty minutes during the day—like so many other fifty-minute sessions, to do everything but learn. Fast forward. Summer hits, or whenever the revered and almighty standardized test scores come out, and uh oh! Damn! The achievement gap went up. Our test scores are flat or went down. But we worked *so hard*. Right? The cycle goes on and on.

We do a terrible job with our beginning teachers. They enter their careers and for several years are below average, really struggling and frustrated, or they are highly paid babysitters.

How long has it been like this? Fifteen or twenty years?

To Change This:

Pay the teachers for a month before the school start date. Have a "teachers academy" for the new teachers in the district. Bring in some dynamic current and retired teachers and pony-up! Let the proven, successful veterans and retirees teach the teachers. Novel idea—I take all the credit— not really. Let's do what they do in business, law, and medicine. Let's have a "get your feet wet" month and make it good and worthwhile. Have education veterans or community members take the newly assigned rookie teachers to the neighborhoods, the churches, synagogues, restaurants, parks, grocery stores, and the recreation centers and let them see and know the visual world of the kids they will serve. This snapshot will prove invaluable for years to come.

The school year officially begins. Now just turn 'em loose, right? No. Have them teach for one, two, or three months with—guess who? A retired teacher or one of these gurus that many districts have who are supposed to be driving the instruction at each school. Let them have a partner who has experience at successful teaching and make them begin what could be a great career, with guidance, instead of what we have been doing. Give the new teachers a support system. Allow them to have an on-call, on-duty teacher assigned to help them any time they need it. Give the new teacher support and guidance for a year or more and the chance to get it right at the beginning. In these turbulent times the profession beats you up enough without additional stress. Lessen the stress of the unknown by pairing the teacher with someone to guide them. Then be there for the rookie as they adapt to new students, situations, and classes. In truth, they should have several years of support as they develop a teaching style that will serve them well and benefit the students.

Myth #5

There are systems in place to help struggling students, and we work hard to catch students before they fall too far behind. We leverage our experience and our resources to assist students who need extra tutoring, support, and services.

The truth:

Yes. Systems, resources, personnel, and money are available to help our struggling children. But this is clearly not a priority. It is essential that we intervene when we spot a deficiency, as it should be. When we first identify a needy student, our lack of action fits in well with our excuses. Our students languish in a system that does not intervene when and how it should.

As we receive the data on our kids, we find they have been grouped into categories. Our free-and-reduced-lunch kids; our ELLs (English language learners); and our children of color. We get these grouped results each time we give one of the hallowed tests. Because the children fall into one of these sub-groups, they are labeled as behind, below grade level, and struggling. We get the data, shake our heads, and never get a plan for assisting them. We have every opportunity to prioritize this, but aside from the fancy rhetoric, it stays the same and the gap gets wider. Thousands of children, in dozens of schools, are allowed to fall behind and stay behind. A district full of boys and girls, young men and women, robbed of their potential by a system that perpetuates this attitude. We have a built-in excuse, which is used all the time. Our asterisk, our reason, our answer is the population we serve. We are quick to give the numbers. *Well, we serve a very poor group of students, most are on free-and-reduced lunch;* or *These are our ELLs—our English language learners.*

We have an excuse that people have bought into for decades, and we use it. Because of the population we serve, we get a pass because our work is so vast that it is impossible to close the gap. This approach has worked, sadly, at the expense of thousands of children who desperately need a chance at this crucial educational opportunity. What's worse, after a while, the very children we serve use their poor test scores as a handicap and believe our words. They are told that it is okay. They accept it because they are rarely told what their dramatic potential is. What makes this catastrophic is our non-response. We allow our children to remain underserved and ignored, and the parents rarely know or understand. Way too often, the cycle of poverty is perpetuated because of this.

Through our failure to remediate when it is most important, the child ends up in this unfortunate cycle with no light at the end of the tunnel. Once high school hits, the child and group become statistics that should embarrass us as an educational system, but don't. They leave us ill-prepared and struggling in many areas because these kids have been cheated out of their free and formative public education.

What should happen?

As a child enters first grade, we get a very clear picture about where they are at. Experts know that at this early age, if we have built a foundation with letter and word recognition, grouping, and counting, then the child is ready for the next educational steps and challenges. A quick assessment by any elementary school teacher lets us know right away. Paul and Lisa are behind. Boom! Sirens, lights, horns...this is urgent!

If we were on our collective toes or really cared, we would jump on it right then and there. We have access to dozens of strategies, volunteers, and specialists who can intervene and be the solution or remedy to get Paul or Lisa up to speed. But hear this. It is okay for a child to fall behind, but it is not acceptable to allow a child to stay behind. It is so simple that it rarely happens in our district, though it does happen in districts that prioritize it.

Let's take the village that grew up under my roof. Six of my seven had a flaw, a weakness, a learning disability, or a speech problem caught by the third grade. By the time they left elementary school they were up to speed, except for one baby with some serious ADD. She went to middle school with a plan. The plan continued in high school, and by the time she did college and five years in the military, it was clear she had learned to manage her disability. We were thankful their school district was committed to assisting all students.

Closing the achievement gap has not been a priority. In our arrogance, we don't take action when we should, and our fearless leaders don't seem to care. Their superiors have not made it a priority. We do not address the deficiencies in our services to a very large group of our children. Our population struggles because we have not given them the skills to succeed or provided support to remediate. We have every opportunity to work with children each day and the tools to assess our work, yet it doesn't happen.

Most of this is common sense, and one would think helping children behind their grade level is a no-brainer. Yet we don't do this. Our work stops when we collect the data. We sit on it and start the excuses. This is one of our biggest sins and may be the simplest to address. Will we? When?

MYTH #6

We teach an ever-changing curriculum designed to meet the needs of our diverse population and serve the learners of this technically advanced generation. There are course offerings that allow each student to carve a unique path for their individual and collective futures. Our courses are updated frequently to make our offerings cutting edge when compared to other school districts.

The truth:

Ask someone at the administration building and they will extol the virtues of our advanced and unique curriculum. They will tell you about creative, imaginative programs, concurrent enrollment, and a wide variety of in-school opportunities and course offerings for our children. This verbiage has been used so long it sounds quite convincing. They proclaim our offerings are progressive and children are achieving at all grades and levels. Without hesitation, they report that the vast majority of our highschoolers take one or more advanced placement (AP) classes.

These proclamations sit well until you wade deeper. First, check out an elementary school. On the surface, the school looks inviting, but you notice large classes and sometimes a volunteer. Some children are distracted and many are behind, across all grade levels. Often a third or more seem detached and uninvolved. The teacher may not even recognize the under-involved student.

Now visit a high school class. With a jam-packed classroom and a tired teacher who is not adept at classroom management, you see on the whiteboard that this is an AP class. Here, many little darlings are on their phones. Some are socializing and a few are actually engaged in the mandated—yes, the mandated lesson of the day. But hey, it is an AP course, and the school looks good in the eyes of the state by having much of the school population enrolled in these courses. Colleges will accept several of these courses if the student has only a better-than-average score on the AP test.

A three is good, a four is golden and a five is really shiny. This means that the child in college does not have to take certain courses, as they have essentially tested out. So how do we do? Our success rates are terrible and embarrassing. At times we bragged about an eighteen percent pass rate, and sometimes it is only eleven or twelve percent. The time, money, and energy spent having thousands in our district take these courses is wasted. The taxpayers must wonder what we are doing with their tax dollars, bond money, and mill levy dollars. Rarely does anyone ask what we are doing. We gobble up the money and life goes on. This has been the norm for a long time, and I am sickened that this has been allowed.

How do we do with our social studies courses? The curriculum, if it's not the diluted AP class, is the same familiar "white bread" curriculum we have taught forever. History is history, except that the history we teach universally doesn't belong to most of our students. We don't teach historical events of the modern age, events that have shaped our country and will continue to define us as a society. We are little more than a generation away from a population of richly blended ethnicities and heritages, and we neither teach nor talk about it. Yet we scratch our heads and wonder why some children just don't fit in.

Our inner-city schools are a wonderful blend of cultures. Public schools in large cities attract students from many nationalities and cultures. Yet our classes don't line up. We do not have current, up-to-date classes that appeal to the learners of this era. Imagine courses starting in the first grade that teach the history of the immigration and assimilation of cultures which has been occurring for decades right before our eyes. Our history, taught early, should reflect the population in our schools. As children move to more advanced concepts, we have the opportunity to redefine how we teach, which is rarely addressed.

We miss the target in math, science, and language arts as well. These courses, often mandated by the district gurus, are flat and lacking. The information age has exploded exponentially, yet our teaching hasn't, and we own it. I have been in many classes and have asked myself the poignant question, "Back in the day, would I have found this class interesting?" How 'bout no. Poor students. Damn, I would want to be on my phone too. Hey, admin and highly paid specialists, as you work behind the scenes, make the curriculum cutting edge. Have some relevance. Make it timely, earn your pay, and keep it current. Time to bust your tails to engage the students and give them a foundation to build on as they advance as learners.

What about the population that chooses not to go to college? What about the children that choose the military? How do we assist them? Are they supported? They damn well should be, because within two years of graduation from high school, eighty-five percent or more of our DPS graduates are either working or have joined our armed forces. We do a terrible job preparing our high schoolers to take this path. We bombard the public with the usual rhetoric and tout the statistics. We brag like hell about the high percentage of seniors accepted to college. Then we ghost the topic. We don't admit that since 2001–2002, graduates from our collective high schools who finished college with a four-year degree is eleven or twelve percent. In a good cycle, maybe fifteen percent. This means that a whole cadre of them are doing something besides college. Let's quit lying. Let's not imply we are a system that prepares our youth for college adequately. We haven't done great at preparing the older students for anything except to struggle. I apologize.

We have been damn good at setting the past generation up to flounder and to feel the stigma of coming from a below-average public school system. A neighboring district tracks their graduates for five years after high school and has nearly a 70 percent college graduation rate for that cycle. We offer a fraction of what is offered in most large metro school districts. Do we still have shop classes? How about home economics? What about a full selection of instrumental music, vocal music, choir, and the ability to choose one of seven or eight instruments and get quality instruction? None of this is happening. Across the street from many Denver schools, suburban counterparts have climbing walls, kayaking, and instruction in five different languages, not just Spanish and French. The sticking point? We got mill levy money to enhance the arts and physical education, but as so often happens, nobody watched the money because they trust us, but they should not. We were given millions, lots of them, to build our programs in music, physical education, theatre, and dance.

At first, we hired three new teachers for the arts and PE and put in an exercise physiology studio. It was cutting edge, and at the time, about six years ago, there were none like it. We had treadmills, twenty-four microscopes to study pathology, and slides of various types of tissue. We had a stress test ergometer to chart numerous functions of the heart. The class became very popular. Students took a class for honors credit entitled Health, Nutrition, and Exercise Science. The class was a hit, and students received a strong foundation. For several years, like clockwork, we had two sections, full classes of twenty-five to thirty, and many chose to continue this in college. But the class was too popular. As they would opt into the class, our Med-Connect program was losing numbers. And Med-Connect was sacred, because Bill and Melinda, or someone very important, gave money for something else, a new flavor of the day.

The curriculum for Med-Connect was a computer class with a lot of watered-down science. After two or three weeks on the computer, the class would fall apart, while the teachers grew frustrated because they weren't really teaching anyway. This is institutional racism at its finest. The children of color who chose to take an honors course and prosper were required to take this sub-par course because the gurus said so. It was a lose–lose situation for both. And what happened to the new exercise physiology lab? Done and gone. Another opportunity to serve the best educational interests of the teens wasted, because someone decided for them. And worse than the wasted money is the waste of the children's potential, again. How's Med-Connect going after five years? It too is done because it stunk.

So, what is its replacement? Robotics. Now I am all for kids that build a damn robot. I wish I were that smart. Hell, my own children couldn't build one and they aren't that dense. Now guess who builds the bots? Yes, the children do, with Mom, Dad, Fido, and a trust fund. Does it appeal to the kid that was loving the hell out of holding up the human skeleton and reciting? Or the kid that was testing his endurance on the treadmill and learning about vital lung capacity? They couldn't care less about a robot.

Our curriculum falls way short of that of the 'burbs. We could change it any way we wanted to, but we take the money, lots of it, and give the children what *we* want, not what they want or need. Are the dollars wasted? Dear reader, you decide.

To Change This:

Let's make education relevant to what we see in our district. We live in a city with a very high cost of living and great diversity. Many of our residents gather in affordable housing units where they share similarities with others. We could deviate from the set curriculum, but we don't.

What about a curriculum that centers around how we all got here? There are countless stories of children who came here for various reasons. Employment, opportunity, leaving famine and hunger, not to mention students who have come to us from war-torn countries or for political reasons. We have children who have never been allowed or encouraged to tell their own stories.

Children are here because we offer a better life for them and their families. They are invisible, and we don't do all we can to include them. We offer ELD (English Language Development) classes which are supposed to immerse them in our language and culture, but we fall way short. The roughly $10,500 per student we receive is used however the authorities choose. The DPS takes the money but does not deliver the services to make these children feel welcome or even comfortable in their new school or surroundings.

What about courses in "our united history" where we tell the story of our population and how we came together? How about math courses which actually teach our students, and hence our families, how to survive in a city where families struggle to provide the basic needs for food, housing, and medical care?

After that, we can incorporate coursework in science that is applicable to what we are seeing in our ever-evolving science community. Genetics, medicine, nutrition, and much of science has evolved dramatically, but our curriculum has not. We are stuck and don't even know it. Millions are spent on guides and course syllabi, but they are stale and stagnant. Time to get off of the computer and actually teach the children.

Each class has an expert, its teacher. Yet this teacher is forced to conform and comply, or else. Imagine the number of classes and hours each teacher has spent on their major or majors. Now think of a system that deems the teacher an expert and asks them to impart some of their knowledge and experience. Currently seventy percent of our teachers merely put the kids in front of the screen, adding to the screen time Johnny accumulates.

There's more. If eighty percent of our students don't do the traditional college track, then it is time to stop. Provide access to the trades which allow money and happiness to so many in our city. It is okay for a child to want to become a welder, mechanic, computer guru, web-designer, or chef. We don't promote these vocations in our hypocrisy. "Every child goes to college" has got to go. How about "Every child should chase their passion"? What about "Each child shall chart their path"?

The work needs to start immediately. The curriculum needs to align to what children need as they leave high school. It is clear to all that they leave unprepared for whichever path they choose.

Lessons need to be presented that emphasize basic skills such as writing and summarizing, time management, speaking, and meeting deadlines. Some erroneously believe these skills are taught now and are inherent to the high school setting. No, there are few deadlines, and rarely do students present or research. Admittedly we don't make relevant, culturally responsive lessons or lessons based on equity. We must ask students to think and problem solve. Included should be deep discussions surrounding the movements and scenarios we have seen during the last decade. Is the Boston Tea Party more important than the movements millions have been part of in recent years? How can we provide the skills needed for post-high school when we expect so little from the students? To say we have watered down education lately is an understatement. If we haven't had deadlines and expectations in place for the last five or six years for our older students, then we have in truth created a problem that won't just go away.

The curriculum specialists should be pressed to make guides which actually require a deep level of thought and relevance to our current societal needs. And we need to get rid of our crutch, allowing them incessant use of the computer or phone.

Teachers too need to leave the electronics behind to give their charges, our youth, a more substantial education.

Dear reader, lets change the rhetoric and do it right once and for all.

Myth #7

Teachers collectively work together to guide achievement and have both input and support across each building. The opinions of the faculty and staff are valued, and prior experience is considered an asset to each faculty. Veteran teachers are embraced and relied upon to assist new, inexperienced, and struggling teachers.

The truth:

Our experts—our teachers—should be the strongest, most persuasive voices as we determine what is best for our children. But teachers don't work collectively to guide achievement. It's not part of our pay grade. In most disciplines, we are told what to teach, how to teach it, and when to teach it. I have been fortunate to have been able to write the district curriculum for two of the courses in the gym, weight room, and science classes over decades, and I taught what I determined was best. I set the pace and did so with complete autonomy. Rarely was I questioned about the content, the routines, or the daily rituals the children latched onto. Each year though, as my designated suit went through the various mandated meetings, they were always surprised at the satisfaction ratings I was given. We met and they scratched their heads and couldn't figure it out.

"Once again, Coach, you have the highest satisfaction ratings in the building," they'd say. At times I had the highest in the entire district. They couldn't understand it. I am tough as heck on the darlings. I require no cussing, no electronics, a culture of respect, and no sagging pants. I tell kids, "Bring your narrow body to class every day and sweat—in science or the weight room. If ya cut class, I'll fail you. If you get three tardies you fail, too. Now obviously there is no fighting, and you can't roll in late stinking of cheap weed." The rest is minutiae, and it rarely needs to be dealt with.

Yes, children want discipline. They crave it. So yes, they are satisfied. It's so simple. Cling to a few rules and don't waver or hesitate when applying them. *After* a few years, the kids will crave the structure and do quite well.

The rest of the building is following the curriculum. They are told what to teach and then are either micromanaged or left alone. Supervised by the teacher-leaders, they are compliant, like sheep, and stay obediently between the lines. Their goal is to stay under the radar, not piss off the administration, and get a five or a six out of seven on the sacred LEAP evaluation.

The teacher-leaders' ability to teach well is not what got them the softer schedule and the stipend. They teach two or three classes a day and are then supposed to mobilize and simply make teachers better. In theory this is fine, except that many are young and not effective teachers. A few have been horrendous and couldn't teach at all. Largely, the veterans do what they do. But are we embraced? Do they love us? No. The veterans are often perceived as threatening in the eyes of the administration. We know the rules and they know that at some point, unless we are tired as hell, we will fight back and have an opinion. Rarely are we asked by admin to work with a younger, struggling teacher. That would make too much sense, though in some districts it is the norm. Veterans are paired with rookies and guide them as mentors. Many of us survived the early foundational years because we had guidance and support and could always go to someone for advice, comfort, to vent, or to celebrate. And now? Nothing.

Teachers today are much different than their predecessors. When I came in, the old timers carried a lot of clout. Admin had no choice but to let them have a say, because they were going to say it anyway. Most of the time they were spot on. They had been in the scenarios and situations the newbies were encountering for the first time. The new teachers often jump right into the friendship role. They want the babies to like them, not realizing they should be respected before being liked. If enough kids respect you for enough years, you become a bit of a hero, and they will always remember you. We don't talk about the power of a teacher very much, but we should Ask anyone. Either positively or negatively, we remember our teachers. Yet we never talk about our dramatic influence and our role as givers of hope.

Don't get me wrong. We have meetings and collaborate for hours. Hell, just ask admin all the way up the ladder. They use the rhetoric, the acronyms, and talk about the collective effort that provides the very best for the children in our buildings. Most of the time the teachers follow like sheep and don't want to ruffle feathers. Our professional development should be renamed "Let's fill some time"; "Let's write on posters"; "Let's watch the video"; and on and on. Have we put our brains together to discuss the marijuana problem facing us and thousands of other schools? Do we talk about the violence at an all-time high among our children and families? Children are now vaping and doing even more recreational drugs. Classroom management? Hell no. We have professional development, which lacks substance. It has been like that for years. I call this "paralysis by analysis." Here's what's deep. Our leadership from the top of the ivory "T" will brag about the intense and dynamic support they provide to our rank-and-file teachers. They talk about how we are culturally responsive and aware. The hyperbole will include how we are trained to be sensitive, warm, and welcoming to all races and cultures. From the outside it will look good and sound inviting.

Trust me, from the inside where I stand, institutional racism is still alive and well and often perpetuated by leadership. And the irony? They don't even know it. Quite often, the group who is supposed to drive these meetings, forums, and discussions are the biggest sinners and phonies.

To begin to break down the inequities that run rampant in our system, we need to listen to the echoes. We need to have eyeball-to-eyeball conversations with those who have struggled the most, but we don't. Their stories are full of events and statements about how they had to overcome racial stereotyping and worse. The students who have risen above our collective mediocrity have the most information, and we never seek it.

We must break down these walls by admitting our past transgressions and decades of failures. We have failed our children, especially our children of color. By thinking we must enable, coddle, and lower the standards to balance the past, we further hinder our youth. If we ever have the balls to send a different message, we might begin to erode the sickening presence of our collective biases. Every time we look the other way as a child does less than what we ask, we lose. Failing to work as a collective body to improve our children who are behind is deplorable. We don't even know what it looks like to create real relationships with all our children. A real relationship with a student means that the person in charge knows about their family, their failures, their fears, their successes, and their passion.

Most teachers and administration are way too out of touch to understand why this would be important, yet it is vital. If the teacher has this relationship, the child views that teacher as powerful. The child is now vulnerable in a good way. No matter what, the student feels a sense of obligation to succeed, to sweat, and to improve so they don't let that person down. Now when the educator lets Johnny know that he fell short, was lazy, or needed to improve, the child responds positively, by words or action or both. Forming this relationship is a true skill and is severely lacking in our schools. Many superficial relationships develop which result in no real meaning or substance. The teachers with the most longevity are able to guide and drive this work. They are still around because they have formed the deep and substantive relationships that are so vital to the growth of a child. Yet they are rarely utilized in this way. Too bad for our many emotionally needy students who could benefit from wisdom passed down from the most experienced.

To change this:

Teachers need to turn off the mute button. We have lost our voice because we quit speaking, we quit questioning, and we have become passive and sheep-like. We need to weigh in on *all* issues which deal with our children and their success. And we need to demand that we are treated as we should be.

We allow the schools to charge us for real-life situations even though the schools face no monetary hardship. Here's an example. Mrs. Smith says she is going to be late. The school does not have to pay a substitute because the teacher has a period one planning period. Out of decency, the teacher informs the school that she won't meet the required start time. Then the timekeeper docks the teacher's pay for *two hours* even though the teacher was only thirty or forty minutes late. If this is a beginning teacher, it may even result in pay being docked. Schools have been doing this for years and it is wrong.

The demand for doing what is best for our students should resonate in every building. But it doesn't because we are afraid. For too long we have done what we are told and not what we as the experts know is best...and there is a difference. A huge one.

Myth #8

School districts stay true to their educational mission and treat students and families in an equitable manner regardless of circumstance.

The truth:

The Denver Public Schools website bombards its readers with the following words: students first, integrity, equity, collaboration, accountability, and fun.

These words, according to our district leaders, are what we espouse, reflect, and live through our daily work. I cry foul. If we did this, we wouldn't have to say it, repeat it, and then give out phony pins with these ideals on them. Every school, all two hundred nine of them, has metal pins they hand out when teachers reach these lofty ideals. Several times a year we have these pseudo-award moments where we celebrate our collective excellence. Yes, dear public, a very special, touching moment—our faculty dog-and-pony show. A teacher raises their hand and gives props, accolades, or praises to a colleague (usually their friend) and the colleague gets a pin that says "integrity" or "collaboration." Then the show continues. This is the district standard, repeated at most schools. The teachers seeking validation display their well-earned pins on their lanyards or in their classrooms. Those who don't need this external validation chuck 'em somewhere and move on. Their goal is to do the actual work, not to get the coveted pin. No doubt, the district leaders hype this up and use this as their evidence that we are living our stated motto. There is a huge disconnect. Instead, our pins might more accurately say underserved, deceitful, lack of equity, top-down leadership, or pass the buck.

Like it or not, this is the reality in our district. Thousands of children and their families are underserved. They survive each day, hoping to meet their basic needs for shelter, food, or the like until the next day. They feel no association with the school which, if things were different, could serve as everyone's ray of hope. The school is a place to send the children, but sadly does not provide what it is supposed to—the chance for hope. If the system at every school intended or otherwise provided hope and opportunity, life would be dramatically better for the children under our watch. Students first? Are they really the priority? Do we, all fourteen thousand of us, work to make their lives and existence better? Do we help their families? Are we accessible and approachable? If the theme were true, why are so many students hungry, angry, struggling, depressed, and stuck in their current places?

Does the district have integrity? Let's see. How are the test scores? Do we retain our new teachers and improve their quality of life? Do we operate on a billion-dollar budget in normal years, or do we have half again as much in our coffers? Why do we have one administrator for every seven-and-a-half teachers? What are our college graduation rates over a six-year period following high school? Are our teachers and staff content with their place in this huge system? Are we straightforward and transparent? Do our families really have a voice? Do we apologize for falling short? Have we admitted we still have institutional racism in many of our buildings? Are areas of our city neglected and underserved? Now, dear reader, answer me. Does this look like integrity?

Equity in education translates to access and opportunity for all students and families. It means that the child in poverty has the same opportunities as the child whose folks make several hundred thousand dollars a year. Equity means that they both see similar situations, teachers, experiences, clubs, and activities. Is all education equal? Not from where I stand. This is yet another falsehood uttered by our large and well-paid public relations staff. They feel better stating it until we all want to hurl. It is sickening to hear we have equity in education and then see the reality.

As you leave your comfort zone and travel to Denver's neighborhoods as I have, reality sets in quick and is quite eye opening. Dozens of schools look nothing like their suburban counterparts. There are a few new buildings, but most are older. Clearly, our maintenance, grounds, desks, classrooms, and physical infrastructure announce we are second rate. In bordering districts, maintenance staff keep the buildings neat and tidy. Classrooms look different, and they are. We contend we are too poor, with too few resources to go around. Who suffers? The children. Should we look like a second-rate operation? You decide, then answer this rhetorical question. In 2018, the highest paid three hundred Denver Public School employees made roughly 41 million dollars. Out of nearly fourteen thousand employees, this top tier made that kind of money. What do they all do? I don't know and nobody asks. Yet if you look at their titles, many rarely interact in a school or with children. Is it possible to make $150,000 dollars in a school system and not link directly with children or families? Yes, check it out. Is this equity? A teacher in his or her fifth year makes $59,000 and works their tail off, while someone who is never in front of a child or their family makes triple that amount. Is this equity? Does the family on the west side of town have the same school choices, class selections, chance at college education, or access that the more privileged families have? After taking a hard look at schools in our underserved or forgotten neighborhoods, you decide. Why have we desegregated our schools?

Who is held accountable? After all, accountability is one of our lofty ideals. The teacher is constantly reminded of that fact. Do this. Do that. More meetings. Post this. Teach that way. Spend ten to fifteen hours a week tied to that computer. Do this while managing your classes, calling parents, having a personal life, and if you get questioned or can't manage, just wait for the fallout. I'm told to be more accountable for documenting my home contacts. Tell me where to squeeze that in. Some weeks I make fifty to seventy contacts with parents, counselors, advisors, students, social workers, the school nurse, or the school psychologist. Now I am supposed to take several minutes per student and enter what I have done on the computer. When? I have asked this question on multiple occasions. It would be easy to keep a log and submit it to the appropriate person who has been told to insist this is done. This could be done concurrently when I made the contact, but for some reason, that is not okay. Why isn't it? This is what accountability looks like at the building level. The principal and his or her staff make it clear.

"Teachers, teach hard and well; give the students your very best; impart your knowledge, and we as an administrative team will eliminate the distractions. Contact parents and respond when they contact you. We will build time into your schedule when you can do this. On several of our in-service days we will free you up from meetings to do this on school time."

Easily said, but it never happens, not these days. Our top-down administration gets pushed from their superiors. Whether intended or not, the message is "Bash 'em and make 'em sweat." They are expendable, and we must be too. If we weren't, teachers wouldn't leave at the constant rate they do, year after year. There are thousands of teachers tired as hell and beyond burned out. They don't have to be in it for very long to feel the constant pressure that becomes part of the grind. What they enjoy most—teaching and engaging youngsters—becomes secondary because of the other demands placed on our shoulders.

Here's a little secret. Nowadays, if a teacher has an appointment or is late because of an obligation with a child or spouse, their pay is docked in the form of a loss of time or loss of money. The school secretary in charge of pay is happy to take two hours or more of your accrued sick time or personal time. This gives our secretary power, which she loves. In these times, there is always a power-hungry secretary, male or female. Hundreds of important people love to bash the teacher. But why? Again, this comes from the top down.

Let me be crystal clear. Not long ago, I was told by the principal and staff to take care of my family. They meant it. If I left to go to the ultrasound during my wife's pregnancy, no foul. If I left during my planning period and got some coverage to tend to my own needs, no harm done, and no loss of time or money. They trusted and valued me. The entire leadership team knew I did many twenty-hour days. Fair is fair; live life and take care of your peeps. We all knew this. If my family was safe and thriving, I could continue to do my work. Fast forward to now. Hell no! You miss fifteen minutes or two hours or come in late, time lost. If I see a parent or work with a family at five o'clock in the morning or on a Saturday, I can recover my lost time. Fair is fair. I can go back and tell the powerful one in charge, and she will give me back some lost time. Right? Oh hell no. Doesn't work like that, so don't go there. Our keeper-of-the-time is so brazen that she did this two years ago. She sent an email to the faculty and staff explaining she would be out of the building and working from the campground and was able to manage her many tasks from this scenic, remote, lovely location. If necessary, we could email her with our needs. She is allowed to work remotely (pre-Covid), managing her emails with no loss of time or pay. Did I hear that right? I did! She was all that! Not only was she that important, but she also had the balls—sorry, the backbone, the chutzpah—to put it out there. What did her boss or any other boss say? Nothing.

I just snitched. I dropped a dime and told you what happens throughout our district and in most of our public schools. My coach I.Q. tells me that "public school" means I go public with the truth and the message.

Fun? This is one of our district values? Just what the hell does that mean? This ain't Six Flags, the bowling alley, the comedy club, or a hike or swim. Yes, I enjoy the heck out of my classes and the daily hustle, but there is no way my colleagues in the Denver Public Schools and our teaching counterparts throughout the nation are having fun. Drop that ideal and replace it with satisfaction or contentment. Teachers work their tails off for low pay and little gratification. There, I said it! My first year as a rookie was pure Hades, my misery compounded by my inept teaching skills. We toss the "fun" label out there because we want to imply that fun is what we are having. But saying we are having fun is an absolute insult. Let's leave that there. I didn't sign up to teach so I could have fun. How infantile.

To Change This:

Let's quit the charades. If we have to give pins, blow up the PR sites, and publicly state our wonderful values, we are falling short. When our students, parents, and tax-paying neighbors start extolling our virtues, then we have really accomplished something. Until then, let's stop this act and say what we really are. The rhetoric is old and beat up. Until we are what we are represented as by our highly paid public relations gurus, we should simmer down.

We are not doing what we say or represent, and as this gets scrutinized and dissected, many will realize we are imposters. Once this happens, we can insist that we stay under a microscope until our mission and truthfulness, and our transparency, improves.

Myth #9

National efforts to align schools and school districts have significantly improved education. Standardized tests, No Child Left Behind, Beyond the Common Core, and other US-based initiatives have had a major impact on education in our small and large public school systems.

The truth:

At the national level we are a system in crisis, yet we won't readily admit it. The truth is that our public schools are struggling everywhere. In a day and age where education should be advancing to keep up with public schools in other countries, we are falling further behind. Despite money thrown our way, special interest groups, and more technology and resources, we are doing worse. Our attempts to educate are like making sausage, or worse yet, hot dogs—we toss it all in and hope the product is good. I love hot dogs and will light them up, and the more nitrates, nitrites, and animal parts they have, the more I like them. But they are terrible for our bodies, and I should cut them out forever. Schools today have become like hot dogs. We throw in more money, technology, testing, "nyms" (acronyms), curriculum gurus, experts, and legislators into this organism, blend it together, and we get this poor concoction with no apparent answers or changes, no nutritional value to raise the organism's function to a higher level.

I would love to say that the efforts to link our public education systems by cities and states have been a positive change. These efforts have been going on for a long period of time. All states give their mandated tests. We have curriculum guides and have tried to make each state system transparent enough to see which classes we all can teach in common or with some similarity. No Child Left Behind had some success, but as educators, we collectively ruined it. What? Yes, you have read this before. In education we are quick to place blame. We blame each other, the parents, society, the system, and these "terrible" children. Education today is harder than ever, with worse results. Yes, our students are different, but not as much as we would like you to believe. At the core, they still want to achieve, they crave discipline, and they are looking for that spark. It is entirely achievable to have respect and civility and to create a great learning climate in every class, yet we don't do that.

As a teaching entity, we have cashed it in. Individually and collectively, we say, through words or actions, "I pick my battles" or "That is a fight I won't have." This attitude, multiplied by several million teachers, has created this dysfunctional system. We own it and can change it, but few have the steam and resolve to wade into this epic battle. We have moved away from basics. We have looked the other way. Our efforts to demand civility or to do battle when children do drugs or join gangs are long gone. Very few of us are still around to wage those battles. Even fewer will take on the technology device addiction for the sake of improving education. Schools look like a cross between the phone store and the sound warehouse. Nearly every kid is wired up with some device, and sometimes several. This is now the way of the world. We better figure this out quick, or this trainwreck will get worse.

Public education has become like the ice cream parlor with acronyms. There are "nyms" for everything. Hundreds of them. Let's choose the flavor of the day. We have SAT, PSAT, ACT, PACT, LEAP, BCC, TDIS, and hundreds more. States have ratings along with local school districts. They have codes, numbers, colors, and report cards. Research on a school will disclose more information than you can imagine, and none of it means jack shit. It is a facade.

I am a parent. Here's what I want to know. What systems are in place to help my kid if he or she has special needs or is gifted? How long have your teachers been at your school? Let me talk privately with two or three teachers and have them be open and honest. Next, how much weed or alcohol are floating through your high school? Prove it. Next, tell me about your social studies classes. This will be telling. Is your school teaching a multicultural curriculum? Does it reflect the population of the school or local community? Do you teach the trades? Does that include how to fix the computer? Are you doing video production and teaching about sustainable energy and those stinkin' drones we will see everywhere? Now, after I go and sit in the high school for lunchtime and one or two class visits, I can decide for my child really well. And I didn't have to research the propaganda or the state department's nauseating narrative. It's that simple, but nearly impossible to see in this educational climate.

What do we know for sure about success in early education? First, we know children thrive and flourish with a strong foundation. If we give the child a foundation, we will have documented success when they start kindergarten. If the family did nothing else, the child who starts in early childhood education (ECE, another acronym) is on equal footing most of the time. But what does this look like? A three- or four-year-old can fall in love with the whole school experience and start school with great social skills and a zest for learning. It doesn't have to cost a lot to provide books, sounds, a few computers—enough to "jumpstart" the child. It can't be high-pressure demands and letter grades at this age, but rather guided exploration, which sparks curiosity and allows the child to develop a passion for many activities. The child can fall in love with reading, music, art, gym, and math, all at the same time. Through different types of learning, this enthusiasm will continue when kindergarten begins.

Here's the rub though. Not every child has access to this, despite massive amounts of federal and local dollars earmarked for this model. Districts are reluctant to provide transportation and high-quality teachers for this. So even at this age, our children of color begin at a disadvantage. A progressive system that truly believes in *equity* will make sure that every child in every neighborhood can start school with this valuable foundation.

Now the stage is set. Kindergarten continues this trend to establish a stable foundation and enlists two or three committed volunteers who nurture the soft skills and the notion that they are creating educational supermen and superwomen. Tell the children they can be like anybody or anything they know or want to be. Tell them they are really good at a lot of things. Have some watchdogs. As soon as *any* child falls even a little behind, send the designated volunteer to do some one-on-one time with them. This is precious time for the student, who often catches up and will stay caught up because someone knew and truly cared. Build on the foundation in the first and second grades. "Read it, repeat it, copy it, and recite it" may seem antiquated, but it still applies and is proven to work. We can't fall into the electronic nanny trap. The daily lives of most children already include enough of this. Even families with financial challenges get caught in this convenient trap. Our kids are allowed to become addicted in the wrong way. We should want our babies to draw, play, sing, dance, speak, and socialize more than we want them to become gamers at seven or eight years old. Why is this model of education not the norm? Why do we underserve so many families who need us the most? This is the question for the ages.

Education needs to change—yesterday. In many places around the country, we perpetuate this nightmare of mediocrity. We want to tout our national educational persona as cutting edge and competitive with other countries, but this is not true. Let's keep it real. Many can go to college and will, but not everyone needs to have an MBA. The working men and women who use their hands or who have a special skill set do quite well in our society. I know many plumbers, electricians, computer programmers, and cable and fiber-optic installers who are as happy as can be and make substantial money. Why are we so in love with the standardized tests? Show me the research that indicates how effective they are.

Multi-million-dollar companies who create the standardized tests make a fortune off them, often from families who see no correlation or benefit. Let's take that money and use it to create a test to determine aptitude for certain skills, talents, or interests. Let's admit that people are getting rich by creating these poor indicators of knowledge. If the tests were so damn relevant, then explain why a hard-working child who tests average or below earns a PhD or becomes a successful entrepreneur without earning the expensive degrees. Our classrooms should align with our current society. Yes, we have phones, drones, hormones, and clones. We have energy that comes from steam, the sun, electricity, the ocean, water, and wind, but where are those teachers and those lessons in our schools? Why is this system in a state of slow or no motion when it comes to educating the whole child?

Why have we let our children off the hook? They rarely speak, recite, do grammar, or brush up on or even learn the math facts. I stink at math, but trying to build a fence, pour concrete, put up drywall, install a microwave or dishwasher or oven or dryer require that I measure. Imagine that! Where has the teaching of great life lessons gone from our schools? Don't teach me on the computer screen what the difference is between deciduous and coniferous trees, show me. Walk the campus and show me. Let me learn about this precious thing called water by letting me feel ice, steam, and still and rushing water. How do we have the gall to still teach only about the Boston Tea Party and those antiquated events and history of the white man—our white country, our white forefathers, and our whitewashed world? Where do we learn about the exploitation of our Indian, our African, our Asian, and our Spanish-speaking brothers and sisters and how we have literally stolen from them for many decades? It needs to be out there; it needs to be stated. How can we make it right when we don't even speak on it? When we do wrong, we must say so.

Nationally, we have done a great job with rhetoric and have created a lot of different words we can say as we advertise the merits of our public school system. In truth, we have done little to meet the needs of our children when they leave us after spending over fifteen thousand hours of collective time in our buildings. The system needs dramatic change and needs it quickly. We should have a national task force to identify what will have the strongest impact on our school systems throughout our country and then make it interchangeable. City-to-city and state-to-state, we should be doing similar tasks to ensure that we are truly serving our children. There should be federal mandates to support one ideal. This ideal is that we follow the different educational laws, and if not, we revise them.

Every child should have access to a great formative education before they enter kindergarten. This should be the constant, even if we have to send a teacher into the home or neighborhood or provide transportation in case that is an obstacle for the family.

A child should be assisted as soon as the need arises. This means that if there is hunger, homelessness, or any obstacle that detracts from learning, the school takes action. The schools have money and resources available for situations of this nature.

To change this:

We must listen to the experts who, like it or not, have lived the school-success experience. These are teachers or former students who used something or someone within a school to achieve something positive in their own life and past experience. The state representative or money hoarder cannot decide what is best for the child or the school. The special interest group can't dictate educational policy either. The people who bank on the almighty standardized tests should be sat on the bench as well. They need to "ride the pine" until they prove that the racially unbalanced tests have merit and substance for all children and provide meaning and guidance.

Let's teach respect and insist on civility. In this day and age, if we insist, stomp, storm, and demand, children of any age will respect adults and their peers. Educational climate can never be achieved with blatant prejudice or racism in its midst.

As teachers, parents, and taxpayers, let's unify and make our education relevant and understandable. We are ready to cross into 2023 with a 1960's curriculum across many disciplines. We can be much more progressive and current with what we teach.

Let's support our teachers. Allow them to learn how to teach, which is the most important teacher metric. Let's support them without the constant teacher-bashing that takes place all over the country. Once this support is in place, the profession will become more appealing, and many will select this valuable occupation instead of shying away from it.

Collectively, let's watch with eagle eyes where the money is going. There is a helluva lot more money than most central administrators will ever admit. Our concerned taxpayers and parents across all cultures need to insist on knowing where every cent is being spent. When you eliminate the huge numbers of wasted dollars spent on consultants, cronies, and people who profit from the standardized tests, change will happen. Suddenly there will be money for children and their needs.

Before we close out myth number nine, let's repeat—we are sorry! We are sorry for our past educational missteps. For the underserved families in every community and city. And for the institutional racism which is still lurking in far too many schools and districts. Finally, we are sorry for wasting the potential of the past generation, or maybe the past two generations. Sorry to be cliché, but we have so much work to do and so little time.

Myth #10

Change in our public schools is difficult or impossible because of the current educational climate. Violence, poverty, rising unemployment, homelessness, and societal problems make it impossible to improve schools and close the long-standing achievement gap. With our troubled society, change in schools is an insurmountable goal.

The truth:

The biggest change must start with our families, then our teachers. We have an extreme shortage of teachers, largely because of the state of the profession. Low pay, lack of respect, constant pressure, and the bigger problem, lack of support. Why would anyone sign up for this? Who wants to get teacher-bashed by the administration, parents, and children who have reset this system to its current model?

The societal issues we have become accustomed to are not a roadblock, but an opportunity. The tough issues in front of us now should serve to clarify the educational mission. We must change to make life better for millions of people, starting with our youngest children. Even with the Covid pandemic, it is vital we take the early baby steps and wholeheartedly change this troubled educational system. As educators, both in and out of school buildings each day, we must commit to change as necessary to help the general public.

It's time to toss out the business model in our schools. Schools are not designed to be for-profit entities. Quite the contrary. Schools are supposed to freely and wisely spend money to provide hope and a better future for millions of children in our country. Schools are not corporations and should not be operated or guided as such. Schools and school systems are in the business of children and people. Shred the corporate model and go back to valuing teachers and staff while honoring the child. Honor the child's right to free and appropriate education, in accordance with the law. Ours is the only major institution which is protected by law in our country.

Dig this. In our country you can practice any religion or choose to practice none. No laws for or against your religious choice or freedom. Choose your god or choose none. Either pray or don't pray.

No law says you have to marry, who you can marry, or that you can't marry. We have the choice to join the institution of marriage or not. The law can't and won't dictate or mandate any choice related to dating or marriage.

Domicile. There are no laws which govern where we live, either. The choice lies with each person to determine their own living conditions. Whether in a trailer, tent, apartment, townhome, car, condo, house, motel, garage, or shed, it does not matter. In our country people can live where they choose or where their income level allows. Not having a hard roof over your head does not mean you are breaking the law.

Same with transportation. No laws dictate how you travel. You can take a car, bus, bike, skateboard. You can walk, run, ride a scooter, or use a ride-sharing service, and all of these are perfectly acceptable and legal ways to travel.

What about our diets and how we sustain ourselves? There are no laws or restrictions about how, what, why, when, or where we eat. We get to choose, without interference, what we do to survive nutritionally and be productive.

What does this mean? All of these important institutions—marriage, religion, housing, and survival—are non-guided and not restricted by law. Yet the institution of education is. By law we have to go to school until at least the age of sixteen or seventeen, and we as adults have to send our children to school. Sometimes this becomes a court battle in a truancy court. It shouldn't really be used though, and I know that this will ruffle some feathers, but if we were serving all our communities and using this institution as we should, the school would be so important and essential that children and families would be waiting at the doors. Could this be our biggest goal or mission?

In Denver, as in other major cities, we have been stuck. Leadership issues, declining enrollment, children who are homeschooled or attend suburban schools, lack of trust, lack of equity, too few teachers of color, and large achievement gaps. Same story, different city. Are we going to let this be the failure and demise of our country's public school systems? We sure act like it. When and where do we stand up and say *enough*?

To change this:

We can't wait. This must stop. It's time. The tidal wave, the tsunami, must be created right now. Change can't be incremental and slow. The redesign must take place within the next year to save this generation. I am not trying to be a drama queen; I am just speaking the truth.

Until the system is stripped of the nepotism, lack of honesty, waste of money, and lack of equity and access, we will only get the same.

Time to butt in and as a large group insist that we become better. And trust me, there is plenty of room for that. We have enough numbers, money, and enough knowledge now as to what the problems are. So let's turn over enough stones to recreate what is positive and most essential for our youth.

The current system is so deeply flawed there is literally no time to lose. We should start the movement immediately, and with thousands of voices demanded that they not be silenced or ignored any longer.

The System

Education. School. Call it what you want, but it is the system; the institution that educators and many millions of children pass through each year. School should be, ideally, for kids. I have spent a total of forty-three years in this system. Does anyone think it's flawless? Of course not. It is flawed, screwed up, and most of the time, it is broken. That's why we educators keep trying to fix it. The more things we fix, the more we screw up. As always, we are rescued by the kids. The reality is, we as educators are clueless. But despite all our crapola each year, kids learn to read. Each year kids continue from junior high or middle school to high school. Each year, kids graduate. Every year, several million kids go to technical school, college, the military, or to work. It's been like that for eternity. Pretty cool.

We keep tinkering with the system and it still goes on. Kids keep moving through it and many succeed. Others, unfortunately, fail. This cycle has continued for decades, and for me, three generations. Imagine the changes and what these old but undimmed and untired eyes have seen. After all the experimentation, mandates, trends, theories, and government interventions, we have the same result. Children learn and grow in a system that most will admit is flawed, yet they end up doing well at life.

The students become good husbands, wives, partners, moms, and dads, but most importantly, they become good people. All of this transpires despite our flaws, yet I am convinced that we as members of the system have created misery and hardship far too often.

I can shed no light on the private school sector, where I have no experience. My hunch is that it is just as flawed, but that it too works. We can't get it right because we don't step back long enough to see why it works. And we don't study what we should do to really perfect this colossal wreck. I am not a cynic; actually, just the opposite. I know that no matter how we try to change or modify what we do in schools, in the end it will be okay.

Here are some examples. Over a quarter of a century, hundreds of studies have been done about what is physically conducive to children's achievement. We went from schools built like prisons with windows to schools built with open hallways. Then we had open rooms and no windows. School rooms have been painted blue, yellow, white, and even pink, because some studies showed that kids felt better in these environments. Some studies show that kids do well in fluorescent light, some in natural light, and some in radiant lighting. We react with an instant knee-jerk when some study comes out that may or may not be valid. Years ago, we ran the school day from 6:30 a.m. to 1:40 p.m., and it worked. Now there is a big movement to start the school day later. Some night owls did a study that showed children need to sleep later. The studies that followed indicated that the late start/high achievement bid has no substance. But have no fear, let's change it anyway. Why not? We have millions of guinea pigs. Let's experiment! Let's take billions of dollars that taxpayers have worked hard for and make constant changes.

No wonder the public perception about education is that we are taxpayer dollar-sucking vultures with a bad return on investment. Our livelihood is dependent on the people we keep asking to bail our butts out. If businesses were run like our school system, they would go broke quickly. Do I suggest that we should operate our schools like a business? No, it still has to be about children and people, but where is the oversight? Who is aware? Who cares enough to expose the waste, the incessant change, and the way our young are exposed to so much that means so little?

About twenty years ago, teachers were told to develop portfolios. These portfolios were one- to two hundred-page documents, full of educators' philosophy, writing samples, lesson plans, and more. The same movement declared we would go to outcome-based education. How innovative. Each kid would make a notebook full of every bit of garbage that some committee somewhere would look at to determine if Tommy was worthy of a real diploma. Or one that just said he attended and existed at his school. And this was the new education. The way to determine how capable and educated our children were. What happened to the teacher portfolios and the kids' masterpieces? Hell if I know. The whole thing just disappeared with no explanation and no admission of guilt. Just gone. Where did all the portfolios and notebooks end up? Did we recycle them? Are they now confetti? This was another grand experiment with the lab rats that cost millions.

The fact is, we don't know and will never know for sure if Johnny does better sitting at a table or a desk. Peggy may or may not do well in the pink classroom natural lighting. Open classrooms and schools may or may not work. Kids can learn at 6:30 a.m. or at 5 p.m. The time of day doesn't matter. In regard to learning, show me a study, and I can show you one that shows the opposite.

Have no fear. After all this maneuvering and waste of money, a few important things are blatantly obvious. Success in education boils down to some ideals that can be summed up in a few words—people, chance, hope, believe, pride, ownership, and loyalty. If we studied these ideals, these principles, and how to learn, teach, and live them, we would be dramatically more successful. Kids, schools, and classrooms succeed or fail due to the presence or absence of these ideals. We are not a system of room colors, lights, or computers. We are not a system of early- or late-shift learning. We are a system of people—for people and about people. With all the new technology, we forget that we're dealing with brains, upbringing, and peer pressure. We're dealing with emotions that are different in each kid we see and teach. It's time for serious reform. It's time to quit wasting money and damaging kids at the expense of our studies, our selfishness, and our stubbornness. Like it or not, we are in the people business. If you want to study lighting, become an electrician. if you want to look at colors of classrooms, become a damp paint salesman. If you want to sit on your flat butt in front of your cool nineteen-inch flat-screen high-definition computer monitor, become a programmer. Education should be about people—about children. Teachers should be hired based on their ability to give hope and to motivate. Our teachers should be selected based on their ability to instill pride. The best principals and teachers are the ones who create loyalty and ownership. Giving a kid hope and teaching a child to have pride when they have had none is more powerful than anything else. Focus on what works. Quit tarnishing the profession with experimentation. Let's change our attitude. Give me a teacher who cares, who is passionate about learning, and who knows every kid's name. I'll take that in the school any day over a tech-head who can't motivate a kid.

Over the years, some of the best learning has taken place in the most unlikely places and circumstances. Oscar, Noe, Will, Janelle, Shuaib, Shakib, Blake, Iran, Sean, Amy, Rondell, Ernesto, Shehila, and hundreds more earned or will earn degrees while overcoming many obstacles, some constantly. Among this named group were many low income or impoverished kids. Guess what? They succeeded! Some succeeded even more despite being raised by one parent who worked two or even three jobs to provide. Some kids overcame tragic events such as the death of a loved one. Some had sad family lives, and they still succeeded. Many know about hunger and homelessness. Success is not necessarily tied to money. If it were, about three quarters of my college-bound kids would not go to college. Kids need to believe; they need to be told and sold on their worth and their value, and some need it pounded into their heads. My study shows that kids with troubled lives surrounded by sadness want to succeed, but not enough of us will tell them they can. Harvard, Yale, Northwestern, MIT, Dartmouth, the army, and the air force are just a few of the places my students have earned degrees. They did so because someone or a few someones believed in them, gave them pride, and inspired hope.

What are we doing to inspire hope? How do we let kids know they have a chance? Are we as educators in this system aware and conscious that we must be motivators? Often, we are in the most powerful position to influence kids' lives. Our job, our work, and our words are actions that can make a kid believe. Take a hard look at your school system—the one you attend, work in, or you support with your tax dollars. Is it a school of hope with vast opportunities for children to succeed? Do you know or care? When you walk into your school or any school, are you greeted by kids talking to adults? Their teachers? Are the administrators, the dean, a teacher, or the assistant principal visible? If you walk in at the start of the school day and don't see any positive signs, beware. Are teachers on task? Are they in the halls mingling with the kids during lunch or passing period? Walk to several classrooms with your visitor's pass and observe.

Are children being challenged and are they listening? Is the teacher interesting or just getting through the day with busy work while in front of the computer screen? In every school in every district in every city, we should be watching. Kids should know they have opportunity and a chance. Nothing is worse than hopelessness, yet much of what we do as a system fosters this and we do little to change it. As you look at the schools, go into the teacher's work area. Tell me what it looks like—I've never been. Are teachers planning and discussing and really working? Or are they griping about the kids, the administration, or the system?

To provide hope, we need to let kids know they have opportunities. Our system needs to change; it does not just happen. Teachers need to be trained differently. The tried-and-true method of training teachers is out of date and out of line. With the typical methods used to train teachers, a college student elects to become a teacher in their sophomore or junior year. They take some methods classes designed to expose them to aspects and techniques of teaching that cover curriculum and testing methods. Cognitive development and other well-researched blah blah blah. The prospective teacher then begins to log hours around kids. They observe classes and spend time on school campuses, because in our profession they need to be exposed to what kids do and how they act. These observations are usually completed the latter part of their junior year. The teacher-to-be gets prepared for student teaching. Student teaching covers a half or a full semester of time during which the student practices teaching. They have a supervising teacher and are also looked in on randomly by the college professor or coordinating teacher. The student-teaching experience is hit-or-miss. Some finish the experience with a sense of reality, and their slap in the face is that they are either unprepared to teach, or worse, find they are going into the wrong profession. The majority gain a false sense of comfort. They anxiously anticipate their first teaching job or become substitute teachers.

This antiquated training system has some flaws. First, at the college or university level, the teacher is most often placed in situations that are cozy and comfortable. A lot of student teaching is done in college cities and towns where the population is vastly different than where the jobs are. Next, the college supervisor picks a good teaching mentor who is good with the kids and enough of a disciplinarian to control the class. When the student teachers have their turn to teach, they can absorb and learn from the mentor over a short period, but the time spent on this is not enough. The student teacher is then thrust into the classroom alone to succeed or flounder. The student-teaching experience rarely allows the teacher to make mistakes or be dynamic, and rarely is this meaningful enough to provide valuable experience.

Here's what the student-teaching program should look like. A college sophomore takes a methods course that is much different than the ones offered now. This class would cover the entire multitude of real-life problems that can a occur in a school or classroom when the prospective teacher can still change their curriculum. They need to know the successes and the pitfalls of the teaching profession. They could be exposed to a class called "Student Populations." This course would provide an honest look at the types of families that our teachers work with and would expose them to the types of students and their needs, which are often dramatically different than the way most teachers themselves were raised. This course might even include a tour into some neighborhoods, both rural and urban, and would educate them on the characteristics of the families and family structures of the populations that educators serve. They should be exposed to school law and what their rights are as a teacher. They would learn how they are evaluated and what benefits are available for medical care, dental care, and vision for them and their families. A teacher usually doesn't get this information until they've signed a contract and started their job. How much sick leave does the teacher get and does sick leave accumulate? What about retirement? Can a teacher work for several decades and then be secure financially?

Student teaching should be a year-long course; alternatively, the teacher starts with observing every day. They should observe for two to three months to see what teachers do that is great and dynamic and what teachers do that stinks. After two months they would venture into one or two days a week of instruction or spend time with a veteran teacher. Their college professor would rate them and give them criticism, both positive and negative, as to how they're really doing. In the second semester they should teach almost every day but be on their own only three or four times a week. They should create lesson plans, be involved in faculty meetings, and should initiate parent conferences. They should make visits into the homes of the students they teach and have firsthand exposure to the lives of the student. They should go to plays, athletic events, and club meetings. They should attend drama productions and concerts to see what goes on in their school. They should jump in, immersing themselves in the educational system to see if it is what the hell they really want to do for the life of their careers. As it is, we do a poor job of training our teachers. Fifty to sixty percent of our brightest who enter the profession these days leave within a three- to five-year window. Most never return to our profession.

This "New Education" is a bust. We are in the 2020s and have entered a new decade more clueless than ever. We are testing the hell out of the kids, collecting data, going on learning walks, and using "best practices." Sounds impressive, right? Not! What we are doing is crippling an entire generation. We watch as children continue to perform three to five years below their grade level. The same kids are often tardy or ditching class. In our district we have a lot of these policies in place, but we rarely hold the child accountable. But hey, the real world will. There are children who are allowed to do as they choose no matter what. We have much-needed drug and alcohol counselors. The vaping trend illustrates that the drugs of choice are always changing, yet forever abundant.

Chapter Eleven

The Tough Times

Imagine about fifty kids hauling, sprinting by me. Then another thirty, then dozens more. Finally, around a hundred and fifty kids crowded outside the school loading dock in a twenty- by thirty-foot secluded area. What a way to start my first day back at GW, my alma mater. I was so excited to be back, and now some kids were ready to pound on each other. I pushed my way through the crowd. I was a stranger to these kids. I was shoved aside and was trying my darndest to stop it before it got too far out of control. In the center, two kids were preparing to get it on. Not Barry White's "Let's Get It On," but the other kind. The big thick kid was a basketball player who stood 6'5" and 225 pounds. His dance partner was a wannabe crip, not hard-core, I might add, but also not too small. He was about 6'3" and 180 pounds.

They were now pissed off enough to start their fight with the instigation of the crowd, who wanted to see the brawl. I jumped between them. In a heartbeat, the crowd grew silent. I was aggressive enough that as I reached up and grabbed their arms, they were surprised and shocked.

Dave, the slenderer kid said, "What are you doing? Who are you?"

"Teachers don't break up fights?" I shot back. "Well, I do." I ushered them back into the school where security escorted them to the office. I have always broken up fights and learned how to use these tense situations. Apart from once or twice, the combatants have simmered down almost instantly. Though it may seem foolish, I have never felt scared in this situation. I like watching boxing and even pro wrestling, but not in the school. I have seen my colleagues hesitate or even go the other way at the first sign of fisticuffs. I don't allow the kids at home to tear into each other, and I won't allow this at school.

A few occasions were much more chance encounters, once as a dean of students. I was in the middle of a gang fight where eighteen or twenty kids were involved in the fracas, and all were suspended. Our principal came and asked me what the heck I was thinking suspending the whole group. I was honest. I explained that even though I was there, I was too involved in separating fact from fiction to accurately determine what every kid's involvement was. Be assured, I explained, they were all there and involved in some fashion. He supported me completely. After five days, the students came back, most of them having learned a lesson. There were no further incidents.

In truth, I'm in a school known more for its academics than its violence. Yet I have seen fights, teacher assault guns, knives, baseball bats, and many other weapons, some not intended for use and others used or attempted to be used in this increasingly violent society. The schools have become a more dangerous place, with a chance of fights and weapons at any time. Still, for the most part, George Washington High School is a safe place, and if the kid is serious about hitting the books, it is very possible to go for years without getting involved in this type of violence. Now, some kids just invite trouble. Of the fights at our school, I would guess that more than half involve kids who show a lot of aggressive behavior. Some kids fight frequently or have this as a behavioral pattern that just won't go away. He or she has probably brawled in middle school and now just continues to do what comes naturally. Other fights happen because of conflict or bravado. Some fights happen because the other kids just wanted to see a fight. Kids who don't fight can be provoked to the point of no return, and they lose it, mostly because of pressure from other kids. Kids that have a random fight or act mad on occasion can be rehabilitated. A fighter, a kid who is intent on fighting all the time, needs serious treatment, far more than the school can give them, and they need to be out of the mainstream. Schools can rarely take that stand, however. We rescue, giving repeated chances, and then an incident—a stabbing, a shooting, or an assault upon the teacher happens from a kid who shouldn't be in the school. Parents have no idea there are dangerous kids at every school that make the school unsafe for the nonviolent kids. The intense mental health support that the kid so dearly needs is not addressed. If it had been, the kid would not have stayed so troubled and conflicted.

Instead, we now have restorative justice. This is a meeting of sorts for the child to elocute and make amends for his indiscretions. These are nice, fuzzy get-togethers, but they don't erase the act and provide no help to the child, adult, or victim who has been wronged. Our most troubled children have been in a system where they have deep emotional needs that have been ignored for far too long. The system has been reluctant to provide true support, so kids end up in high school with far too much emotional baggage to succeed. They needed an intervention by middle school, which most likely they never received. Had they received help then, they would know what is and isn't acceptable. Schools should be diligent and committed to creating a safe environment for all teachers and students.

Bitten

I was on lunchroom duty years ago. Back then, the rule was that kids could not enter the lunchroom with food and drink from outside vendors. I knew the rule and enforced it, and my superiors were clear. Only lunchroom food (gag) was allowed in the school café. Now I'm on duty when a kid comes barreling in with a bag of burgers and a nice supersized soda pop.

"Young man, please don't come in here with your food," I said firmly.

"Why?" he retorted.

I explained the rule. In an instant he reared back, intent on hitting me face first with forty-four ounces of cola. I saw it coming. I batted his wrist away, and most of the pop spilled on him and on the floor. I grabbed his arm. He was covered with cola and a bit sticky as I tried to escort him to the office. He became combative. I was fortunately able to restrain him enough to get him away from the crowd into the assistant principal's office. She was a tough, supportive woman, and was listening to my story.

"Ouch! Damn!" Flashes of pain jolted my nervous system. The misguided kid was clamped down on my bicep, face first, digging in his molars. Growling like a wild beast, he chewed into my skin—not just with his molars, but also his bicuspids and incisors, and even his wisdom teeth. I reared my left fist back, having decided to split his head open, yet in an instant, I changed my mind and grabbed his hair. My grip was strong. As I was doing my best to yank a fist full of hair out of his head, his jaws grew weak. His eyes spun around twice and he screamed. Once separated, the school administrators and security ushered him into an adjacent room.

I was fine. I went to the coach's office and washed my arm off with soap and water and got ready to teach for the rest of the afternoon. The kid went to jail.

I was teaching my afternoon class and in walks the assistant principal. "Coach, we are going to excuse you for the rest of the day."

"Why?" I asked.

"Well, we want you to go and get the bite checked out by a doctor and have a blood test."

"Thanks, but I'm fine," I said. She knew better than to argue. I went back to teaching.

You see, I wasn't really hurt and didn't need a doctor. Next class, I had all but forgotten when midway through the class, in walks the principal. She was and still probably is one really tough cookie.

"Now coach, it is protocol. We must follow procedure. Go to the hospital. We've arranged coverage for you. Your classes will be fine."

"Doctor, thanks, but I am fine, so I'll teach my next two classes." She too knew of my stubbornness and left. *This is no big deal,* I thought. I had a bite mark that was not infected and thought I was free at last. Midway through the next class, in walks a security guard.

"Coach, you have an important call. I'll watch your class until you're done."

Wow, this is getting heavy, I thought. I went to the phone, called the operator, and got transferred to my caller. Damn. It was the assistant superintendent, Mrs. Seick. I had known her for years.

"Coach, how are you?"

"Great," I replied, "how are you?" She is a strong woman, a lifelong educator, and a teacher, coach, athletic director, and principal. She even served for a few years as our superintendent and did a masterful job.

"See, you will go and get that bite checked out, do you understand me?" It was a demand.

"Yes, ma'am," was all I could say. She knew I'd listen, and not because of her rank or title. I respected her. She had no doubt in her mind that I would follow her directive, which I did. I missed one class and had my arms scrubbed and a blood test to see if "Jaws" had given me a disease. The next day, everything was back to normal. My blood test came back normal, and I had another battle wound, and an even better story to tell.

Poetic Justice

This kid was a pain in the bottom. He had brown hair but had done the peroxide treatment on the top, because he thought having blond or whitish hair was cool. Once he enrolled in my class, he became the nuisance I expected. He weighed 150 pounds, played on the soccer team, was loud and cocky, and reminded me of the yellow Power Ranger. I pulled him out the first day, and we emphasized the rules. He mocked, rolled his eyes, and said the right things without meaning them. Daily, the Ranger found someone to pick on and make fun of. Because this is a violation of one of my classroom rules, we got the counselor involved and finally his mom, the advisers, and the disciplinarians. He got the boot once or twice a week. Because of his big trap, these measures didn't change him, he just went undercover. He made fun a bit more quietly, with a bit more subtlety, but that didn't matter to me. He was still making fun.

The kid he finally chose to pick on was a tall, skinny kid from a foreign country who was obedient and polite. He had been brought up well.

Always yes coach, no coach, please, and thank you. He was quite shy and interacted with the class with a minimal amount of dialogue. Though a bit clumsy, he was by no means the most uncoordinated kid in class. The yellow Power Ranger did everything he could to make Stretch's life miserable. You stink; you're a nerd; I wish we could trade you—these were a few of the nicer barbs he threw out almost daily. Each time I caught this I would sit him down, notify the counselor, and go through the proper documentation. This would piss him off. Despite all this, he didn't get any better—he just grew more frustrated. We had at least a dozen documented situations where he had bullied verbally or physically. Mom wouldn't accept the fact that her baby was unable to cope in this class. The school wouldn't yank him out of the class, and I was stuck with him. The year was coming to an end, and I was counting the minutes until this creep was out of my hair.

On the day of our final, we did some fitness testing. After that we divided into six basketball teams for a forty-five-minute basketball tournament. Every five to seven minutes, one team from each court would rotate, depending on whether they won or lost. Stretch's team rotated to play the Power Ranger's team. I thought it would be okay, as there had been no actual fighting between the two. I'm watching the game and suddenly the Power Ranger, whose team was getting their butts kicked, shoved Stretch right in the chest. In half an instant, Stretch reared back and threw a punch that would make any boxer envious. *Crack!*

Now I must be honest. I got up suddenly, and my knee started to ache. I took my sweet time. The Power Ranger was screaming expletives.

"He broke my nose! He broke my damn stinkin' nose!"

Blood was everywhere. Forty kids were frozen like statues. The Ranger looked up, and there it was. His nose was no longer central. It was placed very accurately near his cheek. I had security come and take the Power Ranger and Stretch to the advisor's office. Once there, both kids were sent home about an hour later.

A detective called and said, "Coach—tell me about this assault. I have an irate mom who is filing charges."

"Detective, I'm going to fax you some information." I sent him about eight pages of documentation showing how he had instigated. The kid with his face rearranged had pushed Stretch to his limits. He had gotten on his last nerve. The detective told me he'd get back to me.

Apparently, the detective called Mom back and told her that based on the evidence he had gathered, he was considering filing charges against the Power Ranger. Mom grew livid, but in the end had no recourse. The Power Ranger learned a great lesson. Stretch went back to his usual quiet demeanor. The kids in school, however, looked at Stretch with a hell of a lot of respect after news of this punch made its way through the school.

Nobody saw much of the Power Ranger after that. Stretch came to see me about two years ago in his navy uniform. Because he was an outstanding student in high school, he had gone into the navy and been trained on navigation systems on submarines. I knew he would do well. And after several years in the navy, he became a Navy Seal. I can't wait to see him again. I'm sure he's doing well.

Conspiracy

During lunch one day, my colleague Mr. S. and I were on gym duty as usual. About twenty kids played volleyball and fifty or sixty played basketball. We made sure the kids played fair and didn't cuss. We ran this program in a disciplined and orderly way. I had a meeting one day and as a result missed my duty. When I got back after lunch, rumors were swirling. Apparently, a melee had occurred in the gym. There were thirty different stories about what had happened. The common truth in each of the stories was that Brian (not his real name) was the main instigator and alleged that my colleague had punched him during the fracas. Mr. S. had been placed on administrative leave based on the allegations. His due process was nonexistent, but he laughed, rather frustrated at the whole situation. There were too many inconsistencies. I asked my class questions about the incident and found three good kids who had seen the whole thing. I sent for them later and asked them individually to write down their accounts of what happened. They were reluctant because Brian was a hard-core Blood and would retaliate if they snitched. I asked them to write out everything that happened and told them I would not insist that they sign their names, thereby protecting their identities. They agreed.

Their account went like this: Brian called out another kid by using gang terminology. The other kid didn't back down. A third kid, Brian's friend, got involved and all three kids were fighting. The teacher bounced a basketball toward them and grabbed Brian to break up the fight.

Dozens of people knew Brian had instigated the whole thing. Brian went to the office and claimed he was the victim of the teacher's assault. The rookie student advisor didn't investigate. He didn't get statements and he believed the kid's side. The kid realized he could talk his way out of a suspension, and he carried on, convincing the rookie disciplinary advisor. The advisor went to the principal who, in her haste and without sufficient knowledge of the whole situation, put the teacher on paid leave for the month of December. The rookie student advisor also called the office of the district attorney who then called the police, and ultimately, assault charges were filed against the teacher.

What a crock of garbage. I hoped the truth really mattered, so after the three students wrote their version of what happened, I gave these to the principal. To her credit, she admitted she may have blown it. The hoodlum kid was now getting his buddies to verify that his lies were the truth. Some of his pals wrote statements suggesting the teacher hit the kid. So there we were. The teacher was on leave and the school district was now paying for a substitute as well as the teacher's fifty-five or sixty-thousand-dollar-a-year salary. The district attorney had investigators come and take statements and do interviews. The teacher's union had an attorney who took the statements I had and represented the teacher. This went on until late May of that year. Finally, we went to court for a pretrial hearing. I was called as a witness. The judge asked about my information, and I explained that the three written statements I had were legitimate and that all three kids were scared for their lives of retaliation from the kid who claimed to be the victim.

In open court the judge sternly said, "Mr. Finesilver, please identify your informants."

"Judge, I have the utmost respect for this court. However, I choose not to identify these youngsters," I said. It got eerily quiet.

"Mr. Finesilver, on what grounds are you refusing to give the court these names?"

"Judge," I whispered, "I gave those kids my word—my promise—that I would not surrender their identities, and I must keep my word."

She again asked on what grounds, and I respectfully referred to the Colorado Children's Code. Now I admit I had no clue what I was talking about, but my bologna had baffled the judge.

"We'll be taking a recess for ten minutes," she declared.

I heaved a sigh of relief and sprinted to a phone. After some quick legal advice, I headed back into court. The hearing continued.

"Mr. Finesilver, I just checked the Colorado Children's Code. There is nothing in there to keep you from giving the names to the court. Furthermore, if you refuse, I will hold you in contempt."

I replied, "Judge, if this is the case, I would like a court-appointed attorney." She agreed to my request.

"Okay, Mr. Finesilver, the court will call you within one week with the name of a court-appointed attorney."

At least I was off the hook for a while. A week passed with no phone call. The trial had been set for mid-June. *I'll be damned,* I thought, *I am not going to the "Crowbar Hilton" (jail) yet.* I would not hang my kids, who were honest, out there to dry, and I refused to expose them by revealing their identities. Now I'm a lot of things, but I'm not a phony or a liar. In my second week of waiting for the court to find me an attorney, I bumped into an old attorney friend and found out he happened to be on the court-appoint list. I told him the story and he agreed to get involved. The next day I called and filled them in on the details.

He went without me back into court. The other parties were present. He told them that this situation is not about Coach Finesilver and that all I had tried to do was get to the truth. Why, he asked, was this about trying to punish a veteran teacher? Why is a teacher on trial ready to get put in jail, and all he wants is the truth to come out? Finally, the judge and other parties agreed that the trial would proceed, and I would be left alone. June rolled around, and this case and drama finally went to trial.

The teacher had wisely chosen to have a jury trial. The district attorney, the prosecution, called his witnesses. The first kid, the victim's homeboy, told a story about how the teacher hit the poor kid Brian in the chest with a forearm. The next kid got on the stand and said the teacher had Brian in a headlock. Each of the eight witnesses told a different account. The jury went from confused to amused to pissed off. The prosecution, after a whole day of meaningless garbage and a variety of different accounts of the incident, put it to rest for the day.

On day two, the defense called the principal who spoke of the three statements that were anonymously written, saying that the teacher threw a ball to get the kids to break up the fight. She affirmed that the teacher had a good reputation and had never lost his cool during any situation. The defense called the teacher, Mr. S., who calmly told his story—the real one. At ten o'clock the second day, the defense, after calling only two witnesses, took a thirty-minute recess so the judge could give the jury instructions. He asked the parties to wait patiently as the jury was deliberating. After fifteen minutes, the bailiff summoned all parties back into the courtroom. The jury had completed their deliberations. It took only minutes, and they were done, just like that. Once back in court, he quickly pronounced the teacher not guilty. The jury wondered afterward why more than a hundred thousand bucks had been spent behind the lies of one thug doing everything he could to cover his own butt. What an incredible waste of time and taxpayer money.

We are often falsely accused, mostly in situations like this. Too often, we are blamed. We are the scapegoats. Sadly, this contributes to the lack of respect people have for teachers. Some people feel they must blame someone, so it may as well be the teacher. Now, in the eyes of many parents, it is we who are supposed to raise the kids. The teacher stayed out for the rest of the year and then came back and taught for several more years until he retired. Situations like this go on all over the country, wasting millions of dollars. Only recently have consequences for falsely accusing a teacher been instituted. This is long overdue.

Scared

I was on hall duty at Montbello High School many years ago. Word had traveled that Finesilver will bust you, so my hallway was vacant. Occasionally a kid with a pass traveled by, but always with a hall pass. One day I was on my post, bored out of my mind, when a kid sprinted by me like a bat out of hell.

"Hey," I yelled. About five seconds later, the kid chasing him sprints by even faster. The second one cut to an adjacent hallway. The first kid was going through one of the double doors. Now the fire code dictates schools have a panic bar, which allows the door to open instantly. I followed, yelling for the kid to slow down, but he did not. He reached for the panic bar and missed it. The door was still shut. He kept going, head and face first through the safety glass, which is reinforced for safety with wire mesh. By the time I caught up the kid was suspended, feet barely touching the ground, halfway through the glass. I was petrified. Within seconds, two large pools of blood had accumulated on the floor, one originating from the torso area and the other beneath his head on the other side of the door. In a nearby class, the teacher heard the commotion, and he came out and called an ambulance.

"Get a towel—no, grab a bunch," I said, as he was a shop teacher. In a few seconds, I had wrapped one of the towels around my hand and punched through enough glass to lift the kid, who is now almost upside down and barely conscious. I laid him on the ground and turned him on his back. This was a terrible sight. One piece of glass sticking out above his eye and a large piece protruding from his neck. I somehow decided that the one in his neck should be removed. I pulled it out and took a towel and applied pressure. The glass above his eye was not creating much blood flow, so I left it alone. I checked his torso, found no glass, and shoved another towel over the wound below his rib cage. I held on to both spots for dear life, praying that the poor kid wouldn't die. He was conscious. He kept asking repeatedly, "Coach, am I okay?"

My response was the same each time he questioned. "Yes, just keep talking to me." I had requested a blanket and had the teacher who brought it cover him, as he was shivering, probably from the loss of blood. After what seemed like an eternity, the paramedics came and hooked up IV tubes and various monitors and took him away in an ambulance to the hospital.

One paramedic stayed back. He asked, "Who was the first person on the scene?"

I told them it was me. He moved over to where we could talk privately. I knew then that that the kid would survive, but worried that I had done something wrong. Or would maybe even get sued. After I told him my name he said, "Mr. Finesilver, you did everything right. You saved that kid's life."

A huge sense of relief washed over me. The kid got sewn up and stitched back together. I found out later that he and his friends were just playing around, cutting class. Several months after the accident, the kid came in with Mom to see me. She gave me a thank you card. He gave me one too. The surgeons had done a good job and he told me he would need more plastic surgery but would be back to normal. I felt good about that.

Duty

Duty again. This time I was demobilized and my main duty, of all places, was the 7-11 about a block away from our school. We have an open-campus policy, and I would go there daily to make sure the kids didn't steal, vandalize, or act stupid. It really wasn't too bad—in fact, I loved it.

I had a huge hotdog and a colossal slurpy on this day. A young girl came up to me and said, "Coach. That girl over there has a gun." She walked on, going about her business, not wanting anyone to know she had told. But she still had the urge to do the right thing. The girl she pointed to did not go to our school but was frequently hanging around. I discreetly approached the cop on duty at the 7-11 and a little shopping center and gave him the information. He approached the girl.

"Young lady, I need to check you." She reluctantly agreed. He checked and told her to empty her pockets. She was clean, he declared. I pulled him aside.

"Officer, this girl wouldn't lie to me. You got to check again."

He called her back. She bolted, and he caught her and had her stand while he checked her again. This time he was more thorough. He froze. Then he carefully pulled out a shiny 38-caliber pistol. He checked the other leg. He pulled five or six bullets out that she had stashed in her sock, with one bullet in the gun.

A young girl with a big heart had been encouraged to do the right thing. We will never know for sure, thankfully, whether someone would have been shot that day.

I had a large class of freshmen. The scheduling gurus loaded me up that semester with fifty kids. They were as rowdy as could be but had a knack for following instructions and getting along. This bunch played hard every day, and we enjoyed our tournaments in football, volleyball, and basketball. Fridays were for dodgeball, and the kids had true passion for it. One lovely October day we were on the football field. With only our class, we had four teams playing two separate games of football. I always monitored these games, ever on the lookout for a kid with a hot temper or listening for the forbidden cuss words. This day, about halfway to the class, three cars pull up and eight gangbangers—Crips—started walking to the field where my students were playing. I told them to stop and asked what was going on. They were prepared to collectively jump, stab, or shoot one of my students who, sadly, was mixed up with the Bloods gang. Likely one of the Crips was the brother of a former student.

"Aren't you Mr. Finesilver?" he asked. I nodded. He looked at his homie and motioned with his head. They left, just like that. Took me a while to sort out what had just taken place—another close call. Pretty scary stuff. Schools are touched by this kind of situation all too often.

The kids, some football players, came and found me. "Coach, come quickly," he stammered, out of breath. I was out the door. What a sight. One of our coach's cars, a Dodge Durango, had been trashed. All four tires were flattened, and every piece of glass—every window—was destroyed. The car was barely four years old and meticulously cared for, but it had been the object of some punk's or a group of punks' anger. I sent one kid to get the assistant principal, who in turn sent for the teacher. Big Fred, also known as Coach Harris, saw his car and flipped a switch. He was livid, but composed himself right away. Someone was attempting to get back at him. He was honest and fair but could be somewhat of a hard butt. In time, he got his car fixed. He had good insurance and ultimately cooled down. We all had some theories about who had done the act, but nothing concrete ever came of it. Two other cars got hit in the same fashion. All four tires and all window glass, and to date, almost a year later, these criminals haven't been caught and probably won't be.

I almost got my truck vandalized once. A kid named Chet was in my class. "You have missed too much school," I finally warned him. "Another absence and you'll fail." Senior ditch day rolled around, and he missed again. The cop I had taught ten years earlier arrested him, very drunk and quite disorderly. Chet was not going to graduate. The following day I decided to break the news to him. He beat me to the punch with a smirk and asked, "Am I going to graduate?" I shocked him with my response. "Yes, but not this year." After uttering a string of profanities, he stormed through the hallway to the locker room and made a beeline for the parking lot. I followed him but stopped to make a quick fifteen-second call for a security guard to meet me in the coach's parking lot. I got there and Chet had found the blue truck. He was smashing the windows out. He found a metal pipe and hit the final window. The rear window went, right in front of me and the two security guards. He had made a small mistake. He had picked the wrong truck and knocked the hell out of my colleague's truck. Well, he went to jail and didn't graduate that year or any other year. The teacher whose truck was trashed got it repaired by the school's insurance, and now several years later, has a sense of humor to laugh about it with me. I have heard Chet is somewhere in the Department of Corrections. He was too angry and defiant to be successful back then. He walked around with an attitude that the world owed him something. Occasionally, we see a kid with the cast and chip on his shoulder. Chet wanted the world to revolve around him no matter what he did or how he behaved.

Shaggy

This kid had issues. He seriously believed in the devil and maybe even worshiped Satan. In any event, he was a tough kid to have in school, always writing his messages on desks, his hands, or his notebooks. He drew scary designs, and even some scarier caricatures. His artwork was sick—actually, beyond sick. He featured blood, sex, and renderings of violent acts. He was demented. The plain truth was, he also stunk. His body odor permeated the classroom and lingered long after he was gone. I had him in class. Once he got the lay of the land and discovered that he couldn't sleep and draw, carve, or meditate, he quit coming, and I didn't miss him. He was too strange to even begin to figure out, let alone discipline. Folks knew about his issues, but they never ventured too far into his world. That summer he enrolled in summer school to begin to make up for lost credits. He was obedient for two or three days, but then went back to his usual antics, and his constant defiance and refusal to do work in any academic area frosted his teacher.

He came to me in need of counseling and consequences. I was the summer assistant principal, which means I handled the disciplinary matters. I sat Shaggy down, alternating words of advice with long periods of blocking my nasal passages from the inside. This day he smelled worse than usual. I called his mom and explained to her that he can't draw gruesome pictures while the class is doing something educational and normal. She defended him but agreed to talk to him. The three of us knew this would not matter. Next day, same teachers—same class—different cartoon. This one showed him in the act of torturing someone or something. I called Mom to inform her that he would be sent home for three days on a suspension for defiance of school authority. I also called the administrator of summer school to inform her of the situation. She agreed that we had taken the correct action, including giving him due process. He left, but not before issuing a threat, which I didn't take very seriously. The next day summer school let out at 12:25, the daily dismissal time. As I went outside to make sure that the kids either left campus or got on the bus, a couple of students came to me. Look, Coach, these were in the tree. Shaggy had drawn a picture of me. The picture was not very flattering to say the least. It was covered with swastikas and every antisemitic name which has ever been uttered. He had duplicated about a thousand of these in and put them in the trees, bushes, and on cars in the parking lot. He had papered the school with them. He thought he was getting back at me. I was angry but forgot about the incident. I wonder what happened to him. I probably will never know, but no doubt he will remain very troubled for a long time.

Hey Mister—I Fed Your Kid

Let's call him Bob. Bob was a tall, rangy kid and a great athlete. He liked to hang around with the older football players and me. He would come down to the coach's office and chill during lunch. Sometimes he had lunch to eat, other times he didn't.

As he became comfortable with the guys, on occasion he would ask, "Coach, do you have anything to eat?" Most often I did, so he would nosh on bagels, PB&Js, or crackers. Bob would have some chow and talk among the fellas. They would converse about football, cars, girls, more football, and a little about school. As the kid grew, he matured, and eventually played on the varsity team. He was a skill player, which meant he actually got to touch the ball on occasion.

Around this time the emails started coming from Bob's dad. Dad told me incessantly of his kid's football accomplishments, his football prowess, and how at home they had a "shrine" to display all of the kid's trophies, medals, certificates, and ribbons.

Dad had an agenda. He was not a "team first" kind of guy. Each time I got one of these emails, I would call and invite the dad to come and have a face to face with me. In Dad's mind, the kid was so good that the team should revolve around him. His emails became more aggressive, angry, and insistent. Finally, I'd had it. Dad refused to see me and would not talk by phone, so I ignored his emails. My previous emails had been brief and respectful. He began to email the principal, athletic director, or anyone who would listen or read. He got on these chat forums where he apparently felt validated by his constant analysis of me, the team, our offense, or whatever was on his mind or in his fingers. I had called him on eight or nine occasions. To look him in the eyes as we spoke about his kid made complete sense to me, but not to him. He continued to post, hiding behind his trusty keyboard.

Through the early part of his senior year the kid kept coming around, torn because he liked the guys and the coach (me). This was a safe place. The coach's office in the nether parts of this massive building has been the site of a lot of counseling, fathering, and a bit of psychology. Finally, his allegiance to Dad took over, as it should have. He quit coming around and Dad became more animated in the stands. He was quite critical and among a few other football experts would question and criticize loudly and openly. Even after these outbursts, all invitations to come and meet face to face were ignored.

The mere fact that I fed his kid should have shut him the hell up. I have seven kids and I appreciate any kind words and actions by any parent, teacher, custodian, or coach—point blank, anyone. Even teachers who have chastised or disciplined one of my own Villagers have been thanked profusely. You see, Dad wasn't hurting me by his disloyalty. I never put his kid in a headlock and forced him to come around. He chose to do what hundreds of other great kids have done. Dad didn't faze me with his reticence (or was it cowardice) to have a face-to-face meeting. He indicted himself and hurt his kid in the process. The kid had chosen to come down to the coach's office on his own time, and he always relaxed when he was there. But Dad, through his own insecurity and lack of loyalty, derailed something really good for his poor kid. Dad, I fed your kid!

Grace Kelley or Meryl Streep?

She was quite an actress. She had the lead in several of our school's musicals and also happened to be in the top five of her senior class. Her dad came to Back to School Night and asked me to push his kid. She needed fitness and had not earned gym credit, and she chose my fitness class. Brave child. Dad was pleasant and sincere. Our little actress played by the rules for the first six weeks and earned an A. She got fit in the process as well, during the introductory part of the class.

Second six weeks got tougher. She got some C's on workouts and picked up a tardy or two, ending up with a C for the second six weeks. She knew how to work the system, trust me. Once the grades were entered, she asked what her grade was. I quietly told her. She knew, nodded, and went about her business. She had no further questions. I knew this was a powder keg and didn't care.

She sashayed to the principal, who sprinted to the assistant principal, my evaluating "suit." They got right on it at their respective computers with lots of megabytes. The email merry-go-round began. Our little "Oscar" recipient now had two grown men, who felt really important, worked up into a frenzy. She had cried, cajoled, and pleaded. In their emails, they asked for records and documentation. They questioned my grading and my fairness. They did everything short of changing the grade themselves. All of this over a damn C. After several more emails I drew the line and quit responding. They were no doubt staring at their screens waiting for me to hit the send button. Instead, I picked up the phone and called the old man and explained the situation to him, the same dad I had met a couple of months earlier. He was pissed at his kid. Surprise, surprise. Dad called the principal and his kiss-ass assistant principal and ripped them a new one. His theme was, "Why the hell did you get involved? I want my kid held accountable." The emails stopped. Now what did they do? Apologize? Follow up email? No. They did as so many administrators do—lie in wait and get prepared to jerk the knee and ambush the next teacher in line.

Wedgie, Alan, and the Wild Bunch

They hated me. Wedgie for a couple of years and Alan for three decades. Yes, there are wild children scattered everywhere throughout our schools. You either notice them immediately or they stay under the radar for a while, and once comfortable, they emerge. Wedgie and I formed a bond much sooner than Alan, who carried resentment and hate for a long time, and justifiably so. The "wild bunch" make up a group who are good at heart but do bad things. They either cut class, smoke weed, show disrespect, or bully, and I confront. The confrontation, I confess, isn't always pleasant and used to be brutal. Back in the day, once I caught you, you were on my radar. And I was on your case or your ass consistently with no relief. In my naivete I judged and labeled, which I now know is and was wrong. To judge a child is both unfair and unjust. At fourteen or fifteen, kids do stupid and often unexplainable things, and in truth, I did worse. Yet I judged, and to all of you who were misguided and caught my wrath instead of my patience and bits of wisdom, I apologize. Wedgie was, in my narrow opinion, thuggin' a bit, so I judged and discarded him. I was sure we were done.

Lo and behold, he came back. With Kate Fowler—a saint—he came to my office one morning after being rejected for a year. She gave him the floor. He confessed that all he ever wanted to do was play ball for me. Not for the team, but for me. This was deep and humbling and undeserved. I relented, of course, with my list of requirements, and he joined the team. Wedgie, which will always be my nickname for him, plays at one speed, *full!* Not always lined up properly, or using proper technique, but he played like a cross between a human and a Tasmanian devil, the fiercest animal in North America. The rougher it got the more he loved it. He and his teammates had an instant love affair. I don't recall ever having a player who was happier to just play than Wedge. Recently, he told me he looked upon me as his father. Though I've heard that before, it is always humbling. Now he is coaching. He is a father and a good man who has never forgotten his second chance and how well he did with it. His love of the game inspired others who followed, as well as the coaches who knew him.

Alan was caught up in mischief, wrongdoing, and drama. Although a handsome youth, from the moment we met, when I was just twenty-two years old, we felt disdain for each other. The sneer of disapproval never left his face when we interacted. I thought I was right and just and believed he was a hoodlum, and I treated him like one. I didn't understand his world and he clearly didn't understand mine. I went out of my way to bust him for weed, ditching, and any minor infraction, and he ultimately got kicked out of school. I had heard rumors that he "went away for a while," which he confirmed. He recently explained that while in juvenile detention, an older man was able to convey the importance of Alan changing some of his habits, which had derailed him previously. Alan listened.

As I have reconnected with some of Alan's peeps, I heard of his continued resentment and hatred toward me. It is and was deserved. Yet I kept hearing from his homies that he was working for a local city department and was a great family man. York, who you have been introduced to, has stayed in touch with Alan. I asked York recently to have Al hit me up. That night the phone rang. I confess, I felt embarrassment over my over-the-top treatment of Alan as a young man who needed better. He needed guidance and I gave him none. He craved a male figure, and I didn't even know that.

In our conversation, he justified and validated all I had heard. Shep has been in his job for a long time. He will retire well, but most importantly, he is Dad and Gramps to an amazing family. He put away his baggage to succeed. This journey was made more difficult by me because I didn't understand. No doubt, had I shown a bit of compassion, it might have made his path easier.

Others too, hundreds of them, got the "tough love" treatment instead of the "tough love with understanding relationship." For the last fifteen or twenty it has been the latter, thankfully.

Chapter Twelve

The Suits of Power

Many school leaders love their power. The sign over the doorway, the heading on the school stationary, that desk of real wood, and that big computer monitor validate the very essence of the principal or assistant. But common sense, good judgment, and rich background with students is sorely missing.

I had a hard-working fitness class, and we were in week eight of a sixteen-week semester. The class had built themselves up to handle the rigor of a forty-five-minute session, complete with weightlifting, plyometrics, and other agility exercises. The twenty-five students who came daily were highly motivated and very fit. A young rookie assistant principal sauntered out of the penthouse and brought a little girl to class. The little darling was from a suburban school with a good track team, and our little track star wanted to take a fitness class because her old school was "all that." As we talked in the now foul-smelling room amidst the sound of feet hitting the floor and cast iron weights being tossed around, she informed me that little sweetie was now in my fitness class. I had concerns and I voiced them.

"She has never done these exercises before. It's better to have her start next semester," I said.

"Oh no," I was told. "She is running indoor track. She'll do fine."

I shut my mouth and let the young lady watch for the remainder of that period. The next day she showed up for class ready to "do her thing." As a precaution, I asked her one more time if indeed she was up to the task. She was sure she was. Against my better judgment, I gave her the opportunity. After the second of five stations she began to hyperventilate. I sat her down and had my student assist go to the nurse and the twenty-eight-year-old assistant principal who put her in my class. As they waltzed into the weight room, the little girl grew pale and passed out. Fortunately, both women were there to catch and resuscitate her. I looked at the AP. She knew she had blown it. People in power making poor, catastrophic decisions is normal these days.

The problem is that many of our leaders are teaching rookies and have spent little time in the classroom. Some even think that with their title comes greater wisdom. A few administrators trust the teachers and would have listened before this near catastrophe occurred. This happens all the time.

Who are our leaders? Who are the suits? These days, very few were ever in the classroom at all, or if they were, it was not for very long. Those who were in the classroom got out for a reason. Often the reason is that they caught hell from the kids, the parents, their boss, or all of the above. Yes, our current leaders now are not "in the trenches, paid my dues" educators. If they were, we would not be in this complex cave of educational darkness right now. We would have more answers than questions.

Please listen. Those leading our buildings, and their leaders, are not what you would expect. Imagine telling a lawyer how to practice law when one has never practiced law or even been in a courtroom before. Preposterous, right? Imagine a surgeon who has never operated before teaching a young doctor how to perform the procedure.

But in education we allow people to lead with no experience or with the bare minimum. We, the DPS, just hired a new superintendent who has never been in the classroom. This thirty-something-with-a-fancy-resume has been hired to lead our district full of other "leaders" on common ground when there is none. Why is lack of experience tolerated? Leading people who make the most important decisions related to the education and future of your children is in the hands of proverbial rookies, and this is largely the reason for our continued blunders.

When you parents ask a question, give a suggestion, have a complaint, or need educational direction, now you know that most of the time your respondent is a novice. A decade-and-a-half ago the pendulum swung. Before that, the people leading our schools and the people leading them were experienced educators who had been exposed to all that comes with the profession. Now we have seven hundred or more people in our district who wear the label "admin." About a third were teachers for some years. From this group, maybe a hundred were teaching veterans who made a difference. Finding this diamond in the rough is rare, but they get it. They don't do what the others who share the title do. They don't beat and bash the teachers. They aren't arrogant or hung up on their own self-importance and are masters when it comes to dealing with a child, their parents, or both. They have been there and done that. And some even remember where they started out in the classroom. The rest come from everywhere. Some come from business, and though it used to be a requirement, many have not held a professional teaching license or the principal's license. So how do they get here? Some were guidance counselors and others came in from other professions, so we have this "wonderful" blend of people making good money and important decisions for our children. The public accepts it and doesn't ask about anyone's qualifications. The nightmare has gone on for almost two decades with no public scrutiny or criticism.

So, the highest-paid people in our system are novices with lots of power. They wing it, and because of the title, the pay, and the current business model we operate under, they stay in their important roles. Doesn't matter how underqualified they are for their jobs; this is the way of the world in the DPS. Their interaction with parents—and children, too—are laughable. They become friendly with both groups, and this "you are my bestie" attitude works for them. But when the child needs direction or tough love, things unravel quickly.

These administrators were never in the real educational world—the classroom. Those who were get it, and their first support goes to the teacher. The others have been taught—groomed—to cater to the parent no matter what. They will be the judge and jury once a kid complains loud enough or the parent whines even a little. A complaint against a teacher is often handled with a solution that rarely includes the teacher, and worse, the teacher is vilified, often in front of the parent. Parents get what they want, usually a teacher sanction or reprimand, and the little darling waltzes away feeling quite entitled.

It hasn't always been this way. In the past, a child or parent went to admin and were told facts would be gathered and they would get back to them. The administrator would then collect information which usually ended with young Skippy or Leah being reprimanded for their behavior. The parents were approached by an expert in the field who encouraged them by a reminder that this journey is about the child's growth and development. No matter where the conflict started, it ended up as a win for both teacher and child. Great lessons were learned from many of these situations. This is ancient history now in the era of knee-jerk reactions and hasty decisions by those who have never been trained to support the teacher.

The new breed of administrator has more time than they will admit. Incessant meetings and lots of compliance means they have a full schedule, but how much of that is necessary? Shouldn't they be in classrooms daily supporting the teachers and students? Is it not in their job description to offer their help and guidance? This may be difficult since they haven't been there or done that for some time now. More than seven hundred DPS administrators, including the highly paid central team, could be mobile in our district and support our thousands of teachers, many of whom are struggling. They are unaware of the struggles, frustration, stress, and the new dynamic with the students. We are now teaching students who won't engage or connect because their world is the tiny screen on their devices.

Admins are more hands off than ever. More students than administrators know the good teachers at their schools, especially in our middle and high schools.

Stand Up...Alone

Every teacher, unless he or she is a shrinking violet and stands for nothing, has a confrontation with a kid, parent, colleague, or administrator. For much of my career, when confronted with an ugly situation, someone always had my back. They knew I was a professional and quite fair, often to a fault. There has never been much doubt that I care for the kids I teach and coach. Over the years, when confronted by a kid over a decision a teacher made, the adult stood up for what they believed was the correct position most of the time. Dozens of meetings ended up with fingers, all of them, pointing to the kid and holding him accountable. Even the parent or parents on occasion left these huddles with the strong suggestion that they take control, firm up, or get more involved in the all-important education of their child.

Not anymore. For a decade or more we have stood lonely and alone. Eight years ago we were on the football field with about ninety kids going through minicamp on a beautiful spring day. An uncle, very inebriated and angry, staggers out to the football field. This man cusses me out in front of the whole team. Seems he had a "mad" on because I would not let his nephew participate in these drills. A month earlier the angelic nephew had brought a baseball bat and had shown up to school drunk, intent on using the Louisville Slugger to assault another kid. Based on this behavior and more, I talked to the kid privately and told him we would have to talk further before he could practice with the team. What I passed on to him was consistent with our league and state code of conduct. While the school didn't have the backbone to deal with this behavior, I certainly did. I was hoping to get the kid some counseling for his anger and his other behavior. So his uncle comes out and makes a scene because I won't compromise. Eventually Uncle leaves after calling me every name in the book in front of the team and coaches. He leaves and goes to the assistant principal's office to complain about the mistreatment of his nephew.

The next morning at 6:30 a.m., some of the football team members were at school early, checking in to see what was up. The administrator came down from his Hilton-like office wanting to know what I did to the kid and his uncle. Why did I provoke him? This is the way of the modern-day scared-crapless admin members. I told him to move on, as I was too insulted to answer him. After I dismissed him, I called our school resource officer who took statements from a few of the witnesses and gave the uncle a citation. Now you must be wondering why the administrator who hugged and coddled this drunken uncle wouldn't tell him he broke the law?

He was scared. Scared of a drunken man who had cussed out one of his coaches in front of the team. The gutless administrator had no thought at all to back me, the coach. He had every opportunity to have the uncle cited right then and there for drunk and disorderly behavior. The uncle ultimately went to court and had these charges added to his file and had to pay a hefty fine.

Armed and Dangerous

Kids carry guns, knives, and assorted weaponry to school. Not long ago a teacher at our school was lecturing and a kid turned toward another student, and guess what? Out of his bulky hoodie drops a gun. The teacher, who admittedly should have known better, remarks, "Is that what I think it is?"

Now the whole class knows this kid brought a gun to school. The kid affirms this, and the teacher directs the kid to the office. The kid grabs the gun and through sheer luck ends up in the office and gives up the gun. That time we got lucky. My colleague screwed up. She allowed an armed kid to keep his weapon. She could have calmly sent the kid out and picked up the gun. She could have picked up the gun and called security. She could have sent a dependable kid with a note to get an available teacher or security guard. She did not know what to do and it's no surprise. There are fifty "what ifs," most with a catastrophic ending, that we can conjure up for this very scenario. Bottom line, schools are dangerous places and teachers need to be trained how to handle scenarios such as this.

Should we fret and worry as responsible teachers and parents? No. However, we need to know that weapons are common in our schools. We also need to know our schools house some dangerous and deviant kids, and many are walking time bombs. When I began teaching in schools with more than two thousand students, the most troubled kids were all on the radar. When they became erratic, they were counseled or removed, as they had been deemed unsafe. Each adult knew these kids had to be watched. We were vigilant. We had guts and an unyielding desire to keep our staff and students safe. This has changed. We started caring more about less-important issues and less about the big ones. We gave the right-to-privacy more importance than the right-to-be-safe. We began worrying about the rights of the sick, twisted, and dangerous kids more than the rights of the general population. To hell with the wellbeing and education of the well-intentioned, hardworking kids. This has become our attitude.

We recently had another school shooting not far from where I live at a suburban high school in the metro area. This did not occur in the inner city, but in a more affluent suburb. The gunman died of a self-inflicted gunshot wound, and a little girl died needlessly. This followed a rash of shootings all over the country, and we are left to wonder why. Kids aren't supposed to die this way. Their innocent youth is stripped from them with each of these senseless acts. Isn't it well past time to take a strong look at our schools?

Our superintendent wrote a lengthy letter to our parents and constituents assuring them we were doing everything we could do to make our children safe. He wrote about security cameras, armed personnel who patrol our district, and the bully-proofing of our schools. His words were well composed and well selected by many proofreaders and public relations departments. But we all better take a good look at our schools, because what he didn't say was the most nauseating. He should have disclosed that kids are not suspended for blatant violations of school board rules. He didn't say that there have been threats and assaults on kids, faculty, and staff that are not reported. He didn't mention the violent acts that have occurred, unreported, for many years. He did not mention that we don't really know much about the sick and dangerous kids, because we don't deal with them. We look the other way.

Last year, a group of kids walked into a convenience store intent on buying some rolling papers. They had some cheap weed, and after all, it was lunchtime, their time to get baked. The clerk denied them, and they pulled a BB or pellet gun out and threatened to blow the clerk away. The gentleman had no idea the weapon was not lethal. He hit the floor, scared for his life. This amused the kids, especially the one who had filmed the act. A concerned citizen called the police who came and cited the kids. Board policy is that these hoodlums go through an expulsion hearing. What happened? The little darlings sat in the in building suspension room for a day or so and we called it good. No consequences were given from the school side.

I just read about a kid who we will call Lou. Lou was incorrigible. As a school, we coddled Lou because we were afraid to really clamp down on him. He had no boundaries. He stole, got high, cussed at staff, and had many fights. Once we almost took him to the expulsion hearing which was required by law, but we did not want it on our school report card. So Lou did not get suspended or expelled as required by board policy or state law. He escaped consequences every time. During his second freshman year of high school in a different school, he decided to terrorize and wreak havoc once again. They didn't deal with him either.

Not long after his second year of high school, he realized he was not only above the law, he *was* the law. His life was out of control, and we contributed to the hate and aggression hardwired into him. He was arrested not long ago as the alleged triggerman for the senseless killing of a teenage boy. Now for the million-dollar question. Would his life have been different—maybe better—if we had at some point held him accountable and given him consequences? I dare say it would not have been worse.

Our system perpetuates and encourages this thug mentality. *Give me a break because I'm entitled; I give respect when I get respect;* and on and on. Consequently, we have schools full of entitled kids who are not accountable to themselves, their parents, or their teachers. They skate through high school with a "rescue me" mentality. They get break after break doing what they do with no consequences. They become bold and end up with no rules and a false sense of what the real world is like. Upon graduating, which has become easy, or dropping out, they leave high school unprepared for our cruel world. They can't succeed in college or hold a job, and they can't succeed at anything that requires sweat, hard work, respect, and accountability. The kid continues what he was allowed to do unabated in high school. He is used to being incorrigible and arrogantly believes he is above the law or is the law itself. His rude awakening hits him like a freight train. *You mean, I can't do this in the real world?*

After forty-two years, though sad and painful, I admit I have taught a number of criminals and eight or nine murderers. The depravity many young people own in their teens often carries over into their adult lives. During the last ten to fifteen years, we have actually nurtured and cultivated the lawlessness far too many of our youngsters have accepted.

Not long ago a student was sent to the in-building-suspension room. He was in my class. The staff member who put him there informed each of his teachers he would be gone but was not on suspension. He'd had sex with an underage girl, and one of his sick cronies taped the act on his phone. Yes, the lewd, vulgar act was recorded and went viral online. As you can imagine, hundreds of our students saw this and the school was left to deal with the situation. Because the act took place and was filmed in our school, without question there should have been a suspension, then a ten-day extension, and then an expulsion.

None of this happened. The kid skated through unscathed, without even the required legal citation for unlawful acts and distribution of internet pornography on school grounds. Did we follow board policy? Hell no. He got to chill in the pass room and was not held accountable in any way. Some parent's daughter was violated repeatedly by having hundreds—maybe thousands—of viewers see her innocence stolen. The perverted and twisted kid learns nothing except that the school is too petrified to act. He is given a green light to continue this behavior which becomes more entrenched. He has no reason to stop. We know he is doing this and don't care. We cover it up. In a few years, when he exploits a female or does something of this sick nature outside the protective school environment, he goes to jail. He may become a habitual criminal or sick pervert. When he was fifteen and exhibiting these behaviors, we might have rescued him from himself, but we didn't try.

One of two things would have happened if he were taken to expulsion. He might have received counseling and the women he would have exploited would be saved from his illness. It's true, mothers, fathers, and taxpayers—we have this element among our school's student population. Be aware and be vigilant.

It may sound like I am sensationalizing or exaggerating. After forty-two years I have been in close contact with people who are supposed to mete out consequences. They are frustrated and helpless. Even the school resource officers (SROs) are told to back off. To keep their jobs, they must follow the code. I'm told that our schools now have quotas. A school can only suspend a handful of students per time period to show that our suspension rates are down. Then we tell the public how safe our schools are.

What about the security guards who have been threatened or assaulted? What about the teachers who are threatened, one with scissors held to her neck? She was so scared she retired, though she was young. She ended up with a diagnosis of post-traumatic stress disorder (PTSD). Yes, hell yes, these events take place in our district all the time. Isn't it time we lift up the rug?

Graduation Rates

Our school district has about a fifty percent graduation rate any way you cut it. But we boast of continually improving rates on paper, and for the media we promote a higher rate of graduation. Here's the ugly truth. Yes, more kids who start high school in the Denver Public Schools graduate than ever before. That statistic is up to fifty-six or fifty-eight percent. But in reality, we give credit to students, in several ways, without requiring them to do much—or anything. First, we have a class called Freshman Seminar in most of our high schools. This class has no curriculum and is either not attended or the kid uses it to talk, text, play on their device, or listen to music. Ninety percent of the time the teacher gives the obligatory passing grade for merely attending, rarely giving the well-deserved "fail." This failing grade would lead to a reprimand or worse. A kid starts high school and needs 240 credits to graduate, some in specific subject areas. This breaks down to forty-eight classes spread out over four years, working out to six courses a semester. Freshmen get two freebies in Freshman Seminar. If the student comes for a few days to a three-hour-a-day program in August, he or she gets 2.5 credits, or another half a class. At our school and others, 150 or more freshmen fail two or more classes each semester of their freshman year. Teachers are pressured. *Don't fail too many. Why did you fail Johnny? Loosen up those standards. Make it easier.* The pressure on teachers to pass kids is great.

We have watered down education and pay for it every day. The kids fall behind, but we've created a safety net. By their sophomore year, they can already be far behind. It is possible to have a kid with only freshman or sophomore credit who is seventeen years old. We still don't panic because we have this amazing program called Credit Recovery. Credit Recovery is a self-paced program where a kid can recover credit, often by doing a minimal amount of work or none at all. The teachers are well intentioned. Three years ago, our principal announced in February that more than eighty seniors were not on track to graduate. Each was two to five classes behind the necessary requirement to walk across the graduation stage. The administrator had been told in no uncertain terms that it was up to the faculty to collectively rescue these poor children so they would not be deprived of their day in the sunlight of graduation. By May, almost all graduated, many having done no real work in a dozen or more classes. Many were our chronic hall-walkers, kids who show up in school but walk the halls all day. A couple of the credit-recovery programs had been exposed and busted for this fraud. I have seen kids graduate on time who were up to two years behind on credits. We are proud of our rising graduation rate. It doesn't matter that kids graduate in this fraudulent way—what matters are the numbers we report.

This is not real-world reality. If I screw up on my job, do a poor job, don't show up, gossip, sneak, or steal, do I get job recovery? Does someone wave a wand and allow me to stay employed even though I suck? If I am a poor husband or father, do I get marriage recovery, or am I stuck paying for the consequences of my poor habits and actions?

This past year, a number of kids did not do their obligatory credit recovery. The schools collectively told them "no completion, no graduation." I'm told that by the time the schools started their graduation ceremonies, dozens of kids were given a free pass for doing squat and got to graduate alongside kids who busted their tails and worked for it. The mandate to graduate came from someone important downtown, or so I am told.

We are hypocrites in the truest sense, boasting of our climbing graduation rates as we send these unsuspecting children into college or the real-life work force. It is no secret that many of our children fall flat on their faces in college and need remediation, or they just drop out. Our kids have been allowed to act like jerks and behave however they choose and then they try this with their first and successive employments. Ask around. Any college prof will tell you of the millions of dollars spent on remedial classes because our youth have not learned basic skills. Ask any employer around the country what it is like hiring kids from metro areas. Our educational reform comes with hefty price tags. It is sinful that we rejoice in false statistics and put these incessant lies out to the public. This must stop. Grade us correctly. We fail and have been for a long time. Let's admit our failed past and move ahead with what we know really works.

We know what works, but we keep it hidden. This method is too "old school," too primitive. First, we need to identify what our kids really need. We have kids all over the spectrum. We have kids placed in classes way too difficult for them because *we* get accolades. Our school report to the state education department is better if we have bunches of kids taking advanced placement, honors, and accelerated courses. We haven't cared that the majority of kids enrolled in these classes aren't ready. We just want the numbers. So we brag and point to our college readiness, but our percentage of college graduates who graduate in a timely fashion, about eleven percent in a good cycle, is abysmal. Our leaders don't talk about this and for some reason, no one asks. We ought to be taken to task over this. If we espouse college readiness, shouldn't we have fifty percent or more of our graduates furthering their education and walking the college graduation stage? We don't, and that's the truth.

No One Ever Told Me

I had no clue. Why didn't someone tell me? What started out as a normal day was upended by 6:30 a.m. Sitting at my computer looking at the prep sport results from around the league and state, I hear a knock at the door. I will never forget the look on that kid's face.

"Hey son, what brings you here?" I asked.

"I need to speak with you," he said, through tears. The kid sat down and totally lost it. He couldn't speak for several minutes. After he was finally able to control his weeping, he uttered the ugly truth. His dad had abused him and had been doing so for years. He was angry, ashamed, embarrassed, and confused, all at once. It hit me like a brick. To me, this was a well-adjusted kid, trying to get ahead. I explained to him that, by law, I had to report what he had told me to our social worker or call the Department of Social Services. What he said floored me.

"I know. That's why I'm here; I can't take anymore!"

He went through the process, was removed (appropriately) from the home, and Dad went through the legal system. I don't know the outcome for the dad or the kid but have since dealt with this several other times. With this situation, there is no gray area. If I suspect, have a hunch, or have heard or seen firsthand, I turn it over. I understand if I fail to report it, I am in violation of the law.

No one ever told me children would die. The loss of a child...a student...a player—this topic is raw. I wish someone had told me, in 1979 or before, that throughout my career children would die way before their time. They would leave our earth through accidents, illness, or even by having their lives taken from them through senseless, violent acts. Once you as a teacher go through this, you question whoever you believe in. For me, I have questioned my Lord why. How can the Lord allow a child in their prime—in high school, college, or as a young adult—to be taken? Their families never recover. The loss of anyone creates an irreversible wound, but the wound from the loss of a child oozes and weeps for an eternity. We lost Jeff Clayborn in a motorcycle accident. Jeff had wrestled for me when I was a twenty-two-year-old coach, and we became friends and stayed in contact. His widow showed up at school one morning, got a visitor's pass, and took me out of class to tell me. I attended his funeral the next day.

Matt Hartl had been sick, but all of us thought he was invincible as you have already read. His funeral was heartbreaking. Then Oscar Sanchez. After his illustrious career as a scholar at Yale and then a prominent Denver architect, he lost his battle to ALS. I spoke at his funeral, again unprepared for the reality that I had to eulogize a young man I had known and watched develop into a leader and role model for others. And Derrick, and Tara—so many as only babies, all way too early. My heart breaks.

And just last week, though I found out last night, we lost Temi. My baby, and just a baby in her forties. Once again, I was blindsided and left empty with no reprieve. She was my student, student assist, and breakfast friend who joined me and Coach Nye once a week at 5:00 a.m. to hang with two coaches. She came to Denny's, always a breath of fresh air, with eyes that danced and a zest for life rarely seen. She had sickle-cell disease. I knew she had pain because she told me. Her knees and elbows would swell, and though she didn't complain, those who cared knew of her discomfort. And yet, she smiled! She went regularly and got transfusions. This eased her pain and gave her several days of relief at a time. And yet, she still smiled. At her twenty-year reunion, which I attended, she came and illuminated the gathering.

Temi was very comfortable with making all of us content. She was quiet and attentive. She expressed her love and gratitude frequently, and she smiled. God once again decided to take someone very special who was widely loved. Once again, I am numb and have no answers, only questions. And once again, I am angry. The man or woman upstairs didn't follow the script. We are supposed to leave before our youngsters. They are supposed to mourn and shed tears with our families. Why? I don't have the answer. I wish I did.

Violence. As if losing kids before their time isn't enough, if you are in this profession and committed to the youth you serve, you will deal with acts of violence within their families. You will see firsthand, too often, young people and members of their families who can't escape the nasty talons of drugs and alcohol. We must accept this as fact and then learn to deal with it and support students and families who are exposed to it daily. In truth, we all have baggage we carry that sits on our shoulders. No family is perfect, well-adjusted, and always happy. Grief, drugs, alcohol, depression, anger, and more have touched all of us and our families. Long ago, I learned to accept this and not judge.

Moral dilemmas. Will you take on issues you feel strongly about? Will you allow a kid to bully because you don't want the confrontation? What will you do when you see or hear racial epithets directed to an individual or group? How will you handle cheating on a test? Will you allow kids to posture, then fight? What about the kid you bust with weed or drugs, or the kid that comes to your class high on narcotics, meth, or other deadly substances? Are you gonna watch and curl up? What will you do?

One mother called me and reported her kid's indiscretions because she considered me their father, father figure, or someone who should help. She called when her sons were disrespectful and lazy, when they did not come home before her curfew, and when they were caught watching porn late at night on her computer. Her daughter once got so full of herself I had to intervene by phone and promise (not threaten) to come over and call the law myself. Baby girl believed me and quickly straightened out her act. Yet I was never told or prepared to deal with this. The job description didn't include this.

Depression. Why didn't someone tell me to notice the signs or symptoms of depression? I have taught many children who were clinically depressed, yet in my naiveté I couldn't tell or didn't know. I could have helped; I could have been more kind. I could have lifted them, but I just didn't know.

Anger. Someone should have told me about anger. I have seen a lot of it. After more than a dozen years, I began to understand it. I should have known the reason some kids lashed out, became combative, or carried anger for years. Only when it erupts are we forced to react. Often, the kid can't explain the sadness, loneliness, and rage that builds up.

Many times, the kid is angry, doesn't know why, and can't understand his suppressed thoughts. Most of the time this rage is tied to a loss like death, or to jail, drugs, violence, or the abandonment of a parent. Often, they are abandoned by Dad and sometimes Mom, a parent they never knew or knew only briefly. Now, when I see the signs and symptoms of deep anger, I ask what has proven to be poignant. Asking the questions "Who are you mad at?" or "Why are you so angry?" always elicits the same reaction. Always. The youngster pauses and says they don't know, or they become defensive and rebut with "I'm not angry!" Then the slammed doors begin to open. I explain that they are indeed angry and dig a little deeper. Most of the time they want to talk about it and do so with a sense of relief. Someone has cared enough to push a bit and allow them to have a revelation of sorts. It is deep and powerful to pull away a layer of defense and to allow and enable a kid to begin to understand what has derailed their ability to deal with others, to cope, and to have any real chance of success. I'll admit I slacked off when I took psychology. I should have paid attention.

A teacher worth their salt never stops teaching, guiding, advising, or parenting. That's right, you're on duty 24/7, and it doesn't end. I have been giving out my phone number for forty years, and yes, I still have a landline. It cracks me up when one of our suits, young enough to be my son or daughter, asks me why I haven't logged my calls or parent contacts. Our district and school leadership puppets their requests and requires us to get on the computer to enter our conversations with parents or guardians. They don't and won't realize that I don't have time to log this.

How can I log over a hundred, but more often upwards of two hundred contacts a month? They may have this kind of time, but I don't. I decided long ago it's more important to be 100 percent accessible and available than to sit my fat ass down at the computer to play their compliance game and drain my time, taking me away from my job. Hey—get over it and yourself in the process. To any admin who has ever questioned me on this, take your high-paid ass to a wedding, or break bread with a student and their family. Go to the workplace or home, to a funeral, a bar-mitzvah, a graduation party, or any other event or situation. I have been to or been a part of these countless times. We all should.

Institutional racism. Nobody told me institutional racism exists in our public schools and is insidious among our faculty and staff. Our teachers have a double standard, and our leadership teams may be the most blatant sinners. Rather than feel an obligation to empower our youth, many feel sorry, and through their constant enabling, they make it very clear that "You have less, and I will help you wallow in sorrow rather than challenge you to rise up to be great." That message is delivered daily and is part of the message that is crippling our youth. Our public schools are full of these messages, both intended and unintended, and nobody intervenes. Why? The children themselves don't want pity or sympathy, yet that is exactly what we are trained to do. Make it easier, relax the rules, accept this, don't fight that battle, all hindering and paralyzing the youth. We are too caught up to recognize what we are doing. Because of this, our children expect to have it the easy way and to be rescued, enabled, and coddled. Our students are too young and inexperienced to understand the consequences of this and find out too late—way too late.

The real world isn't like school where we have mechanisms and systems in place to relieve the pressure and stress of true accountability. The youth leave our secure and inviting clutches and the door to the real and brutal world outside smacks them between the eyes. *I gotta work and actually sweat and toil at my job, my college, or in the military? What? You mean, there are real deadlines? Real consequences? Wait, I have to be on time? What? They review my performance? I actually have to do my work or fail that college class? Uh-oh, I am not used to this because during my four years in high school I always had a nice soft landing spot.*

Incessant meetings. No one ever disclosed that there are incessant meetings, lots of them, rarely with substance. The school leaders are told to collaborate and have opportunities for teachers to use their voices. So they wing it and do some of the most bizarre activities and boring presentations, always with the holy grail—data. Yes, any teacher who has been around the block will parrot the infamous DPS mantra "We are data driven." Many times a year we are presented with data. Pie charts, graphs, numbers, stats, scores, screens, papers, pamphlets, and posters, all to show us what we already know. The achievement gap. Test scores. Satisfaction surveys. Opinions. On and on. There are better ways to use our precious time.

Revolving door mentality. No one told me the profession included a revolving door mentality. I knew the students would come and go, and I expected this cycle. But teachers and administrators constantly changing, often without notice or explanation? And agendas—so many of them hidden, and people whose jobs include being the heavy, the snitch, and the punisher, even those in leadership spots.

Grief. I never knew children would lose a parent, sibling, or someone so close to them that they would crawl into grief and never leave that dark place for years.

I didn't know I would have to go to funerals, give eulogies, and look into the eyes of family members who had lost a child way too young and far too soon, never knowing what to say. Children are abused, neglected, hurt, and carrying wounds and scars of the worst kind—those deep within their hearts and souls, appearing so often to the outside world like everything is okay when it is not.

Little acts—big dividends. Nobody early on told me that little acts pay big dividends. This realization started by accident. My people feed people. Jewish folks, especially, take pleasure in surrounding most every damn thing—event, milestone, wedding, divorce, death, or engagement—with food, and lots of it. After about five years in this vocation, I started supplying food by chance, not to be righteous or Mother Theresa-ish, it's just who I am—a "fresser" (Yiddish for "eater"). I got hungry, and in truth I have never, not once, had a bad meal. Something about having food with a parent, student, or lots of them is cathartic. Two years ago, I did food my style every other Friday. "Cones With Coach" evolved into burgers, chicken, burritos, doughnuts, popsicles, ice cream sammies, and more. Every other Friday about a hundred kids threw down, and the invitation was open. One administrator (now gone) found out I was feeding the kids doughnuts with a layer of ice cream sandwiched between them and layered with Hershey's [syrup or candy bars?]. A utensil was needed to eat this. He questioned whether it was good to feed the children so much sugar. During the next "throw down" I ran a test. As I was doing my food thing, I took several cardboard baskets and sandwiched ice cream between two huge chocolate chip cookies, then drizzled the chocolate syrup over it. I asked Mitzi, my helper, to take some up to the penthouse home of our royal admin. She complied and then gave a vivid description of how the administrator who questioned my choice of corn sweetener was the first one done, with chocolate dribbling down his lip.

If you teach and expect from kids what you expect from your own children, or what you would if you did have children, you will be golden. "No, Felicia," (our oldest), "you can't talk when the teacher is talking" should hold the same value, meaning, or consequence for all of your students. "Mary," (our middle daughter), "it is not okay to get angry and snatch a kid" (a freshman who pissed you off when he grabbed something from the café that you managed). "You can't leave your post and bring him to justice by dragging him by the neck to return the item while the school security camera is running." "No, Becca," (our baby girl) "you don't pass notes in English class without consequence." Becca's mother got this call and Dad reacted by showing up at the school and sitting in her class and even taking and failing a quiz on the parts of speech. Zach, Mitch, Matt, and Josh got the two rules for school when they were close to starting the high school experience. The first is the most important.

The teacher is always right. Even when they're wrong, they're right!

In a nutshell, that defines the biggie in our home. Do what the teacher says, and you are fine. Don't whine, complain, cry, or plead when it comes to a teacher. You comply with those requests, and in the process, shut your mouth and learn something along the way.

The beauty and the satisfaction. The validation that comes from teens who become very successful despite their stumbles and struggles. In five years of college, not a word was said about any of this, or guidance given on how to actually make a difference.

I never knew. Someone should have told me before I ever started this journey. We don't tell our bright-eyed future leaders in the classroom these things because it's hard, it's uncomfortable, and it's raw. Yet by not telling them we make them suffer more when they have to deal, cope, or go through it.

Resilience. Nobody shared with me as an impressionable college student that kids are resilient and will battle through insurmountable odds to make someone proud. Giving hope is far more important than giving knowledge. Lessons on embracing the inevitable sting of failure are well learned and critical, because like it or not, we all have failed or will fail. And failure is powerful. How we react to it, respond to it, rise above it, or let it be the victor defines us.

Chapter Fourteen

The Real Heroes

Who says a child can't be a hero? These unsung and often forgotten youth can make an indelible impression if we open our eyes to their challenges and see what they have overcome and accomplished. They exist everywhere. We fail as educators to see the beauty, often right in front of us. We see the obvious—students of the week, great athletes, fine musicians, artists, actors, singers, and of course the valedictorians and the intellectually gifted. We often don't see the Dannys or the Faiths, but we should, and I have.

He Got Rid of the Chair!

I brought a large class in from outside where they had been playing soccer, and there he was. I was shocked, startled to see a young man in a wheelchair in the weight room. He had just put some dumbbells down, caught in the act of lifting weights. He expected a teacher-like tongue lashing and he was ready. Instead, he was asked the obvious question.

"How did you get in here?"

"Do I have to tell you?"

Surprised at his response, I said no. We left it at that. I was sure he knew he couldn't be there unsupervised. I was wrong. The very next day, I come in after my class ended and he was back. He had maneuvered himself from his wheelchair to a seated press machine and was working hard. I was really confused. I always lock and secure this liability-prone space.

"Son, how did you get in here?"

"Mister, do I have to tell you?" he said, answering a question with a question. Again, I said no.

Here is what I was thinking. If he had somehow gained access and was doing something good and positive, why would I stop or hinder that? I asked the obvious. "What class do you have now?"

He had an open period, so I asked why he didn't take my class legally. He chuckled. I could tell what he was thinking but wasn't saying. It was the wheelchair and the disability. He assumed I didn't think he fit. He was wrong. I wrote a note indicating that Danny was okay to take my class. This request was granted, and in time, Danny was in class and every bit a wild child as my rowdiest student. The next week he again surprised me.

I was about fifteen minutes into a boxing lesson with about thirteen kids. They were using heavy bags, speed bags and dumbbells, to increase their power. We were interrupted, and Danny was not bashful.

"Hi, Coach. I am here to box, so teach me." He had purchased his own gloves and was ready, and yes, quite able. Yet I was unsure of his disability and guidelines, so he helped me. "Coach, I am going to jump in and hit both bags, but I may need to take a break or two."

There it was! He had decided he was going to stand and hit both bags. As he rotated to the speed bag, which is quite a challenge, he got up, faced the bag, gloves on, and did as well or even a bit better than the other beginners. Then he took his turn at the heavy bag and understood the importance of stance and hand position more than the rest of the crew. Danny became a different person, externally, after that lesson.

Suddenly, he belonged. He had met an individual who didn't or wouldn't believe and accept the limits others had informed him he possessed. Danny flourished. He kept getting out of the chair. To box, play goalie, go out for wrestling, keep boxing, and on and on. After several months he was spending more time out of the chair than in or on it. I waited until October to find out more.

"So, how long have you been in the wheelchair and what does the doctor say?"

He had been disabled since the fourth grade after broken legs and a hip issue. He stayed confined and accepted his disability most of the time. He said both his parents and his doctor approved of his newfound passion for activity. I had a conversation with our school nurse who affirmed that he was okay to try new things. By March, Danny was in the gym two or three times a day, loving his new existence.

I thought the disability was such that he would always have some type of tether, a constant tie to that wheelchair, but in May I found out different. Coach, "I am going to leave the chair at home tomorrow," he said.

I tried to hide my tears but couldn't. He couldn't hide his either. We took a moment and gathered our emotions in a manly way, and the next day, ten minutes before class, he once again appeared and was walking, well-balanced, with no sign or indication that the chair was anywhere nearby, and it wasn't. He got tired, understandably so, after so many years in a seated body position. He endured and spent the last weeks of the school year as mobile as any other teenager.

This year? The only problem is the monster that has been created by this situation. Danny wants to miss, ditch, and forget some of his other classes and stay in the gym with me several times a day. We decided once in class and once as a student-assist per day was the limit. He would come after school and would join the wrestling team once again this year. Daily I am reminded of how little things can often help anyone—child, adult, it doesn't matter—find hope and meaning. Danny found himself, through something small, in a colossal way. And yes, he got rid of the chair—forever!

Faith

She was tiny and eerily quiet. This pretty young woman with beautiful large brown eyes was barely audible when I took attendance for her afternoon class. She was so shy that as I called her name each day, she blushed and forced herself to answer with the obligatory "here" or "present." She would look down or away when asked something directly, and this didn't change for many months. I was sure after the first quarter and not missing a day, Faith would opt out of physical education. She was clearly uncomfortable and had not come out of her shell. Yet she worked out like a tyrant. Others grimaced or openly complained, but not Faith. When others backed away from the challenges of pushups, weights, cardio, and planks, she didn't waver. She didn't blink when she was sweating and in great discomfort. I shouldn't have been surprised, but I was. The next quarter started and there, like clockwork, was Faith. As the workload grew, so did her confidence. She started to lift more, and her cardiovascular capacity increased. The harder the workouts became, the more she relaxed.

She began to come out of her comfort zone and on occasion would respond with a sentence or even a question. In November she came out for wrestling and had her first boxing session with eight of her classmates. The boxing room is a converted storage space. Picture a room in the summer with a temperature of ninety degrees or more, and in the winter the heat accumulates as it sits above the boiler room. In a nutshell, the room has no ventilation and no heating or cooling, and none is needed. Over the last twenty-five years it has become the perfect place to teach boxing. Picture this—a large fridge, some weights and kettlebells, dusty mirrors, an old stereo, and boxing. Speed bags, heavy bags, boxing mitts, and gloves are contained in a tight space to define who has become the ultimate grind for a high school student or faculty member. The gym has been a place of comfort for many, and Faith was no exception.

This wonderful lady "found herself," discovering her hidden talent in the most unlikely place, the boxing room, her haven and safe space for almost nine months. At 117 pounds, give or take, those pretty eyes gained confidence as her persona grew larger. When she "gloves up" she is poetry, in a strange sense. The room where she blossomed allowed her to become not just good at a really tough sport, it brought her into a new and different world. Her eyes, at times doubtful and lacking in confidence, are now much different. Faith glows and emulates a newfound confidence. She spills optimism and hope. She has become the best in the school at boxing and will soon break all records, some held by students from previous decades. Her work on the speed bag is phenomenal. Another youngster from Texas stopped her mid-workout and asked in a serious tone, "Are you kin to Mike Tyson?" She is not, but she strikes like it. Faith has become comfortable drenched in sweat, with muscles aching and heart pounding from this brutal training.

She works out with 14-ounce gloves on the 100-pound heavy bag and finishes on the 120-pounder. When she is done with that, she does the most grueling cool down, hundreds of additional punches holding dumbbells, and jumping jacks with dumbbells above her head. Each day she comes to train is wonderful because of her personality and her attitude toward life. Faith asks for nothing, yet gives of herself as an athlete, role model, student, and now as a symbol for all that is positive in our youth of today. She is full of hope and purpose because she chose to achieve greatness. Any sadness or doubt I once observed has all but disappeared. This wonderful eighteen-year-old will continue to chase dreams as she has proven to all of us, but mostly to herself, that there are no limits or boundaries. Through sweat and agony this young woman has set goals and will continue to dream of greatness. Faith is a hero to many, yet doesn't even know it. She will leave a legacy for all of us.

Chapter Fifteen

School Sports

'86

Based on our 1985 season in which we won most of our matches and sent several kids to the state tournament, 1986 was supposed to be huge. In our league of ten schools, we finished third and returned every wrestler except one to the existing team. Even though I coached this group many years ago, I have a vivid recollection of the kids, their nicknames, mannerisms, and events during that magnificent season. This group is forever etched in my mind and in my heart.

Before the season began, we met and outlined our goals and spoke of expectations for the year. My counterpart and mentor, Coach Hall, was by my side as always. We looked at this ragtag bunch of kids and spoke as we always did of academics, citizenship, and loyalty. They had heard it before but knew better than to interrupt, act bored, or let their attention drift which would have "frosted" Coach Hall, who in turn would have stuttered out some fierce orders and directions. Then a stinging session would take place that no one would soon forget. These sessions would make the marine's boot camp seem like a picnic. So, more than seventy pairs of eyes were riveted to our every word.

After we covered the basic disciplinary rules, we explained in no uncertain terms that our number one wrestling goal was to win the Denver Public Schools' city tournament in February. Anything else would not cut the cake. They knew; they had the same expectation as well. They were well-aware of what was ahead of them to get to that place. The prize? Only game, with sweat, toil, and blood. They were game.

Our practices included stretching, performed military style, with every kid on the team counting together, loudly and proudly, in unison. Then came Coach Hall demonstrating techniques, counters, and wrestling situations. He insisted the kids go through their moves together, by instructional numbers. The double leg was taught like this. One—change levels. Two—shoot with your right knee ending up between his heels. Three—gable-grip behind the thighs. Four—turn the corner. Five—run your feet and cover down. Incessant repetitions would follow, and they would drill till everybody got it right. Yes, thirty or forty times and then once the move was covered it became a part of our daily work to continue to refine our technique.

After fifteen to twenty minutes of instruction came the live wrestling. Kids would be put in groups of four and then they would go through "grinders." Grinders, or baseball wrestling, went like this. One dude came out and stayed until each of the other three had been able to tangle with him numerous times. Then the next, and twice more, until each member of this wrestling quartet was exhausted. This was just for takedowns. The same format took place for top- and bottom-style wrestling.

They were good. Stan led us off, then Danny, Garrett, Liz (short for Lizard), Paul, Chris, Johnny, Sam, Danny, Sammy, Rodney, Chi (short for Chicago), and then Truth, short for Turmenne. They were supported by Heiu, Sam, Paul, Andrew, and dozens of others all on a quest to be the best in Denver as a team. They didn't have the best technique, but they were the most disciplined, the most in shape, and the raw-bone toughest. What they lacked in experience they made up for in the pride they showed on and off the mat. They began to gel, placing in some major tournaments against the best Colorado has to offer. We stumbled against our rival, the league's best. John F Kennedy was good, but I thought we could beat them in our dual match. Three weeks before our league tournament, we went to their house where they proudly displayed the banners of their nine or ten league championships. The stage was set, and we didn't wrestle well. We got beat, no excuses, by twenty points, and after the match all eyes were upon me. I had circled that date as our tune-up for the league tournament.

And we had failed. I had failed. So what did I say? I told them we would learn from this and that the prize (a city championship) was still our largest goal. They were surprised. They expected to be criticized and told of their wrestling flaws. That would not have worked. So we went back to work. The next day, yes, the Friday after the Thursday match, we were back in the practice room. That day defined what Coach Hall and I expected all along. After stretching, we had a nice conditioning session. Not really, the session was brutal. Some of our guys looked tired out on the mat, and rarely did we see that. Clearly not in shape, with three weeks left we knew that could and would change.

Coach Hall was masterful that day. His stuttering was more pronounced and within minutes this 22- by 40-foot room was humid with the perspiration of dozens of wrestlers doing drills, pushups, wall sits, and right-and-lefts, a brutal drill designed years ago by a drill sergeant, no doubt. The room smelled like a cross between a herd of goats and my sock drawer (which smells worse). This was not the typical day after an evening match routine. But we had goals and dreams. After two hours of this we adjourned with specific instructions about the start time for the next day, Saturday practice.

Coach and I decided to let them sleep in, so we called for a 7:00 a.m. start time instead of 6:30. I am sure they savored that extra thirty minutes, right? They were there in full force, all in attendance, and they knew what to expect. After warmups, which on this day included rope climbing, sprints in the vacant gym (the basketball team came at 9:00), and twenty minutes of spin drill for mat balance, we were ready to start wrestling. In groups of four, they went through a grind which only the toughest teams go through these days. Each wrestler was challenged and thank heaven nobody quit. In those days quitting was rare, as parents back then wouldn't allow or tolerate quitting without a good reason.

Amidst blood (mostly from the nose), sweat, and slobber, the team endured what few teams could have that day. Liz, Chi, Sam, and Rod were pushing Danny, Paul, Chris, Garrett, and Johnny. Truth was quiet as usual and working as hard as an undersized heavyweight is able. Coach

Hall and I had set the tone for the next week's routine. We couldn't relent or back off. The team was bright enough to know that if we did, it would show we thought they were weak. They were good before the JFK match but were not quite ready to win the title. We left no stone unturned to change that.

On Wednesday afternoon, the week of the league tournament, we started to taper. The conditioning would ease. They were ready physically, and now the mental side had to kick in. The rest cycle ensued and on Wednesday and Thursday it was review and light drilling. Weigh-ins for the event were Friday at 12:00 noon and we arrived fresh and ready. As the crew lined up in their briefs to weigh in, they looked primed. Toned and muscular, they wore the telltale signs of brutal preparation. Bruises, welts, and residual swelling told the story of a team that had been worked and then allowed to recover to get ready for the two-day tournament.

The first round went well, with no surprises. Eight of our twelve wrestlers won, and we had two pins. We were ahead on points but in a tight race with Kennedy, Lincoln, and West High. The first round of the next day would be the determiner.

On Saturday morning, I could tell our mindset was right where it should have been. We were in the driver's seat with seven who were still alive in the tournament. We had three who were in the championship round, wrestling to become city champs at their weight. Three or four were on the backside, which means they had a chance to place third or fourth out of the ten spots. Would we stumble or would we become one of the few teams from the east side to win the league title? The team that day was unbeatable—and that day and night have been etched in my memory ever since. We had five on the winner's side and others still alive to place in the top four in our ten-team league. Three made the finals—Lizard, Sam, and Rodney. In the wrestle backs, Johnny, Chicago, Garrett, and Danny were going to wrestle for the third-place spot.

Danny was first and came through with a solid third-place finish. Then the 126-pound match announced Terry "The Lizard" Lyles. At 126 pounds he was as strong as a man and seasoned to wrestle—and wrestle he did. He won convincingly and earned his second league title. By that time I knew but kept it a secret. We had accumulated enough points to clinch the title and no matter what happened, we would leave North High School as the city champions.

Garrett took third place and then came the classic match between Sammy and a kid from Thomas Jefferson who had wrestled Sammy a month earlier. They had tied. The kid was tough and experienced. Sammy was, no doubt, still miffed at his lack of success in their earlier match. He took charge early and by the second period the kid knew the outcome would be different this time. Sammy was superior in every way, and if my memory serves me correctly, he pinned the opponent in the second period.

Johnny Aragon also took third, and the stage was set for the classic matchup between two seasoned 167-pounders. Rodney Wright (who sadly recently passed away) was to have a classic rematch with Thatch, one of several brothers from East High School. They too had battled to a tie in their earlier match. We all knew this would be a proverbial bloodbath as they "metered up" (shook hands) at the center of the mat. When they tied up, Rodney asserted his brute strength and got the first takedown. And he didn't stop. The match went the distance, but this time the result was much different. Rod was our third champion that night, and by then they had updated the points. After Chicago's (Anthony Miller's) placement match we had scored 120 points and the next closest team was John F. Kennedy with 102 points. At the end of the tournament, we were fairly low profile as we accepted our trophy as DPS champions. It was a bit of history that night. Rarely had teams from the East side been champions. And for a school with no deep history and wrestling tradition, it was even more remarkable.

We had a large contingent of fans, families, and our younger wrestlers wanting to celebrate. I hurried to a public phone and made a call as the team was enjoying some moments with those who had supported us.

I called the Godfather's Pizza in Montbello. After asking to speak to the manager, I made an unusual request. Could we come in and eat unlimited pizza with unlimited sodas for a discounted price? He somehow realized this was a special occasion for me to make this request. He agreed, but said we'd have to be out by midnight. So we drove across town back to our neighborhood, convoy style, to celebrate with our families and loyal supporters. The night was a blur, but we had over a hundred or more who wished the team well and ate pizza. The majority stayed until the anointed hour, full of thick dough, greasy cheese, and far too much fatty pepperoni. I even had to borrow forty dollars to pay for this night of celebration. My dad hit me up with a fifty-dollar bill and in total, I think we spent 110 dollars to feed our entire crew, and we ate well!

What a feeling, celebrating a group who had never been known to accomplish something of this nature. A far cry from the administrators who hired me as a young twenty-two-year-old coach and said, "Coach, just field a team. You won't win because this is going to be a football and basketball school." I knew they were wrong, and I didn't have to prove it. A bunch of tough, inner-city, grinding, sweating teenagers had made a statement that reverberated across all of Denver. They had proven what dedication, sacrifice, blood, and tears would do over time. This was one of the finest moments in my coaching journey.

What is clear is the impact that has been made in a large community. Those who wrestled or played on the gridiron for all these decades are united as a large family. As a group, they have been admired and even envied for what they stood and still stand for, for what they represented, and for what they endured.

Word got out shortly after I figured out this coaching concept. The kids at Montbello and then George Washington were held to a different standard than other city or suburban schools. You *were* going to study. You *were* going to be a great citizen and give back time to your community, and you would represent your school and family in a positive way.

If you ditched school or came to class tardy, or even missed one of our Tuesday and Wednesday night mandatory study halls, you simply did not compete. You would miss a game or a match. No discussion. This was accepted by our student-athletes and their parents as they signed the team policy agreement, which I made and still make a requirement.

Over time, resentment of the rigidity of the stringent rules evolved into great pride. Hundreds and maybe thousands of athletes who met these lofty standards are now huge successes, partially shaped by their collective identity. They are linked forever. As our perennial t-shirts say, they are "Bound by blood, sweat, loyalty, and pride."

It has been (I am not done coaching) and will always be a special feeling to be on the sidelines or in someone's corner. To be present and teach the lessons of failure, success, adversity, resilience, and persistence has been monumental in my love of this profession. To watch young men and women "chase dreams fiercely" and know that I have contributed just a bit is what keeps me going and loving what I do. Though so many come back and say or show their thanks, they need to be shown my gratitude. They have chosen to join my family, and without blinking they accept the rigors and grind that accompany this often bumpy journey. I am the one who has been the recipient of too many (more than I deserve) beautiful snapshots of eternal success. Please accept my deep love and admiration; it is well deserved.

Games, Matches, and Jocks

I looked quickly at the clock. One minute and eleven ticks left in all. We were at midfield, fourth and two, with two long yards to go. The score was 7–6, and we were ahead. This was 2001, in what ended up being DPS's championship game. We had around 2,500 fans in the stands, a big crowd by city-ball standards. If we punt, we give them the ball and a minute to score. If we don't punt and don't convert, we hand them the ball at the 50-yard line. They had called time out. Our "brain trust" was divided. Damn, I wanted them to tell me what to do as I ran very slowly, I might add, (packing too many pounds), to the huddle. As I got in the huddle and looked at the crew, all twenty-two eyes on me, the decision was easy. Their look gave me confidence, and I sensed their toughness. They had physically knocked in the teeth of the crosstown bullies, and hey, why stop now?

"Men," I whispered, "you have just made three first-downs in a row, now make one more!"

I glanced in mid-sentence at their defensive leader, a 230-pound beast of a linebacker, who I still see. Once we made eye contact, he became seriously pissed off and yelled, "Bring it on, you punks!" He had kicked a lot of butt for a lot of years. Dave thought his team, the Spartans, were the best, and had said it loudly and publicly.

I looked at him one more time, then at our eleven, and said, "Run 24 isolation and put that hotdog on his back." Our fullback, John Feeney-Coyle, who became an all-state linebacker, nodded while wiping a combination of sweat and drool from his face. I jogged back to the sidelines a bit quicker, still feeling the 300 pounds that sat squarely over both of my worn-out knees. Once I got to the sidelines I turned, knowing that as long as it took my slow ass, the crew would already be at the line of scrimmage. They were. Down...precision...everybody locked into their stances. Set! The quarterback, Brandon, reverse-pivoted and put the ball in the gut of our tailback, Dre Wilson! John F-C got off the ball low and hard, just how coaches love their fullbacks (guards in the backfield). What happened next wasn't pretty if you were a Spartan, Spartan fan, or Spartan parent. As Dre ran through the hole, he had to slow down because John had his helmet right in the middle of Dave's umbilicus. To the left, our guard Carey had his helmet on Dave's right love handle. Even Swifty got some. He played the game with a passion rarely seen.

Dre could have planted and gone for ten, but he was never wired like that. He chose to be the closing force that put Dave flat on his back, then planted, and while doing so he cleated Dave in the inner thigh or even the testes. I suspect the latter because I heard a high-pitched scream indicating that someone's balls were being violated. We needed two yards and got eight. Dave ended up with turf burn on his lower back near the area girls get a tattoo called a "tramp stamp." We still had 34 seconds on the clock.

Kneel down? Hell no. One quarterback sneak for 5, another fullback trap for 5 or 6, and it was over.

Our celebration was not too insane or out of control. These moments never go away. In truth, the seasons blend together, but after twenty-nine years as a head football coach and forty years in coaching, it all blends together in this amazingly satisfying way.

I confess, if you are waiting for me to tell you about all the state championship teams I coached, you are about to get really bored. We had some chances on several occasions but fell short as our city teams often do. Our kids won many league championships and went to the playoffs significantly more than a dozen times. Trust me on this one, what our kids accomplished is far more remarkable in many ways than that of the many teams who won the coveted state championships. They represented a school, a section of town, and a community in a manner others envied and still talk about. They collectively dropped hundreds of gallons of sweat. They got worked! They had to toe the line in school—as students, as citizens, as young men and a few women—before they ever proved themselves on the field. What the players and I were at times ridiculed, made fun of, and even mocked for is now the legend—not of Steve Finesilver, but of George Washington football. Hundreds and maybe a thousand or more form a fraternity of students who survived and excelled year after year at doing what few teams can ever hang their hats on. The traditions, routines, discipline, aura, rep, and prowess as true student-athletes is now the standard of what every team, regardless of sport, school, coach, or situation covets and envies and will likely never have.

In 1979 I developed a philosophy that never changed. As I became both a head football and wrestling coach, there were constants, predictable as the sun coming up and setting daily, with no deviation from the few laws that accompanied every kid who joined these teams. On our teams, respect would be shown to every adult they interacted with. Clerks, teachers, secretaries, lunchroom workers, parents, cashiers—each one would be referred to as "mister," "missus," "sir," or "ma'am." When answering a question or giving an instruction, it had better be "Yes, Coach" or "No,

Coach." No verbal interaction could ever just be ignored, and heaven help the one who violated this edict. Homie, yo, whatup, G, dog, fam, and these other ridiculous salutations were for others, not us. Violate this and get lit up. Hundreds of pushups, gassers, up-downs, and sometimes all of those would ensure that this was never again violated. Enough said.

Next, you were going to be present and on time. What exactly does this mean? You came to school daily and operated on G-Dub or Coach Fino time. Class at 7:30 actually meant you were there, with your low-key, respectful self in your seat, with your mouth shut, at 7:15, and yes—I frequently checked. Missed class or tardy? Okay, test the system. Miss a game? Games are precious. No deliberations, no negotiations, you've lost one out of that small and short time-wise window we call your "athletic career." Make missing class, practice, study hall, or a meeting a habit? Fine, find another team. Study halls were part of our agenda. Not like the aptly named free-for-alls I see now. We held study halls each Tuesday and Wednesday night from 5:15 to 6:30 p.m.

Starting in August and continuing throughout the season, our students run like the military. You'd be in your seat with space between you and the next kid—no music, no talking, no phones, no bullcrap—or ya didn't play. On our squad you were in a posse of more than a hundred who were expected to perform in the community and be pillars. Our kids went to elementary schools, made breakfast for their teachers, and did volunteer work for seniors around our school because we had (and still do) something special. Our leadership team within the school had a guarantee that a hundred-plus students would emulate or demonstrate what was expected of everybody. Many principals from this era felt the team set the tone for the entire school and community.

The power of a coach, not just in athletics, is often life changing. The speech coach, drama coach, voice coach, and music coach share common ground with the basketball or soccer coach. They encourage and also suggest, criticize, admonish, and correct to get their desired result. And what is that? This elusive creature called *potential*. This is what separates an ordinary coach from a great coach. The great coach bridges the gap between average and great. He or she knows how to tap into this mysterious trait called potential. They often see it when nobody else does. But how? I wish I had the answer, but I don't.

Coaches are like volunteer talent scouts. They see and find talent where others can't and don't. Once they see it, they grow and nurture it. Coach Lanham, the esteemed wrestling coach at Duke, is a prime example. Each and every year he and his dedicated staff qualify hard-working grapplers for the prestigious NCAA championships. No big deal? It is rare that Duke gets a "national name"—a kid ranked in the top fifty or even the top hundred. Yet, his grinders come out of the Atlantic Coast Conference with four or five of the top fifteen teams in our nation. And he molds and sculpts All-Americans from athletes who were average by college wrestling's tough standards. His tough love approach works, and his blueprint is different. He has no scholarships. Let me say it again. He has no scholarships! Either the incoming freshman pays for school or gets financial aid based on the family circumstance. Every other school in the conference is endowed with 9.9 full scholarships and a budget at least two times the size of Duke's budget.

Coach Lanham has had success at the highest levels. Yearly his wrestlers compete in the tough Atlantic Coast Conference. He takes good wrestlers and makes them better. He takes good people and through his unique approach makes them finer—as people, as humanitarians, and as contributors in society.

Standing in the gym, on the sideline, and being part of a kid's life as "Coach" is a very special role, one which I take quite seriously. I knew when I started coaching that I held great power. I could build a youngster up and tried like crazy to do so. I also on occasion went too hard and tore down a kid's spirit. Though not intentional, at times I was no doubt a bit too impatient or cutting with my words. As I aged as a coach, I was able to be far more positive than negative and realized that I did not have to demean or devalue a kid...ever. Our children have and will always listen to a coach, often more so than they do a parent. The ability of a coach to influence a player is unbelievable. Every coach, whether they intend to or not, leaves a legacy. This legacy is either a positive one or a poor, tainted one. The coach impacts each kid in some way. Good coaches put education, morals, family, and faith way above winning. Winning through cheating, illegal recruiting, or bending the rules is hollow; empty. It is possible to win by playing within the rules and being honest and up front. Others, I am ashamed to say, lie, deceive, and cheat to win. In the last decade I have seen more and more coaches who infest our profession and seek to win in competition at any cost. These frauds and phonies are always exposed, and they leave kids' careers spoiled by their own selfish deeds and actions.

Loyalty

He was a golfer. Now I have nothing against golf and even watched it once for about two minutes. I have never tried it and don't plan to. Many years ago, we had an athletic banquet at the end of each sport season. The fall sports would have a banquet for men's soccer, gymnastics, tennis, volleyball, and the other seasonal teams. Our team took part, but we still held our own more intimate dinner for our team, friends, and families. The banquet was over, and I gathered my belongings and noticed Pascal waiting. Since it was about 9:00 p.m., I asked the obvious.

"Son, do you need a ride home?"

"No sir, my dad gets off of work and will pick me up at about eleven o'clock."

"That's kind of late," I said. "Call Dad or Mom and see if I can give you a lift to the house."

He did, and they consented. I had just agreed to be the wrestling coach and was inviting any kid with a pulse to join the squad. Once in the car, I quickly congratulated him.

"Pascal, I am so excited that you have decided to join the wrestling team."

He was surprised, explaining he had never seen wrestling and knew nothing about the sport. Once at his house, I dropped him off and told him I would see him for our first day of practice a few afternoons later. How crazy is that? He showed up and to be honest, had no clue. He toughed it out his first year and won—well, actually, he won zero matches out of eleven or twelve. I was the head coach, and the next year, after picking my successor, I supported him in the stands and watched the team improve. Pascal got better, winning about half of his nineteen or twenty competitions. His senior year, through toughness and commitment, Pascal nearly went undefeated. He was humble and modest and had grown and developed, hour by hour, in the weight room. He entered the state tournament after winning his region as a virtual unknown. He shocked a bunch of people by winning each match and ultimately made it to the state championship match where he was to face a brute of a kid who had wrestled internationally and had about twelve or thirteen years of experience under his belt. The kid put every move, counter, and hold on Pascal, yet couldn't score until late and only scored a single escape, making the score 1-0 in his favor.

Pascal, dejected but undaunted, became a symbol that night for many others. Work hard, do things right, be resilient, and success will follow, were the lessons he demonstrated that Saturday night. I left the arena with great pride, not knowing that Pascal was being interviewed by members of the media that evening.

When I awoke the next day to read the Sunday paper, I was brought to tears by Pascal's words. He had been asked how, after only wrestling for three years, he could have fared so well and competed so fiercely. His response was, "I really did not like wrestling at first, and wasn't very good at it, but Coach Finesilver asked me to wrestle, and I never wanted to let him down." All I had done was to give the kid a ride home and some bits of encouragement and look what happened. What an incredible gesture of loyalty!

Now the story gets better. Shortly after reading those kind words, I sent for Pascal. He came down to the coach's office and we had a very frank discussion. I explained in no uncertain terms that with my help he was going to college. He very respectfully informed me that he planned to do so and that his parents had been saving up to pay the enormous fees. I pledged to help him get recruited and, in the process, save his parents lot of their hard-earned money. He thanked me, yet he didn't really believe this would take place. Each day we called coaches and helped get him on the radar. It was already February, and we were trying to get him placed in a good school as a college wrestler for the next fall. After nearly fifty calls and many rejections, California-Bakersfield called and at the time was nationally rated. They just so happened to need a kid to wrestle at 190 pounds, and Pascal had the frame to step into their lineup in the not-so-distant future. They scholarshipped him and he became a two-time All American and wrestled his senior year for an NCAA Division 1 title.

Pascal continues to do well, and we stay in touch. After many years of struggling and refining his business plan, Pascal oversees a large medical staffing organization. He is doing quite well and stays connected to his roots, to his community, and to those in the wrestling world. What an intensely loyal young man who no doubt learned loyalty the best way a kid can, from parents who value and demonstrate it.

Chapter Sixteen

Jobs by George

Damn. I did not think I would get selected. They were looking for administrators for summer school in 1992, and they held interviews and picked me. I was to be the assistant suit at GW for seven or eight fun weeks in the summer. Not too tough, but this required having to be vigilant with kids from two or three different schools. Around three hundred kids took an assortment of classes to get caught up on credit.

We were starting to see a gang presence in Denver. The Denver Police gang unit had a list of around eight hundred known gang members who were affiliated with the gangs trying to get a foothold. Among our summer school kids there might have been eight or ten wannabes who were at the first of several steps to move up the gang hierarchy. They kept their noses clean during that summer, and I became the summer school principal for the last several weeks while the nice woman in charge transferred to become the new middle school principal at a nearby school. That short time went well with only a couple small flare-ups—a drop of weed, a bit of alcohol, but no fights, vandalism, or stealing.

After this experience, I decided two things. First, I would never wear a shirt and tie in the summer—my days of summer school leadership were over. Not my idea of fun or fashion.

The media decided to name the next summer "The summer of violence." They blasted the children in the city with reports that gang members would be recruited and next summer there would be bloodshed. Sad, but unfortunately, it ended up being true. I marinated over it, and instead of throwing my hands up in despair, decided to start Jobs by George.

I wrote up a proposal and began to solicit people who had property, apartment complexes, or warehouses, and I made appointments. We were going to provide jobs to inner-city youth doing intense manual labor, kind of like how I grew up. The crews—a supervisor and several students— would report at 6:20 a.m. for a meeting. Then they would go out and perform tasks such as weeding, construction cleanup, or anything labor intensive. After working for seven hours from Monday through Thursday, they would come in on Friday and do community service.

I felt I needed to dress up to meet the business owners and CEOs who might hire us. I had my college sport coat dry cleaned and the polyester brown size 52 regular was looking pretty sharp, although a bit '80s style. But it fit well, and at least it wasn't a sweatshirt or t-shirt. After each presentation and request to hire our youth, I got either a quick rejection or the "lack of budget" speech. A couple of owners cut right to the chase and said bluntly that the teens in Denver would never do manual labor or the required community service and certainly would not wear the JBG uniform, jeans, and the shirt with our brand. It was a great plan, but with sixteen rejections I had to up my game.

I persisted, and yes, on my seventeenth appointment, changed the attire. Now I wore a mid-'80s navy sport coat and tan slacks. It must have worked. Mr. Robinson, who owned Robinson dairy, listened. After hearing the introduction, he declared, "Done! We are all in!" I was shocked and grateful when he said he would get the other dairies and bakeries on board as well.

In 1993 we hired eight students to work at the dairies and bakeries, and one crew daily worked at an apartment complex. In 1994 we hired eighteen students, and we were off and running. We kept growing and began to work for numerous home builders, including Richmond Homes, who has been our biggest employer to date. We have done only labor, and hard labor at that.

Al Blum, who owned large apartment complexes, helped by hiring a crew the first summer. A wonderful human being, he ended up coaching with me. He is Becca's godfather and has been our true champion. As we became a 501c3, he became the chairman of our board. Coach Blum guided me through the business end of things with budget, insurance, and all the things I had no clue about. He would not let me put anything on credit as we purchased tractors, weed mowers, sealcoating equipment, and more. For many years we have had more than eighty students from across the entire Denver metro area in our program.

Fast forward to 2022, our thirtieth year. We may be the longest-running non-funded youth employment program in the nation. Our teams have performed over ten thousand jobs, and we have employed over two thousand students and logged thousands upon thousands of community service hours. The crews have shared more than two million dollars of pay, and many have earned expense awards from five hundred to eleven hundred dollars. We have provided profit-sharing bonuses in cash to many deserving students.

And we have never changed the original philosophy. No-calls and no-shows mean no job. One tardy allows you to do pushups and sit-ups for thirty minutes, and the second will get you put on the "bench." We have hired young men and women who are persistent and resilient, and they have performed admirably as JBG crew members. Our past JBG family of workers are among the most successful in their respective communities. They relied on us to provide their first or second job and now have become advocates for our program. Many have insisted their children join the JBG family.

Despite the societal changes that have occurred, JBG has remained constant. My goal is to find an understudy to perpetuate and continue this program and work with me for a couple of years, then take the reins.

The Jobs by George journey has been amazing. Thank heaven I changed into that navy blue sports coat.

Chapter Seventeen

What I Have Taught

After more than forty-three years, I hope I have taught something meaningful. As I look back and quantify all the classes in a variety of subjects, I have invested thousands of hours of discussion in the classroom setting and even more of exhaustive physical training. Lessons on health, nutrition, the systems of the human body, and much more have been well received over the years. Sessions with plyometrics, weightlifting, speed and agility training, and cardiovascular endurance have formed the foundation of my fitness classes for decades. And the students have jumped into the deep end without exception, along with my pushing and prodding on occasion. But this is not all that has taken place.

Life lessons. I want to believe that along this path kids have learned some lessons that reach beyond the classroom or gymnasium walls. I learned something long ago that has driven and inspired me:

> *"People will not remember, over time, what you did or said. Those memories fade and become unclear. Yet people, especially the students and athletes we coach and teach, will remember how you made them feel."*

This is fixated in my brain when it comes to my teaching approach. How I make a child feel determines so much of what is important. Do I check in with them? Ask about their families? Offer hope? Am I a good role model? Do students look at me as someone they can come to or even be around? I am not a therapist and don't have a degree in psychology, yet for many I have been a quiet listener, and I have realized over time this is often what is needed most—someone who sits with them, shuts up, and listens.

We talk a lot in class about the importance of self-identity. I try to honor who each child is and where they came from. Every child has a story, and their stories have proven to be powerful. Their journeys often explain and define how they behave and where they ultimately go later in life. And I, along with any other educator, can change the path of that journey. With a little patience, fatherly advice, honesty, and food when Johnny or Tina are hungry, a lot can transpire. I am human, with my own flaws and blemishes which the children, past and present, know. I make mistakes and acknowledge them. And in spite of that, I and many others have made a difference. The transformation from childhood to full adulthood is breathtaking.

Our teacher training has to change. Our learners have way too much going on in their lives at all levels to keep training teachers with this antiquated model. Our teachers burn out quickly in this profession that pays too little for far too much stress and minimal support.

We are never told that our job won't fit in the little box as we anticipate. I have been on call and on duty around the clock and accepted a long time ago that there would be little rest from the grind of helping children grow up and find themselves.

I hope I have taught children resilience, persistence, and useful skills as they wade into the complexities of adulthood, but these questions can only be answered by the children who have been in the system with me.

I have learned much more than I have taught or ever hoped to teach. As a teacher I have the power to mold, shape, and add to the story the child will tell and live out as they blossom into what they really can and want to be. I can be a source of support and a believer in the potential lying hidden, even though others may not see what is under the baggage we all cling to and haul around. I can be constructive with my criticism and give genuine praise when a child most needs it. I can be the one to share celebrations with, along with fears and failures. I can knock down or elevate the spirit of a youth by my words and actions. I am powerful beyond what I ever anticipated in my role as an educator. The power a teacher holds is immense and immeasurable, yet most of my colleagues don't see the profession that way. Millions of teachers over the years have never leveraged their extreme power to change a life, and the ones who have repeatedly go unnoticed.

By my actions, I hope I have learned. It is hard to be a good listener in an era where children go weeks or months without engaging an adult in a deep way. Yes, I have seen much sadness and strife, but far more at the other end of the spectrum.

I have shared celebrations, births, success, marriage, quinceaneras, college admissions and degrees, and young men and women who have become military officers.

And I have seen the wonderful evolution of many fourteen-year-olds who battled the real world to become good people and even better husbands, wives, fathers, and mothers. I have met and taught the children of children who are one or two generations removed from my teaching roots.

I'm Flawed

Yes, I'm deeply flawed, and I admit it. I know it is wrong, yet I keep repeating the same behavior. Then I have a revelation. It is wrong.

Yes, I get angry at the Lord. In my religion, it is God who at times, too often lately, gets the brunt of my anger. I question why. "Again? really? But he or she was so young." I question death and continue to funnel my anger to the Being who I mistakenly believe decides that people should leave us on earth. I am wrong. Yes, with each episode of an untimely death, I blame, question, and second-guess a supreme being who provides us with so much beauty. I can't understand why death happens far too often and far too early. Recently, with Big Rodney, I promised myself I would do better. I will, from this point forward, grieve and cry for a while and then remember. I promise to try, though it will be hard. Derrick, Jeff, Temi, Tara, Rodney, Darrell, Angie, and so many more. The longer I teach (or try to), the more embedded I am in a community of my broader family, a large one. It only makes sense that death touches us, and me more often. I resolve to celebrate the lives of those who leave us on earth and remember not their passing, but rather their lives and how they chose to live.

Heartmates

They reside in my mind and share space together, quite prominently, in my heart. They were teammates and still are, and no doubt are wreaking havoc with their antics way up in heaven. I'm sure they have looked down on me for years and scrutinized my coaching, wondering why I have gotten a bit kinder and softer, yet in time they will figure it out and understand. They are bright like that. They grew up different but were all carved and cut from the same cloth. I love them and miss them and pray two different themes daily. I pray for their families, and then I pray and give thanks that I was able to share them.

Matthew was only fourteen, and we met in the hall near the main office. It was August. He walked by and I said hello. He stopped. I learned he was a freshman named Matt, and that he was a baseball player. He had never played football, and I didn't care. I invited him to come out for football, and he said he would think about it. He was encouraged to come out that very afternoon, and he didn't. But he came out the next day, looking athletic but lost. At 6'1" and about 180 pounds, it was clear he could run. He was strong and had a deep gas tank, probably a blue-collar dad and mom who had him doing chores and playing all sorts of games— in the yard, on the playground, and at the baseball park.

Within a few weeks he was a starter on the Junior Varsity team as a tight end and linebacker. He had settled in and had good training by Dave, Miles, Bru, Merg, Larry, Oscar, and Brian. He was soon acting as primeval as the rest of the bunch in the locker room. He had found a new home. As we spoke in our coach's meetings, we knew he was destined for greatness. Yes, we knew even before he did. I met his mom and dad, and I was right. They were working-class parents with an older daughter and were thrilled he had found a new passion. They came to the games and were always supportive and among the first to congratulate the team and coaches, whether we had won or lost.

By his sophomore year, Matt was over 200 pounds and about 6'2". He had been in my weightlifting class. By this time, he was the best at about five positions and had become a starter on our varsity team. He started a routine late that year where he came to the coach's office at night about twice a week after practice. In my bachelor years I would go eat after practice, usually fast food, and then come back to watch film and work on college letters. Matt would often join me with his buddies. They would hang out with me, eat food, eat more food, and then at 8:30 or 9:00 head home after time spent winding down with cronies who enjoy being together. As this ritual continued, early in his junior year, he had a new thought. Intrigued by the whirlpool next door in the training room, one night he asked if he could try it, with his entourage all there. I said yes and let him in with a brief tutorial on how to operate the steel tub that circulated steaming hot water.

We left him alone, and the kids ate while I watched film on the upcoming opponent. After a bit, we were into our own world and suddenly I remembered we needed to check on Matthew. I sent one of his teammates to see if he was okay and had wrinkly skin, as the whirlpool will do that. The kid yelled for me. The yell was one of amusement, not concern for a comrade who was hurt. I hurried in and there was Matt, in his state of bliss, taking a bubble bath. Yes, in the whirlpool, with bubbles everywhere. I had never even thought of this. A bubble whirlpool? This continued twice or thrice each week, and he gained nicknames from this and ultimately settled for—I don't know why—the confusing nickname of "Twinkle toes."

He could flat-out play. He could play football really well and got better with each practice. By his junior year he was among the best players on our team and rated best in the state. At tight end he could do it all, and at 6'3" and 220 pounds, he was a huge key to our nine- or ten-game wins. He could run, throw, block, tackle, and catch. He was on the radar at every

Division 1 school in the nation, and I met with his parents. I explained that maybe he would have to decide between football and baseball and assured them football offers would be coming. Arizona, Wisconsin, Northwestern, and dozens of others came calling and offered full scholarships. Even more baseball schools offered recruiting trips and full assistance. He had to decide.

He came to me, mid-summer before his senior year. I was surprised he had decided on football. After the stress that accompanies these decisions, he decided on Northwestern. They had begun to win some games, and he loved the school. He loved the football side along with playing in the prestigious Big Ten. After being named to the All-Colorado team, he left for Illinois and started his journey at this highly respected school of academia. He soon became a starter on their squad which was projected to have their best year ever, and they did.

His dad called after an early-season game against Michigan. They had not beaten the Wolverines in over forty years, and guess what? Not only did the Wildcats win, but Matthew caught the winning touchdown pass. Yes, I write this with tears flowing freely. I have a picture on my desk of that catch and the football they gave to him and which he in turn very modestly gave to me. This journey led him and his team to the Rose Bowl where he attended the Heisman ceremony as a guest of his teammate, Darnell Autry, who was a Heisman contender.

Then we got the news. Matt had cancer. I will say it or write it again. Matt had cancer, the same cancer that had taken his dear mother's life a few years before. He underwent treatment and had to give up football. He dropped from 240 pounds to 180 and had only one lung functioning fully. The tumor was near his other lung, prohibiting it from functioning, and he was having a hard time breathing. He was declared a medical, non-returning redshirt. What this means is that he was able to stay on scholarship but was unable to play ever again. After a series of procedures, he went into remission and began to recover. They could not keep him out of the weight room or off the field, and those closest to him wondered why. They knew he would never play again. Right?

But Matt Hartl was planning a comeback. Like everything he did in life, his comeback was done with grit and desire found in few people. He went back to the doctors who declared him unable to play, echoing their original prognosis. He would not take no for an answer. They held firm. He was undaunted; he would not give up. He contacted the university attorneys and asked them to advocate for him. They went to court with him to overturn a rule that had never been changed. Once an athlete held this medical designation, none had competed again in NCAA history—until Matt. He won. Several doctors cleared him, and he was told he could resume the team with many restrictions. He did not quit working, and his weight crept up to 210, then 217, then 236, and he was once again named a starter before they were to play the Oklahoma Sooners. Yes, he played with one functioning lung and a 110 percent functioning spirit and was introduced as the starter in the Northwestern stadium in front of more than fifty thousand fans, each wearing a shirt with his caricature on it. The shirt said, "I'm back!"

What a moment for him and all of us. He played and finished his career as one of the finest players in the conference. He was to graduate in May of that year, and he did, with honors. Prior to that, he was voted as the topmost inspirational amateur athlete in the United States and appeared on national television for his numerous accomplishments.

Then, it happened.

Dad came to see me at practice shortly after Matt's graduation. He gave me the news. We cried together as he told me that the cancer had returned. I was blindsided once again. Though Dad had said he was going through treatment, I was worried. It was so unfair. Matt passed after an epic battle shortly after his graduation.

I miss him. A lot.

I am warmed by the thought of him and what he has meant to me and my family. I see him running for touchdowns, hugging his parents after the games, in that damn bubble whirlpool, and his penetrating blue eyes, always ready for battle—in school, baseball, and football—but most often in life and the way to best live it.

Oscar

I eulogized him in a packed chapel. I would speak a sentence or two from the heart and then the family member next to me, also shedding tears, translated in Spanish. The day before, I was caught off guard when his sister came to my class asking to see me. As I left the weight room and stepped into the hallway, we both cried and hugged. The relationship that had started with embraces for happy occasions had now turned into the act of comforting and nurturing each other at his passing. Yet, what Oscar Sanchez accomplished in his way-too-short time on earth was monumental and among the most inspirational paths you could chart.

You see, Oscar started with a dream. His seeds of hope were no doubt planted by a family who had pride and a love of learning which Mom and Dad knew would provide quality lives for Oscar and his three sisters. He was recruited, more like "voluntold," that he would play football. He resisted for several days and then appeared for a practice and hated it.

I told him he had to come back or I would keep bugging him, and he believed me. He was solidly uncommitted until he met Davie and Kyle, two of our best, and once he hung out with the rest of the "fam," he was all in. Picture this very withdrawn 6'3" bruiser with our football regulars who were at first more familiar and far more athletic. By then it didn't matter. Once that team thing enters your persona, you are usually hooked. Then, as is almost always the case, you get better together. And he did.

By his junior year he had lifted for a year and was playing offensive and defensive tackle. He was really good and was an All-State player. He also had to kick for us. He was barely average, but as the best we had, he helped a lot on extra points.

But his real story begins as a student and an amazing person. Not to mention as a gifted artist, which I did not know until I saw his artwork on display in the main hallway. Imagine this. A young man who could draw, paint, and sketch, carried a 4.2 GPA, All-State in football, and able to communicate in two languages while practicing a third, as I recall. As he and I became close, we had a conversation I will never forget.

"Oscar, what are you thinking about for college?"

"I am going to Colorado University, that is where my mom wants me to go."

I shut up, but it began to gnaw at me. I asked if I could go at some point to talk to Mom and the family. He agreed, and finally I was offered an invitation.

Fernando went with me. My college buddy translated while I explained that Colorado University offered a great program in architecture. But, Fernando explained in Spanish, Oscar could expand and go to Purdue, Rice, Stanford, or an Ivy League school and likely get full financial aid.

Now I digress. The meal was sensational, but I only really remember the huge amount of flan I consumed. Somewhere between my third and fourth serving, Mom began to cry. She said if I would guide him, she would allow him to leave to seek a degree out of state, if indeed that was best. Within two months he had gained acceptance to every school he applied to, and finally, after much deliberation, he chose Yale. I made a promise to him that spring, and he honored me by naming me his graduation godfather, a very high honor. I promised I would be at his graduation, and I was. Watching him cross the stage was an unforgettable moment. A young man, my godson, graduating from Yale. The day and environment were surreal. I had a meal with his family, and he told me he was going to graduate school again for free because of his excellence within the School of Architecture. He got his master's degree at Yale, then took a job in New York City and stayed while passing the grueling tests to become a certified architect. Then he worked a year in Boston before deciding to come home.

In Denver, he rented for a while then enlisted me to help him find his own house. With my realtor, he found a property that he wisely put in his and his parents' names. They collectively held the title. I gave him furniture, including what had been the Finesilver's dining table. It was a heavy walnut table which obviously had seen a lot of food come across it. He was set and climbing the company ladder with bonuses and incentives which he quickly gave to his parents to make their lives easier. In a sense he was taking good care of the whole family by his presence and his ability to help financially. He came to see me at school. I grew worried.

As we spoke he seemed a bit out of breath and out of sorts. He said a doctor was suspicious he had ALS—Lou Gehrig's disease. I stayed strong and then read up. *My God, please don't let this happen* was the opening to my prayers for months. Those thoughts, though divine, didn't matter. He confirmed our fears and said he had five years or a bit more. I was floored. He was so strong for that first eighteen months, I was sure the diagnosis was incorrect. Then he began to fail. He was always coming by the house, fishing with our family and watching the Finesilver village grow, as we had been close, as family members should be. At about four years, he was losing weight and really slowed down. His speech changed, and at the five-year mark he came to the house in a wheelchair with a machine that would speak his typed words. We had a fine visit, the best you could expect. He said he had his affairs in order and had a fund set up for the family, and they would get the house. Even in ill health, he made sure to take care of his family. When he left, I broke down. I didn't know if I would ever see him again...and I didn't.

Before giving the eulogy, I was so confused. I did not know how I would hold up or what to say. I decided at the last moment to talk to him and with him.

"Well Big O, what is the view like from heaven? I know you are there and can see us." There wasn't a dry eye, I noticed. My words were being translated to Spanish by the translator, who also was crying.

"What were you thinking when you got in the tub and removed the plaster cast with your dad's help because you were sure the broken leg was already healed? You didn't have enough money to have the drain unclogged, but we survived that.

"Why did you decide to take a two-day detour and leave us so worried when you were coming home from Boston? You were in a 20-foot moving truck touring the Black Hills, Mount Rushmore, and the Dakotas with a van full of your past from the last six or seven years of school and life. When you made it to Denver, most of your furniture and architect supplies were broken, but to you it was worth the journey. Why didn't you tell us about the firehouse you designed, the first one in the country, with a completely open glass structure so the engines were always on display? In New Haven you were celebrated, as an undergraduate, for your creativity. We miss you because we love you. We love how you loved life and your family and friends. When you were about fourteen, we learned that with you there was no moderation—you had one speed and that was full bore, pedal to the metal. We don't fully know why you left us, but we do know this. Our Lord made you very special, and we will always hold you in our eyesight and in our collective hearts. You chased greatness with everything you did and never wanted notoriety or recognition, and you always took care of your family, a hundred percent of the time."

As I concluded, I felt a small sense of peace. I prayed that the family would heal and again thanked God for the incredible gift of Oscar...my godson.

Chapter Eighteen

The Mommas

Mothers are wired differently than we are. Yes, mothers have a different mentality than our half of the species. Our mindset with our babies is to have fun, create mischief, give a bit of advice, and after eating a nice meal (usually not well-balanced), call it good. We don't bother with or care much about the details. They are just that—details—and not very important in our world.

But not the Mommas. Nooo. They are ready and primed. Always coiled to spring and attack with the sharpest tongue, or with claws and fangs with a bigger threat. Mommas are the ultimate protectors, adept at navigating this threatening world. Their babies remain babies well into adulthood. While Pops sees them as grownups, Mom acknowledges their growth but still protects them like they have and should. There are some tough jobs out there, yet not one is as grueling as the round-the-clock task of motherhood. Just one day as a mom will wear your tail out. Moms answer the bell day after day for years and spend decades to give their offspring the best that exists. I would be remiss if I didn't acknowledge our mothers and tell the stories of four of the most dedicated I've known. They, mostly flying solo, raised more than one child and led them carefully and methodically (maybe with a bit of hysteria) into adulthood and then let go a little and watched them soar. As their little ones grow, they rarely take credit. A bit tired and worn out, the mommas care about only one thing. If the children are happy and healthy, the mommas will, on occasion, take a sigh of relief and get right back to the vigilant task of continued love, devotion, and support.

Mrs. Sitty

She came to the games. She came to the school. She was ever-present and insisted that her children, Yaya, Methe, and Brook study, read, and respect. After Brook, the oldest, became a sophomore, I learned Mrs. Sitti didn't drive, but that was false. She didn't have a car. She drove on the rare occasion her relative let her borrow a car, and only then.

She either walked or took the bus. Mrs. Sitty, with dark, piercing eyes, would bring the children to school, check in with me, make me food, and shortly, we closed each conversation in person or by phone with "I love you." And we both meant it. The bond between us will link us forever. She was often in our home, and her children were around the village frequently. She was livid when she caught Brook watching nudity on her computer. I supported her and had a fatherly talk with him about the inappropriateness of that act. If her children were not reading or doing their work in school, she would call me. On speaker I provided guidance and they listened. When Methe got too full of herself on a Sunday afternoon, I intervened and lectured this sixteen-year-old about respect for her mom, no matter what Mom's expectation was. When I heard they went twice a month to the mall and freely spent Mom's hard earned money frivolously, I became heated, the pseudo-father to three children who have since become very successful and embedded in my heart. As adults, they have flourished. Brook has a college degree, Yaya works in city and state government, and Methe, like her siblings, has a degree under her belt and is quite successful.

Mom would not relent. She never gave up on what she expected from her children. She knew I supported her a hundred percent and was always ready to jump in by phone and in person. I would be remiss if I didn't include my love of Ethiopian food developed by this fine family. One of the children brought me several plates (more like platters) of cuisine with names I still can't pronounce. I once took this care package home and radiated it in the microwave. The kitchen soon filled with the scent unique to this culture As I sat at the table salivating from the smell, my son Matt jumped onto my lap. We shared bites of the most amazing dish—meat from the lamb, onions, lentils, potatoes, and a blend of seasonings I have learned must be purchased at the specialty store. With gusto we devoured this dish, and soon, the rest of the children gathered around. Matt was fine, satiated, and I was sweating. Beads of sweat originated deep in my scalp from the spices and the tiny red peppers found in this dish. Droplets accumulated on my cheeks, chin, below my eyes, and around my upper and lower lips and the children were marveling at how I was able to produce this large amount of perspiration so quickly. And I didn't care.

Over time, Mrs. Sitti has become one of my all-time heroes and my bond with Brook, Methe, and Yaya is everlasting and eternal. I love them and believe they love me back. I am proud of them, but mostly I hold Mom in the highest esteem. I am in awe that Mom never gave up or became tired. She had decided that despite their obstacles, as a family they would have what they wanted and envisioned. When the bills accumulated, she was undaunted and worked more. When the weather was inclement and the several-mile walk to work frigid, she put on another coat. When it took Brook a bit longer to get his degree, she made ends meet to pay for extra time in college. No one, including me, will ever know what she really went through to provide for her children, but she did provide. Mothers don't come any more dedicated or true to their values than this beautiful woman. How lucky I am to have shared a small part of this wonderful family's journey. Mrs. Sitty is my mom of the year, every year.

Genet

I called her Mrs. Ali, but to her dear family, she was Auntie or Genny, short for Genet. Her family members, the family you just read about, somehow connected us into a larger family which has intertwined over the years. Nonetheless, we were close by the time Denavion had enrolled in my class his freshman year. He had been told, no doubt over his protests, that he *would* take my fitness class. This tall, handsome fourteen-year-old had been informed. The whole family had taken a class with Coach, so he was to "man up" and survive.

For Denavion, it was survival. He didn't fit in with the older students, who took every opportunity to ridicule and needle him. When he slacked off during the grueling lifting sessions or the hated plyometrics, his older classmates put him in check and snitched freely. On occasion he pouted amidst the sweat and toil he was forced to be a part of, a situation he hated but was powerless to change. For over a year he had no voice and no options but to endure what he hated and then, like so many others, came to love. Sammy, three years his senior, was all over him and reveled in the fact that he too had to take the class, sentenced to this fate by his older brother Daniel. Denavion was sore for months, forced to work out with the older guys because of the family connection. It was clear he counted the minutes until class would end.

And it got worse. His sophomore year he had some tardies and the school notified Mrs. Ali. Her words to him, then repeated to me, were heart-stopping.

"I am tired of this. You are now a Finesilver."

She called and told me and then he came, teared up; he knew. He thought he already had it bad, but it got worse. The intensity doubled and he had to come at lunch daily to do push-ups, mop the weight room, study, listen to a lecture—he caught no breaks. His sophomore year was wasted, in his mind. His social life had been squashed by his mom's mandate. He had no free time, and neither mom nor I would relent. We figured six months was a fair sentence. The class and other fitness students loved it. The weight room was spotless, and Denavion was good with bleach, disinfectant, wipes, mops, and rags. Mom and I spoke each week and compared notes. Midway through his six-month sentence she came to see me, vibrant as ever. She brought Chick-Fil-A. Genet was in rare form, laughing and full of life as she had been at our Thanksgiving table the year before, and lunch was delightful. We needled Denavion and he took it well, knowing this routine would end with lessons learned.

Genny became ill. Before Denavion's senior year she confided in me that she had gone into kidney failure and would start dialysis. I checked on her and she checked on me. We were like that. We supported each other and knew that Denavion's senior year would be stressful, but we were aligned together, and he had, to nobody's surprise, grown up well. He carried a 3.5 GPA and decided to play football as well as his beloved basketball. Though playing in the midst of the pandemic, young D found he was designed for the game. Not only that, but he had also trained with the gridiron crew as a youngster in the weight room. He had a helluva season, and by mid-year was hearing from some schools because of his grades and prowess between the stripes.

Mom and I were in touch daily, as he was to decide not just where he was going to school, but where the financial burden would not strain Mom and her limited financial resources. As she endured the dialysis and the fatigue that accompanied it, she let me know she also had diabetes. Damn, life was throwing her more curveballs. That made me push even harder to make sure Mom could provide enough money to maintain her life and medical obligations. Carroll College, in Montana, ultimately came through and put together a financial package that covered nearly everything. We all shed a tear as he committed to school, football, and leaving this dear woman in July to begin to carve his path. Genny took a turn for the worse and by mid-summer seemed more tired than usual. She needed another procedure. Denavion was adjusting well, and we spoke often. He knew he had support from his biological people and from me.

I got the call in a Thursday faculty meeting. Methe was calling, and I left the meeting to take the call.

"Coach, this is Methe."

My heart sank.

"Genny is in the hospital, and I know she wants to see you."

I explained I would go to the hospital later that afternoon, but I could tell Methe was conflicted. Then I knew. I left school and cried on the way to the hospital. I broke down, knowing that Genny, my little sister, was very ill. The more I told myself to be strong, the more I cried and was really torn up when I arrived at the hospital. I saw Yaya first, and he took me to the waiting room. Denavion had just arrived in town. We sat waiting to see his mom, my beloved Genny, and we embraced, trying to gain strength from one another. As we went in to see Mom, we again cried, though we both tried to maintain our composure. It didn't work. I hugged Mom as she was ready to come out of her hospital room and sit on the outside porch at the hospital with her closest friends and family members. What an outpouring of love for this beautiful woman. She had pulled her hair back and looked as flawless as ever, just a bit frailer. Being around her on this day with the sun shining brightly gave us a lift, but we all knew. She had become weak and wasn't going to be with us much longer. Yet those surrounding her and those she had touched deeply would always have her and we would keep her at the very top of our hearts. She passed shortly after, and at her funeral was another outpouring of love from her community. Hundreds of people came—those whose lives were made better because of this mom, sister, niece, pillar, and absolutely beautiful soul with a spirit that will never be duplicated.

I think of her daily and I am saddened because I can never embrace her again and tell her how much I love her. Yet through the sadness, I get these amazing snapshots of her zest for life and how much she gave of herself to make others happy, even though she was very ill. Her legacy will last an eternity through the lives of others and through her strong, inspirational son, who continues to achieve and grow, and who is my son too—Denavion.

"I miss you my dear, and I love you. As you look down from heaven, be assured that Denavion is fine. Your village on Earth is fine. Though we miss you daily, you will never truly leave us, as you are not just embedded in our minds, but even more deeply in our hearts."

Lori

Big Swift came around as a freshman, and little Swift, "P'nutt," came around in the sixth grade. Hence the phone call. It is not unusual for a younger sibling to tag along with an older sibling, but every day? A bit different, to say the least. So I called Mom. Mrs. Swift, known by friends and family as Lori. I had to check to make sure that Lil' Nutt was okay to be hanging around on the daily. She said yes.

Out of curiosity, I asked, "Can he run through some drills with us?"

"Of course, Coach, he would love that. And let me know if you have any problems with them." And she meant it.

So, picture this. One brother legitimately in high school, and little brother, maybe eighty-five pounds, holding a pair of dumbbells, both sweating and toiling, learning the system and immersed in the football lifestyle. Yet after a summer with the older fellas, Nutt had learned the system, on both offense and defense, better than the varsity veterans. So as a seventh grader he was like a coach on the field. We leveraged the expertise of this seventh grader to help teach our system, and he fit in everywhere. Life was good. And then Big Swift had a violation, or let's call it a misdemeanor. Maybe a tardy, laziness in the classroom, I really can't remember. Nonetheless, I called Mrs. Swift and keyed her in. She was working two jobs at the time. I reached her at her job at Denver Children's Hospital.

"Mrs. Swift, I need your support," I said. As I informed her of the violation, she calmly told me that she would take care of it and did she ever. Big Swift was apologetic the next day and assured me Mom had put him in check.

Now picture Mom, with soft eyes and quite diminutive at maybe five foot three, yet raising the guys while Dad was in Oklahoma City training fighters who had chosen boxing as their sport in which to excel. Mom was raising two teenage boys and working two or three jobs without complaint so they could flourish and chase dreams of their own. Their path was noteworthy, as they have both become educators in Denver, with Nutt at our school. But this is about Mom. During the dozens of conversations we have had over the years, she has never wavered.

Every request of mine for support or permission has been approved. Whether it was big brother or little brother in trouble, she was consistent.

It is no surprise that both are very successful as educators, men, and role models. Mom insisted they play by the rules and follow her script for them. The script included what they should do at home, in sports, and at school. Dad would come into town when he could, and he too stood for all that was and is positive with young men. He instilled hard work, and they have always maintained their close relationship with their dad, though he lives several states away in Oklahoma. Lori now has grandchildren. It is not surprising that they are a bit spoiled and tremendously loved by this devoted woman. She still keeps both Swifts in check and provides the perks that grammies often give to their grandies. She hasn't changed and won't. She personifies "Mom" and all the obligations and responsibilities that go along with that tiring, yet all-important task.

Ms. Love

Talk about a huge personality, Ms. Love has been a fixture at our school. How lucky we are as staff, and how fortunate our families are to have been able to know her. I know her well. She trusted me to work with her older sons and now has made sure I have connected with her baby, Gigi.

To say that DJ, Devante, and Deondre were a handful would be insulting to the family. Like so many other wild children, I was able to tone them down, but not totally. DJ was the first, and he may have been the most accepting of the agenda the students were asked to follow. He loved his fitness class and flourished in weightlifting, jumping, and all that is required to be successful in the course. He is still on the record board for his superior vertical jump.

Deondre was quiet compared to the others, but in time he too jumped in knee-deep. Before long, the routine in gym class became a normal, fun part of his day. He accepted the rigors and the disciplined behavior. Mom had told all of them what her rules were for school, and I gave them separate instructions for my class. By the time Devante enrolled, they had no doubt imprinted him with stories of class, classmates, and their own successes, including their occasional forays into the land of pain through pushups, squat jumps, planks, and other activities students are unable to hide from. I got a call in the coach's office from the administrator in charge asking me to go to the pool lobby, a secluded place where bad things can take place at the school unnoticed. Sure enough, there they were, Devante and Deondre, in 14-ounce boxing gloves, the main event, trying to beat the stuffing out of each other, on camera no less. I broke them up, took their gloves, and made them do an inordinate number of pushups. Weeks later, I told Mom. True to her nature, she thanked me for this kind act of helping with the tough task of harnessing the energy of rowdy teens.

She raised four wonderful children, unrelentingly. I am speculating a bit, but I know she has had hardship and obstacles that most are unaware of. My hunch is that the challenges many of us face with finances, housing, relationships, grief, depression, and sadness have hit her and her family at times. I know she has been in pain, forced to use her military background, her stubbornness, and her promise to herself to never quit. She is unfazed—the consummate professional. Few know of her hardships and likely never will. How fitting is her title. Ms. Love loves, and once you enter her circle (which takes a while), there is no finer friend or loyal teammate.

She is kind and courteous to everyone who enters our school or calls the switchboard. Our staff loves her. She has had this illuminating effect for years on our staff, students, and parents. She makes time, no matter how busy, to help navigate the complexity of the school setting.

As a mother and now grandmother, she is a rock. Ms. Love anchors her family like she does her colleagues. She keeps us safe and asks for nothing. Years ago, someone wisely asked her to be the first person to greet our school family. As students, parents, staff, and visitors entered our building, she greeted and directed them to the main office, their day brightened by this wonderful woman. Ms. Love is an ambassador of love and professionalism and keeps her family, all of us, in her line of sight at all times.

Chapter Nineteen

A Little Humor

The Naked Swimmer

Coach Gurian was at GW for over thirty years and could teach many skills, but his forte was his ability to teach swimming. He loved it! It must have been '91 or '92, and he was intent on teaching his classes, all of them, how to swim. His course load included two Team Activity classes for the student who had skills but was not good at swimming. I was in the gym when Coach Gurian explained to the class that for several days, though they were not swimmers by any stretch, he was going to take them to the pool. They were excited to do something different and liked the thought of some variety in the daily routine.

The day came. Coach Gurian lined the kids up in the shallow water, hands on the deck, to work on the swimmer's flutter kick. They dutifully complied. One young man remained in the bleachers wearing his towel. He had not chosen to swim just yet. Coach Gurian did not want him to be left out. He encouraged, cajoled, and suggested, and the kid wasn't having it. He remained sitting, yet after several minutes he did stand up—progress was made. Coach asked again and there was finally a response.

"Mister, you sure you want me to swim?"

Coach nodded.

"Are you sure?" the kid asked one last time. This time, when Coach nodded, the kid agreed. He flung off the towel and was wearing only what he'd worn at birth fifteen years earlier. The class stopped kicking and fluttering.

Coach stated, clearly and loudly, "Everybody in the locker rooms."
They hurried into their gender-specific locker rooms. The kid was not
done. He jumped in, yes, naked as he could be, and started swimming.
According to Coach, he wasn't half bad. By then Coach had called security
for assistance and they came in three deep along with a random assistant
principal. They looked at each other, not knowing what in the hell to do.

Finally, the anointed one, the wannabe principal, grabbed the rescue
stick. Every pool has one of the long aluminum sticks with a safe curved
hook on one end. He was going to try to snag, catch, or hook the kid. But
the kid hadn't tired yet. The kid allegedly decided then to do the
backstroke, and finally the assistant principal gave up trying to catch this
teen. In time, the kid got tired and came to the side, breathing heavily, and
climbed up the ladder where he was quickly thrown a pair of sweats which
he—thank heaven—put on. He finished dressing and was led upstairs to
the office of discipline. I have no idea what happened to the nude
swimmer, but needless to say, the incident was the talk of the school, for
years.

The Almost Naked Swimmer

Let's call him Pericles. No, I didn't or couldn't make that up. That was
his name. He came to my class and introduced himself. He walked in very
casually as I was ending my class. I had the students in rows, and the girls
saw him before I did, with my back toward the gym doors. He created
quite a stir, and they were not bashful.

He is sooo fine. Who is this new guy? was the theme. His long hair was
pulled back and his stubble gave away his age as seventeen or eighteen. He
had a nice suntan from the beach in his home country of Greece. He was
very respectful as I explained the rules, including the required green shorts
and plain white t-shirt. He agreed to the terms and conditions. The next
day when class started, he again made a noteworthy entrance. It contained
more rhetoric than the previous day. He was indeed in the required
apparel, but it was not exactly appropriate for fourteen-year-olds who

were marveling at his muscles—all of them. His t-shirt was a size or two too small, but worse (or better if you were a post-adolescent female), his shorts barely covered his derriere and barely reached the top of his thighs. And no, they were not baggy.

As I was trying to figure out what to say, he knew and said again, very respectfully, "Coach this is the t-shirt and shorts that you said I had to wear."

I nodded. "Pericles, the shirt is very tight, and those shorts are bun-huggers." He looked confused.

My assistant found a baggy pair of green shorts which he threw over the bun-huggers and we were good to go. He played kickball and fit in well, and the girls requested he be on their team the next day. I assured them they would all have a chance to be on a team with the new guy.

I was wondering, during the kickball game. I had seen on his schedule that he had swimming the next period. If he walked into my class with shorts that tight, what would he wear to his first day in swimming class? I went to the pool during my planning period. I greeted my colleague who was shocked because I rarely entered this space.

"Coach, what are you doing here?"

Coach Gurian had been my teacher back in the day and was quite sharp—the consummate professional—so I had to retort with something good, right?

"I admire you and want to learn from you." He was puzzled, wondering why I was there. His class of twenty-five were in the pool, warming up with some flutter kicks and holding the gutter to anchor themselves. They were obedient and adept at the required warmup by this thirty-year veteran educator. Then, it happened.

I heard a scream and looked down from my chair on the deck, seven feet away from a class of flutter-kicking teenagers. The girl who screamed grew silent as she dropped her jaw and opened her eyes as wide as possible. Pericles entered, walking gracefully, slow and stately. He was tan and muscular. Now imagine this. He was wearing a leopard-skin thong! Even his buns were tan, which we all noticed as he was getting ready to jump in with his classmates. I should have helped, but I couldn't. I was not only going to enjoy this unforgettable moment, I was going to enjoy the heck out of it. I started to laugh, then couldn't stop. Soon tears streamed down my face and I was kicking and pounding the table. My brain was ignited! This kid in a thong was entirely confident he was fine to proudly display his buns and tan in this way.

Coach Gurian said, "Pericles, what are you wearing?"

That made me laugh more. Young dude was in a thong.

"My swimsuit," the young man answered.

Coach, still flustered, said, "That is not a bathing suit—you're practically nude!" By then I was pounding the table with both fists and loving this time with my colleague.

Coach grabbed a towel and tried to wrap it around this student who was confused as to what rule he had violated.

Pericles, now holding the towel around his own waist, said, "In my country, this is a bathing suit!"

I tried to stop but could not. My jaws were sore and my face still contorted after three or four minutes of hard laughter. Here is this kid, confused by our American rules and swimwear guidelines, who had caught the teacher off guard and created a hysterical class with extremely happy females who had decided that this was now their favorite class.

Pericles finally learned to navigate our system and methods and was a delight. He loved both classes but really enjoyed "dodge ball Fridays" the most. At the end of the year we took pictures, as he had to return to his home country in June.

Vocabulary Lesson

The day started off well but got much better. A young lady had prepared a very detailed presentation on the keto diet, which over the years has become one of the more popular ways to slenderize. Good diet, but like so many of the others, it didn't work for me. I actually gained three pounds after a month of the food, which I had consumed like a glutton.

Her presentation was thorough, and she clearly knew her material. Her visual was a tri-fold board with cool graphics, and she was telling the thirty-seven other students about our glycemic index, amino acids, protein counting, and more. They were "all in" as she created a nice flow and interacted well with her peers. As she wrapped it up, I knew I had to follow her very intellectual presentation and keep the class involved. We all gave her a hand for a job well done and I jumped in.

"So, what have you done that has been interesting in science lately?" Three hands went up and I called on one who explained that their class was working on dissecting a mink. Others confirmed this, so I seized the moment.

"So, what do mink have in common with a human?" They knew we were mammals, carnivores, warm-blooded, and that we have some similar anatomical parts, such as four-chambered hearts and similar digestive systems.

I was happy to be blessed with a class that was hard-working, bright, and attentive. Their sense of humor showed that day and that too made me happy. As we got into the digestive tracts of many creatures, we learned that the mink has a large intestine, a small one, and a stomach like ours. I then asked about the digestive tract of the dog. They didn't know, so I tossed out this tidbit.

"The dog has a very rudimentary digestive tract." They were confused. I described the much smaller and primitive system and closed with "The dog eats it and twenty minutes later excretes it." They got the picture.

Next, I asked, "Tell us about the digestive system of the cow." They were lost, and I was happy to inform them that the cow masticates. They all stared, except for one young man whose eyes grew larger. He froze, then scooted forward.

"Coach—say that again?"

This time, with more emphasis, I proclaimed, "The cow masticates!"

He blurted out, "How often?"

I was so proud inside. I felt I had really reached out to everyone, including this large football-playing linebacker whose mom I had taught and whose grandpa was a friend. They were all awaiting my response, but mostly Angelo (not his real name). I whispered, "The cow masticates every time it eats!"

Angelo scooted forward even more. He asked because he had to know. "The cow does that every time it eats?"

My turn. "Yes, the cow masticates frequently."

Angelo was caught in the moment and then started blushing and marveling way too much and then it sunk in. Actually, a young lady sitting next to Angelo said, "Bro, Coach said *masticates*. Not what you do, *masturbate!*"

I bit my lip and the class lost it. Angelo was stunned, but not nearly as embarrassed as he should have been. I was happy as class was ending and went to my office and laughed again until my cheeks hurt. What a fine teaching moment none of us will ever forget.

Chapter Twenty

The Wrap

This story is about to wind down, or is it? The sequel lies in your hands, along with thousands of us who will challenge the system and ask—no, demand—transparency and change. Will this be the catalyst for change in this system which has abused its powers for decades and now cheats what is most precious to all of us? The futures of millions of both pre- and post-adolescents teeter on what we do now.

Our children have been deprived of what they need, crave, and desire the most. They have become faceless and have lost their identities over time. It is worse than ever now at a time when children are most vulnerable. Post-pandemic, they are wounded, and we are left wringing our collective hands and wondering what to do. But now is no time for a pity party.

Is there strength in numbers? Heavens, yes! The power of thousands of voices in each city and millions throughout the country will drown out the politicians, board members, and those who have created and perpetuated this system but who need to be part of the change. Yes, the change must be dramatic. It can't be business as usual with small, incremental change. Slowly we have allowed our educational values to erode, and over decades we now have this convoluted mess. Public education is spinning now, led by those who can't seem to focus on the obvious needs. So many entities want to put their hands, opinions, and values into a system that is supposed to be there to serve children. How did we get so far off base?

Where do we start to right the wrongs and steer this colossal ship onto the correct course? We start with embracing what works and what has been proven through the decades. We know our youngest children need an all-important foundation. Let's take money, volunteers, and a huge chunk of our resources and revamp the system to be consistent throughout. What that should look like is that every child, in every school, has the opportunity to get the attention that only our more advantaged students have been given. At the age of four or five all our children should have spaces for socialization, centers for manipulatives, and introductory reading, writing, and most important, the ability to have their basic needs met from the moment they set their tiny feet into their classrooms. Children who are hungry, cold, sad, or troubled simply can't perform or progress in any way.

Our staff should be diligent to make sure each child has food, warmth, attention, and counseling, if necessary, to jumpstart them into this twelve- or thirteen-year journey. Whether the parents have the time or financial resources to supplement this does not matter. No more excuses.

Let's staff our early education centers and our elementary schools with the finest specialists available and give each child a fresh and happy start. And no, money is not a hindrance. Millions, even billions, are already allocated to make this happen, but we don't use them effectively. Our waste begins early and often. Money from programs like this, often federal dollars, goes elsewhere, and this must stop. Imagine all of our fours, fives, and sixes moving to the next grade with each other, prepared to learn together, even though they learn at different paces. Have the experts ready to embrace those who fall behind or need emotional support. Have the volunteers ready to assist those who have a learning disability or a physical condition which requires attention. Give them every chance to play on a field that isn't tilted.

Now our littles have the skills, including emotionally, to move onward. They are used to being embraced by a system that honors them and their families, previously forgotten, ignored, or both.

Two days ago, in the middle of teaching, a young lady walked in. We were in the upper weight room. She sat down quietly, and I asked my student-assist to take over to see what this unknown child needed. The large class continued to work out. Interruptions like this happen a lot.

"Coach, I need you to help me." She was barely audible and was tentative and embarrassed, and I could tell she had rehearsed.

"Honey, what can I help with?"

She whispered, "Will you teach me to box? I heard you do that." She was fidgety, awaiting my response.

"Of course I will, but are you supposed to be in class?" She explained she had a free period. I had her take some hand protection out of our boxing storage, and as class ended, I gave her a short tutorial. Let's call her Ann. Ann listened intently as I covered the boxing basics. I was happy she had reached out, but I didn't know her story.

She did well and said she would be back. Like clockwork, she returned the next day, still quiet, but a bit more confident. I was watching a few lifters who were getting some sets in as I was waiting to leave for a meeting. She put on the gloves I had left her the day before, and we began lesson number two. She had improved, and now she became lost in concentration on her new craft. As I told her how well she was doing, she blushed, uncomfortable with praise.

She asked for a moment to call her mom. I asked to say hello. I confirmed that Ann was with me, and we had a nice chat. Mom explained that Ann had been angry, and that boxing and joining the wrestling team would be good for her. When we hung up, I continued the boxing lesson until Ann and another young lady who had joined her were tired, sweating from the rigors of this intense training.

As Ann was getting ready to leave, she asked if she could train the next day. Knowing she had a free period, I consented. I asked, based on what Mom had disclosed, why she was so angry. She hesitated.

"Where is Dad?" I asked. She paused and after an awkward silence told me that her dad had passed away when she was six, and she has never been able to "figure it out"—her words.

At that moment I was the one at a loss for words as my eyes welled with tears. "My dad died when I was fifty, and I still can't figure it out." She nodded.

Though separated by many years, Ann and I shared the same emotions and now felt a little more comfortable with each other. I don't have a crystal ball, but I imagine this wonderful child will join so many others who found their "grind" in this most unlikely place, the boxing gym, like her new friend Faith. Once again, I was reminded of the importance that we not just teach, we understand and listen too.

I tell that story to tell this story. Needy children are everywhere, and I hope and wish for education to change, as you know, for this and many other reasons.

My fear and doubt that this system will ever change has now subsided. The anger I have felt for so long has turned to hope and optimism. With you, all of you, we are going to voice together what needs to be said as we share.

Let's share the stories of children abandoned by the system that is supposed to care for them and propel them to great heights. We must talk about uncomfortable subjects such as inequity, bias, and mismanagement.

Your voice is mine and mine is yours as we challenge, question, and demand change to better serve our families. Our faculty and staff are essential and must deliver on the promises we need to make. We must promise, both inside the system and outside, that things will be different.

Let's leave the past methods and flip the entire script. Time to put the students and families first and see them clearly, and not as an afterthought. Instead of operating schools like a business entity, we will force change in the way we treat people, especially our families and children. Then those who manage the system must be scrutinized, evaluated on their commitment to the education of *all* children as well as in their treatment of staff and faculty. The "layered-up" system has been the thorn in the side of the public schools for far too long.

The way our system conducts education now, with the message "I am your superior, so what I say goes," must stop. We educators all hold the same power, but we support our children in different ways. True voice, which we must value at the core, means we all work together to provide what we deem best for our youth. And yes, they belong to all of us.

Let's stop the excuses. Children whose families have less are now the majority in our system and must be treated as such. The achievement gap, the opportunity gap, and all of the other gaps are the result of historic flaws by those who lead. Our leaders, until now, have not been accountable to narrow the accessibility gap. New buzz word? Maybe. When each child has access to what is offered to other children, the bar will move. This is the essence—the nitty gritty. Across the board, equity must dictate that the funds, quality of facilities, availability of programs, and commitment to change and excellence must be consistent. We can no longer tolerate anything less.

We must seek transparency. Real numbers will show that we are losing students in Denver and other major city school districts because of our inadequate education. Yes, it's a bitter pill, but it is the truth, so let's fix it. If we offered up enough innovation and change with a humble apology for our previous sins, families would come back. The flight from the city schools would stop. Time to issue a heartfelt apology and mean it by showing a different attitude.

Finally, we must embrace our uniqueness. The diversity we see must be celebrated. The recent world events have led to new residents in many neighborhoods. This has created unique communities. Time to celebrate our customs, foods, music, stories, and more with the energy created by the new families in each neighborhood. Gatherings at the schools should become the norm and allow us to connect on a frequent basis.

So much work to do, but now, more than ever before, so very necessary.

End Notes

I never thought I would get here. More than twenty years, and I am ready to put this in the hands of my dear friend Mrs. Grabau and let her work her magic. Yes, it is magic. She took this on with no idea of my quirks, stubbornness, and lack of technical skills. Not to mention, writing that looks like I had never taken basic grammar classes or paid attention when I should have.

A connection with Kendra, one of my dearest students, now chasing life and doing so well. Kenny knew of the book and was the one to tell me about her talented grandma, who for months has toiled with the dubious task of getting this ready for you, the reader. This would not have happened without Kendra and grandmother. I will always be indebted to both of you.

I want to offer thanks to my early students who are now living in their fifth or sixth decade of life. You were the ones who accepted me when I was most flawed, clueless as to what I was doing. But you gave me a chance, and in the process I learned far more than I ever taught back then. You taught me to be honest, not to judge, and to realize that teachers are needed and trusted. Though young and fiercely convicted, you showed me how I could make a difference, and I have tried.

In 1987 they said I couldn't go back home, but I have. I returned to George Washington, the scene of my own high school experience, and over time it was no longer a job, but an extension of my life. I haven't worked as a teacher; I have lived as a teacher. And yes, there is a difference. My family has expanded and will keep growing, just as you have children and grandchildren who will expand our village. Teaching, coaching, mentoring, giving you your first or second job—all this has been a life-changing experience. Hats off to you.

You have all been successful and risen to great heights. You have accomplished so much, both individually and as a group. The seeds of your dreams were planted in some unlikely places. You have brought great pride and vibrance to the communities where you have stood your ground and planted your feet.

Moms and dads; grandparents and guardians: You have trusted me with your most prized possessions. You have embraced what I have said and done and helped reinforce the lessons in life so essential to young people. You have invited me into your lives and allowed me to share in your childrens' journeys. I appreciate you.

To my friends, colleagues, and fellow staff members: You have endured and survived my pranks and endless supply of junk food, but you stood side by side with me. We have taken the hits together with changes in methods, rules, policies, and procedures. And guess what? We are still standing and now have hope for a better education. I salute you, and I am grateful.

To the children in Denver: I promise to do what I can to make your lives better. I will continue to fight for change and insist that our schools become places where you shape your dreams. God bless you.

Steve Finesilver has been a teacher and coach at George Washington High School in Denver, Colorado since 1987, the same school he attended as a youth. The city of Denver has undergone tremendous change during his forty-four-year tenure. His intensive lifelong experience guiding, mentoring, and assisting children and families gives him direct, unfiltered insight into how our struggling schools can be helped, for the health and benefit of our children and our society.

Coach Finesilver has invested in the lives of youth and their families by starting two programs. Jobs by George, founded in 1993, is likely the longest-running non-funded youth employment program in the nation. Denver Youth Initiative is gaining momentum and will impact our city and youth as well. This book is a twenty-year project that will have wide-ranging appeal to parents, students, current and future educators, and the public. Coach Fino believes that together we can be the voice of change and improvement in our large-city educational systems across the country.

Besides his work in the schools, he and his wife have raised a village of their own, investing in the futures of their seven children and embracing those in their community.

Get involved: Denveryouthinitiative.org
Speaking engagements: Contact Coach at finosbf@yahoo.com

It's Time!

A movement is coming. A crusade, a demand, an education revolution is upon us. As this writing circulates and awareness grows of the critical need, so will the revolution.

No more silence. It's time for uncomfortable questions, and we have but a short window to provide answers. The Denver Public Schools hierarchy is going to, with all voices resonating, acknowledge and answer. The longstanding questions about inclusion, budget, equity, and the dreaded gap in achievement will be directed to upper management.

Our children from all parts of the world will begin to see staff and educators who share common ground. Why? It will come to the DPS leadership as a demand, not a request. We will make a promise, not a threat, to finally take action. We will leverage what is already in place to diversify our staff and those who work in our schools and district. We will actively recruit the most talented people to work with us. If this requires bumps in pay to attract these candidates, then so be it. The money will be found. Each of these demands will require a short time period, but not an insubstantial length of time. Our district leaders will respond and answer publicly to the voices of the media, our government leaders, taxpayers, children, and parents. Upon encountering the typical stalling or delays which have been part of the response when things get cloudy, actionable methods will be used to speed up the process. This is our promise.

The curriculum will be revised. This antiquated educational system will be revamped to include what our children really need—and what they deserve. Our experts, who have been ineffectively utilized for far too long, will work tirelessly to change the outdated methods, techniques, and standards. Imagine a hundred specialists coming together to do right by our children of all ages, with a deadline to make these changes.

We will attack the achievement and the accessibility gap in ways we never have before, aligning student and adult mentors with our children who show early struggles. These individuals will "adopt" children, sometimes more than one in a family, thus making a difference immediately. The schools will be directed to find the children who are struggling the most and give them support, across the board. No more handwringing and data-spewing rhetoric in the form of tired excuses. There is no reason, no excuse, to allow any child to fall and stay behind.

Changes will be made about building access. School and community leadership will come to the table and strategize about how to make neighborhood schools the focal point for gatherings, classes, events, and more. We will give the schools back to the communities who fund our very existence. Then the hyperbole about "great schools in each neighborhood" will mean something.

Innovation will replace stagnation. We will have a series of grants and funding to create school settings and learning spaces that are different. Starting with ten grants by geographic location to fund various projects, we will create hubs for activities that are conducive to children's growth. Maybe a bike park and a new video or music production lab. Let's give new families coming to Denver something different than what other locales offer. It is entirely possible that our schools would be selected because of innovative offerings not found in suburban schools. Families would move into our neighborhoods because of the quality of our amenities in the school setting.

Hopelessness will be replaced by attention on what is taking place. Those who have been justifiably critical will see change. Our school population will likely grow. We will recover families whose choice to leave the Denver Public Schools was valid, and we will ask them to return. We must promise to do better. As an entity, a collective team of 14,000 or more DPS families, we will agree to do better. This means we will acknowledge our flaws and blemishes but not dwell on them.

Let's be optimistic that we can jumpstart all of this. A village will be needed to invest in these changes, but the reward for doing so is immense. What is more important than the existence and education of our children? A large portion of our city is tired of false hope and broken promises. They cut ties with the DPS long ago and had many reasons to do so. But we want you back. Scrutinize what is taking place and view the changes. The money will be found, trust me. Our business community is largely made up of DPS alumni who want to be loyal and invest, simply put, in our children. They haven't yet been asked to come forward, to lean in and make this dramatic change together, but they will be. They want to be embraced and encouraged to open their arms, and we will give them every positive reason to do so. Much is at stake and change needs to happen quickly. We have lost so much valuable time, and sadly, more valuable potential from our youth. No more. This will be a new era.

Will you be part of the team, the voice, to orchestrate this change? Are you convinced we must do better and that we can and will? Do you recognize the flaws, the inconsistencies, and the hypocrisy of our past?

If you have given your affirmation, please reach out. This cannot take place without your voice and your desire to uproot the systems contributing to our school system's demise. Your courage is needed to take on this Goliath-like task. Once we begin to rework this layered bureaucracy, we cannot turn back. Please join the movement. We need you. Its time!

Upcoming Books

Stay tuned for ***Beating The Odds***, a companion book that tells the true stories of Denver children who have taken on life and earned happiness and success. The following amazing individuals will be included.

Kenya McGuire-Johnson—vocalist
John Platt—Sony Music
Otis Hamilton—United States Marshall
Robert Hayden—Business owner
Michelle Griego—News Anchor
Kevin Corke—News Correspondent
Marybel Gonzales—News Anchor
Stephen Brackett—musician, artist—The Flobots
Elias Diggins and Robert Pablo—Denver Sheriffs
Javon Jackson—Musician
Liz Phillips MD
Theo Wilson—Writer- Poet-Public Speaker
Jason Shankle PhD—Author
Greg Primus—Orthopedic Surgeon
Nina Tombs—Teacher/Mentor
Sheldon Reynolds—Colorado Elementary Principal of the Year
Helios Villaneuva—Manager, Firestone
Vaughn Henderson, Kendry Jackson, Shaun Drumgo, Denver Firefighters

Out of Nowhere: Shermie

The story of a common man who did uncommon things, Sherman Finesilver, born in 1927, grew up on Denver's west side. In his words, he was lucky to be "poor" and not "really poor." He rose, through hate and antisemitism, to the Federal bench after flunking out of law school. He rubbed shoulders with dignitaries, kings, queens, and presidents, yet he never forgot his humble beginnings and he never changed.

He used the lessons he learned through failure to allow himself to gain national prominence in the field of law. He spoke all over the country and inspired thousands. His story could be anyone's story of success and happiness.

Made in the USA
Columbia, SC
27 July 2023

20875723R00173